Semiotic and Significs

Semiotic *and* Significs

The Correspondence

BETWEEN

Charles S. Peirce and

Victoria Lady Welby

EDITED BY CHARLES S. HARDWICK
WITH THE ASSISTANCE OF JAMES COOK

Indiana University Press   Bloomington and London

Copyright © 1977 by Indiana University Press

All rights reserved

Published in Canada by Fitzhenry & Whiteside Limited, Don Mills,
Ontario

Manufactured in the United States of America

Library of Congress Cataloging in Publication Data

Peirce, Charles Santiago Sanders, 1839-1914.
  Semiotic and Significs.

  Includes bibliographical references.
  1. Semiotics—Addresses, essays, lectures.
  2. Peirce, Charles Santiago Sanders, 1839-1914.
  3. Welby-Gregory, Victoria Alexandrina Maria
Louisa Stuart-Wortley, Hon., Lady, 1837-1912.
  I. Welby-Gregory, Victoria Alexandrina Maria Louisa
Stuart-Wortley, Hon., Lady, 1837-1912.   II. Title.
P99.P4   1976   412   76-12369
ISBN 0-253-35163-4   1 2 3 4 5 81 80 79 78 77

This book is dedicated with love to my mother
Ida Mae Hardwick
and to the memory of my father
Paul M. Hardwick

CONTENTS

APPENDIXES   155

Preface

An edition of Charles S. Peirce's letters to Victoria Lady Welby was edited and published by Irwin C. Lieb in 1953.[1] This collection has proven to be a valuable contribution to Peirce scholarship. The letters were written at a time when Peirce was doing some of his most intensive work on the theory of signs and are an excellent introduction to this aspect of Peirce's philosophy. In these letters, Peirce presents some of his more complex ideas in an informal and relaxed manner strikingly different from the style of his published works. The letters have the added value of revealing the personal hardships Peirce faced during the latter part of his life.

Lieb's edition of the correspondence has been out of print for a number of years and has been relatively inaccessible. It seems altogether appropriate, then, to make these letters available once again to Peirce scholars and to others interested in the history of semiotic.

The present edition has been expanded to include the letters from Lady Welby to Peirce. The justification for including them is twofold. Lady Welby was, in her own right, an important figure in the history of semiotic. Although her work is not as extensive as Peirce's, she nonetheless made a substantial contribution to the development of semiotic around the turn of the century. Also, including her side of the correspondence contributes to an understanding of Peirce's letters. Much of what he had to say was in response to comments and questions contained in her letters.

A number of other items have been included in this edition which should prove to be of added value. One of the most important additions is a long section on Existential Graphs, which was not included in Lieb's edition. In response to an interest shown by Lady Welby in logic, Peirce introduced her to his system of logical graphs. This material is important in that it serves as an introduction to Peirce's system of Existential Graphs, and supplies examples of problems with answers.

Lady Welby's article on "Significs," originally published in the eleventh edition of the *Encyclopaedia Britannica*, has also been included, as well as two "essay-lets" (as Peirce called them) she sent to Peirce during the correspondence. These items have been included not so much for their originality as for their importance in establishing the relationship between her work and his.

Two letters by Juliette Peirce, and one letter by Mrs. Henry Cust, Lady Welby's daughter, have been included simply to add some understanding of the personal relationship that developed between Lady Welby and Peirce during their correspondence.

Peirce's letters to Lady Welby are now in the Welby Collection in the York University Library, Toronto, Ontario. Lady Welby's letters to Peirce, along with a number of essays and papers by Lady Welby, are in the Peirce Correspondence in Houghton Library, Harvard University.[2] In Peirce's correspondence there are also draft copies of letters he either sent or intended to send to Lady Welby. These have not been included in this collection, since many of the ideas Peirce dealt with in them are incorporated into the letters actually sent.

Several of the letters from Peirce were published prior to Lieb's edition. In the Appendix of Ogden and Richards's *The Meaning of Meaning,*[3] C. K. Ogden gives a brief account of Peirce's theory of signs. Ogden quotes extensively from three of Peirce's letters to Lady Welby.[4]

An edition of Lady Welby's later correspondence, published by her daughter Mrs. Henry Cust in 1931,[5] contains several letters from her correspondence with Peirce. The letters included by Mrs. Cust, however, give only a partial indication of Peirce's work in the theory of signs, and many of them are not complete. Part of one of the most important letters from Peirce is omitted as being "too long and technical for quotation."[6] The letters included in *Other Dimensions* are as follows:

(1) Peirce to Lady Welby, December 1, 1903 (p. 8 below.)
(2) Peirce to Lady Welby, December 1, 1903 (p. 10 below.)
(3) Lady Welby to Peirce, December 22, 1903 (p. 13 below.)
(4) Peirce to Lady Welby, May 7, 1904 (p. 19 below.)
(5) Peirce to Lady Welby, October 12, 1904 (p. 22 below.)

(6) Lady Welby to Peirce, November 20, 1904 (p. 37 below.)

(7) Lady Welby to Peirce, December 4, 1908 (p. 63 below.)

(8) Peirce to Lady Welby, December 14, 1908 (p. 66 below.)

(9) Lady Welby to Peirce, January 21, 1909 (p. 86 below.)

(10) Peirce to Lady Welby, March 14, 1909 (p. 108 below.)

(11) Lady Welby to Peirce, April 1909 (p. 130 below.)

(12) Peirce to Lady Welby, October 11, 1909 (p. 133 below.)

Mrs. Cust includes excerpts from two letters from Lady Welby to Peirce which are not in Peirce's correspondence. One follows Lady Welby's letter to Peirce dated December 22, 1903, and the other is written in reply to Peirce's letter dated December 16, 1904. Complete versions of these two letters are included in the present edition, along with a third letter from Lady Welby to Peirce dated November 8, 1906. None of the three letters are in Peirce's correspondence, but draft versions of all three are in Lady Welby's correspondence.

Several items relating to Peirce's correspondence with Lady Welby are included in the *Collected Papers*. Peirce's review of Lady Welby's *What is Meaning?* is included in Volume VIII of the *Collected Papers* (8.171-175) along with a number of other reviews. There is also a short note in the *Collected Papers* which refers to Lady Welby's book *What is Meaning?* and to her three-part distinction between sense, meaning, and interpretation.[7]

The next item, on the definition of a sign (*Collected Papers* 8.177-185), only mentions Lady Welby in the last paragraph and does not have any direct relationship to either the review or the correspondence.[8]

Two of Peirce's letters to Lady Welby are included in the *Collected Papers*. One is the letter dated October 12, 1904, and the other is that dated December 23, 1908. The October 12 letter is published in its entirety. It is one of the most important letters in the correspondence. In this letter, Peirce attempted to outline his whole theory of signs. It is also a letter Lady Welby reproduced and sent to a number of her friends and colleagues, among whom were J. Cook Wilson, Bertrand Russell, and C. K. Ogden. The December 23 letter is evidently a draft of a letter later sent to Lady Welby.[9]

One final note on this collection of letters. The main purpose in publishing the correspondence is to provide important source material which should open the way for a more comprehensive study of both the work of Lady Welby on significs and that of Peirce on signs. The introduction is admittedly sketchy and incomplete. A more comprehensive account of the work of both of these important figures will have to wait until this and other primary source material has been made available. But the introduction will at least, I hope, allow one to see the major outlines of the work of both Lady Welby and Peirce at this particular stage of the development of their ideas.

This edition of the Peirce-Welby correspondence could not have been completed without the help and encouragement of a number of institutions and individuals. With the assistance of a grant from the American Philosophical Society (Grant No. 5330–Penrose Fund, 1969) I was able to do preliminary research related to the life and work of Lady Welby. Grants from the Humanities and Social Science Research Committee, College of Arts and Sciences, Texas Tech University, enabled me to continue work on this project during two summers. I also wish to thank J. Knox Jones, Graduate Dean and Vice President for Research, Lawrence L. Graves, Dean of the College of Arts and Sciences, and Henry C. Thomas, Director of the Organized Research Committee, College of Arts and Sciences, Texas Tech University, for their support of the Institute for Studies in Pragmaticism, under whose auspices this project was finally brought to completion.

I am indebted to the Philosophy Department, Harvard University, for their kind permission to publish Lady Welby's letters to Peirce, and to Mr. Reverdy Whitlock, Whitlock's, Inc., for permission to publish Peirce's letters to Lady Welby.

I owe a special debt of thanks to Professor Irwin C. Lieb for his help and encouragement in preparing this expanded edition of the correspondence. It was Professor Lieb who first encouraged me to undertake this project. Without his generosity in allowing me to use his notes to the Peirce letters, the preparation of this edition would have been much more difficult and time-consuming.

James Cook provided valuable assistance in preparing the manuscript for publication. With his help, a number of new notes have been added to the previous edition. I am especially grateful to him for undertaking the difficult task of transcribing the section on Existential Graphs.

Mr. Hartwell Bowsfield, Archivist, York University Library, was especially helpful in supplying information about the material contained in the Welby Collection. I also wish to thank Sir Oliver Welby, Denton Manor, Grantham, England, for graciously spending his time with me discussing numerous ideas related to the life and work of Lady Welby. And I wish to thank Professor Max H. Fisch, who has read successive versions of this manuscript and has offered a number of helpful suggestions and comments. His expert knowledge of Peirce and his generous assistance have been invaluable.

Finally, I wish to thank my colleague, Kenneth L. Ketner, Director of the Institute for Studies in Pragmaticism. He has followed the progress of this project from its beginning, and I have profited from his advice and counsel.

NOTES

1. Irwin C. Lieb, editor, *Charles S. Peirce's Letters to Lady Welby* (New Haven: Whitlock's, Inc., 1953). These letters, with omissions of "purely incidental passages," are reprinted in Philip P. Wiener, *Values in a Universe of Chance: Selected Writings of Charles S. Peirce* (Garden City: Doubleday and Co., Inc., 1958), pp. 380-432.

2. References to the unpublished manuscripts of Peirce will follow the order given in Richard Robin's *Annotated Catalogue of the Papers of Charles S. Peirce* (Amherst: The University of Massachusetts Press, 1967). Thus, Robin, Ms. 280 will indicate manuscript 280 as catalogued by Robin. References to Peirce's published works will be to the *Collected Papers of Charles Sanders Peirce*, 6 volumes, edited by Charles Hartshorne and Paul Weiss (Cambridge: Harvard University Press, 1931-1935); Volumes 7-8, edited by Arthur W. Burks, 1958. I will follow the convention of citing volume and paragraph. Thus, *Collected Papers* 8.345 will refer to Volume 8, paragraph 345.

3. C. K. Ogden and I. A. Richards, *The Meaning of Meaning* (New York: Harcourt, Brace and World, Inc., n.d.).

4. Ogden quotes from Peirce's letters dated October 12, 1904 (p. 22 below); December 14, 1908 (p. 66 below); and March 14, 1909 (p. 108 below).

5. Mrs. Henry Cust, editor, *Other Dimensions: A Selection from the Later Correspondence of Victoria Lady Welby* (London: Jonathan Cape, 1931).

6. The part omitted is from the letter dated October 12, 1904. Unfortunately, this part of the letter contains one of Peirce's most cogent statements about his theory of signs. The letter has been reprinted in its entirety in *Collected Papers*, 8.327-341. Reprinted in this volume p. 22 below.

7. This appears to be from an unpublished manuscript dated March 28-29, 1909, and was one of several attempts by Peirce to write an introduction to a collection of essays on pragmatism. See Robin, *Annotated Catalogue*, p. 78. The essay has no direct relationship to Peirce's review of Lady Welby's book.

8. The material included in *Collected Papers* 8.177-185 is taken from a forty-sheet letter Peirce intended for William James (see Ralph Barton Perry, *The Thought and Character of William James,* Vol. II, Boston: Little, Brown and Co., 1935, pp. 438-439). The draft is in the Peirce Correspondence at Houghton Library, Harvard University (Robin, *Catalogue*, L-224).

9. See note in *Collected Papers*, Vol. 8, p. 231. In most cases, Peirce drafted his letters to Lady Welby with great care, rewriting them several times before sending them. Although there are passages common to the version in the *Collected Papers* and the one reprinted here, there are nonetheless differences. In the draft version, for example, Peirce goes into much greater detail with regard to the discussion of signs. A complete list of Peirce's drafts in the Peirce Correspondence, Houghton Library, is included here in Appendix F.

INTRODUCTION

I

The correspondence between Charles S. Peirce and Victoria Lady Welby began in 1903 and ended in 1911, shortly before her death. It occurred during the last years of both of their lives. Lady Welby died in 1912, and Peirce died in 1914.

It was the most difficult time of Peirce's life. He had been living in Milford, Pennsylvania, since 1887. By 1902, the year before the correspondence began, Peirce was in debt and was living off the small amount of money he obtained from writing reviews and articles. By 1908, he ceased contributing reviews to *The Nation* and lost his principal source of income. "By 1909 he was a very ill man of seventy, compelled to take a grain of morphine daily to stave off pain."[1]

In addition to the rather large number of articles and reviews he wrote for *The Nation* and *The New York Evening Post* during this period, he continued to work on his book on logic, which, unfortunately, he was not able to complete. He also gave the Lowell Institute lectures in 1903, part of which were published as "A Syllabus of Certain Topics of Logic";[2] he read a number of papers before the National Academy of Sciences; and he published his articles on pragmatism in *The Monist*.[3] These, along with his article "A Neglected Argument for the Reality of God,"[4] were some of his most important published writings during the time of the correspondence.

Lady Welby became interested in Peirce's work after reading his articles on logic in Baldwin's *Dictionary of Philosophy and Psychology*.[5] She saw in his work similarities to her own, and she initiated the correspondence with the hope, no doubt, that she would find someone sympathetic to her own work in semantics. Recognizing the strong similarity between his work and hers, she had Macmillan and Company send a copy of her book *What is Meaning?* to Peirce.

Peirce was more than sympathetic. He read *What is Meaning?* and reviewed it for *The Nation*.[6] More importantly, he reviewed her book along with Russell's *Principles of Mathematics*, to which he devoted but one brief paragraph, and acknowledged both books to be "really important works on logic." Peirce sent Lady Welby a copy of the review, along with some other reviews he had published in *The Nation*, and the correspondence began.

It is evident from the review that Peirce was favorably impressed by Lady Welby's book. Lady Welby herself thought his comparison of her book to Russell's work was, to say the least, extravagant. Nonetheless, Lady Welby truly appreciated Peirce's positive evaluation of her work. Her work had received only moderate recognition, due partly to the unique nature of her ideas and partly to the difficulties of her style.

That her ideas were unusual may, in itself, have appealed to Peirce. He noted in his review that her book might be "too feminine" for some readers. But he obviously saw that she too was breaking ground in an area that had occupied his own interests for a number of years. And he surely understood the difficulty she encountered in expressing ideas that went against accepted traditions. Whatever the case may be, Peirce did have considerable respect for her work, and even though he disagreed with her on a number of points, he was never condescending, nor merely indulgent of some of her more vaguely put ideas.

In these letters there is a sympathy, cordiality, and tolerance that reveals an interesting side of Peirce's personality. There are a number of references to his financial difficulties in the letters, and almost constant references to his bad health. Yet there is no discernible note of bitterness or complaint. Even though he felt that the importance of his work had been overlooked, that his pragmatic doctrine had been misinterpreted, there is no indication in the letters of resentment or bitterness. What is revealed in his letters is the heroic struggle of a man confident of the importance of his work, a struggle heightened by his failing health, burdening debt, and the prospect of continuing poverty.

II

Victoria Lady Welby was born in 1837.[7] She was the daughter of the Honorable Charles and Lady Emmeline Stuart-Wortley. When she was christened, Princess Victoria (for whom she was named) and the Duchess of Kent stood as her godmothers. Only five days after the ceremony, Princess Victoria became Queen of England.

Her mother, Lady Emmeline, developed a passion for travel during the early years of her marriage. When her husband died, she continued to travel, taking her young daughter Victoria with her. From the time she was eleven until she was eighteen, Victoria traveled with her mother on journeys to the United States, Canada, Mexico, Spain, Morocco, Turkey, Palestine, and Syria.[8] It is difficult to estimate what effect these extensive travels had on the young Victoria, but they constituted, as she remarked to Peirce in later years, her only "formal" education.

In 1861 Victoria was appointed Maid of Honour to Queen Victoria. She spent almost two years in court in the company of many great men of her time. "Lord Derby, Lord Palmerston, the Duke of Newcastle, Mr. Gladstone, 'Dizzy,'—each in his turn would take the young Maid of Honour in to dinner, and, as it would seem, devote a thoughtful attention to her unorthodox views on foreign—above all on American—policy."[9] Surely it was unusual for a young lady to have been able to discuss foreign policy from the point of view of one who has seen so much of the world first hand. Even though she was quite young at the time, she had been to America, both the northern and southern states, and had formed definite opinions of people and the conditions. From her experience, she was persuaded, "in spite of the prevailing cant, to defend the slave-owners against the false charges of cruelty which were brought against them, and to paint the lot of the slaves in the true colours of happiness, in which British liberalism dared not look upon them."[10] In expressing her bold and unorthodox views, she displayed, even then, a strong intellectual independence which was to characterize her more mature years.

Victoria married Sir William Welby-Gregory of Denton, Grantham, in 1863. During the years that immediately followed, she devoted her life to her husband and family.

During the early years of her marriage, she was sympathetic to the various evangelical religious movements characteristic of the times.[11] Her first book, *Links and Clues* (1881), had strong evangelical overtones. It was extremely unorthodox in character. Indeed, the mere publication of a book on religious instruction by a woman was enough to raise eyebrows of the more orthodox believers.

Links and Clues was not an overwhelming success. She sent copies to friends and relatives, and to a select few clergymen whose opinions she respected. But the book was misunderstood and misinterpreted by those who she thought should have understood it; and it was a source of embarrassment to some of her relatives and close friends who thought it unseemly of her, a woman, to presume to write a book on religious instruction.

The disappointing reception of *Links and Clues* turned her thinking in new directions. She became aware of a fundamental problem—the problem of meaning. She came to realize that religious expression was severely limited by the use of outmoded forms of language. To her, religious belief was a living, vital aspect of human experience—one that must draw upon contemporary experience—and must be cast in contemporary forms of expression. In a letter to Bishop Talbot she said: "When the Fathers of the Church, the great Divines of three centuries ago, are quoted to me, I have always the same answer: are you able to tell me positively of your own knowledge, that what they said then, they would say now, here in this room, knowing all we know and belonging to these times?"[12] What we fail to take into account is that forms of expression change with man's changing experience. If we cling to expression characteristic of earlier times and related to different conditions and a different understanding of human experience, we cannot help but be misled and confused. The question of religious belief, then, became secondary, and her interests shifted to a study of language and meaning, for there, she thought, lay the fundamental problem that must be solved before one could fully comprehend questions about religious matters.

III

From 1885 until her death in 1912, Lady Welby's interests were almost completely centered on problems of language and meaning. Although her interest in religion persisted, she undertook a serious study of science and philosophy. In doing so, she discovered that the problem of inadequate expression was not characteristic of religion alone. William Macdonald, an associate and close friend during her later years, noted that she had

> an almost romantic aspiration towards, an entirely simple and wistful yearning for, the intellectual life as she conceived it to be, among the wise and the learned, the thinkers and the teachers of mankind. When in the course of her married years she began to make her way, with however little assurance, into the El Dorado of the mind—this region mild of calm and serene air—she found it, to her bewilderment, quite other than she had thought. Here was a world of confusion and outcry indeed, as though Comus and his rout held festival within the pale: in every direction antagonisms, controversies, misunderstandings, sectional interests even in science and metaphysics, and all the little ironies or vulgarities of animosity, partisanship, prejudice and stupidity, just as they exist in courts and cottages! The discovery, presently made, that the

greater part of this turmoil was caused by difference about the
sense of particular words first brought home to her the conception
of language as conditioning and enabling all our thought, and
therefore as largely constituting as well as limiting our actual being
as intelligences.[13]

Her basic thesis was that language follows experience; not
the other way around. Thus she began a program of study to
better understand the scientific discoveries and the more advanced philosophical doctrines that seemed to characterize the
times. Rather than attempt to clothe present discoveries in
the garments of the past, she sought to weave new cloth, to
devise new patterns, from present discoveries. With reference
to religious belief, she decided to begin at "the other end."
Rather than attempt to reconcile science with religion, she
sought, through science, to restructure religious belief.

One of the first attempts to deal with the problem of
inadequate expression was in a pamphlet she had privately
printed in 1891 entitled *Witnesses to Ambiguity: A Collection.*[14] The pamphlet was little more than a collection of
passages extracted from her extensive reading in philosophy
and science. In the introduction she stated that her object in
printing the collection was "to help in making known a state
of things constantly ignored and even denied; but which is a
main cause of much of barrenness in current discussion, of
confusion on matters of pressing importance, and of hopeless-
ness as to the possibility of any real solution of 'enigmas'
which perhaps depend on some unrecognized survival of, or
change in, meaning."[15] In 1892, she published an article in
The Monist entitled "Meaning and Metaphor."[16] And in 1897,
she published an article in *Mind*, in two installments, entitled
"Sense, Meaning and Interpretation."[17]

In each successive article she began to develop carefully the
central themes of her new science of meaning, which she
called "significs." In very general terms, these themes can be
stated as follows: linguistic confusion, in all forms of intellectual endeavor, is very much in evidence; what is needed is
the development of a "linguistic conscience," an awareness of

the need for linguistic reform; the cause of much intellectual confusion is the use of outmoded forms of expression and misleading metaphors and analogies; and, finally, there is a need to recognize the organic, or growing and changing, nature of language.

The main thrust of her appeal was to urge the development of a new science of significs, one whose methods of analysis could be brought to bear on science, philosophy, sociology, and psychology. She was not, however, interested in developing a new language, or in formulating an ideal language, in order to avoid the pitfalls of inadequate expression. Most urgently needed was a more adequate understanding of the flexibility of language. We must get away from the conception of language as a system of fixed meanings and recognize the "plastic" nature of language—that language grows and changes in response to the need to express changing experience.

Lady Welby had a more than adequate understanding of the important scientific discoveries of the late nineteenth century. She was also very much aware of the conflicts that arose between science and religion. But rather than perpetuate the conflict, she sought to show that science was not antithetical to religion. She saw in scientific discoveries clues to new forms of expression that would transform religious beliefs into something more meaningful. Where others protested the conflict or clung dogmatically to traditional beliefs, she sought to cast belief in a new mold.

Lady Welby also argued against the doctrine of "Plain Meaning" and against the tendency to see language as a logical system of precisely defined terms. To her, language was merely a tool, the servant of thought and not the master.[18] This view, though not so original now, went against the more widely accepted views about language and meaning at the time. There were many who agreed with her about the need for linguistic reform, but few were willing to accept her overly "plastic" conception of language.

She thought a great deal of confusion and misunderstanding was generated by the survival in our language of outmoded metaphors and analogies. The confusion can be cleared up not by precise definition of terms, but rather by the use of *new* metaphors and analogies more closely related to current experience and current discoveries. This involved a more acute awareness of what we really mean by the terms we use, and an understanding of how these terms are used in various contexts and situations. The more we begin to explore the various uses of language, the more we become sensitive to the subtle variations of meaning that may either hinder or enhance our understanding of various forms of expression and, in turn, that must render expression more adequate to the demands of changing experience.

One must begin, she argued, with an analysis of meaning. For in attempting to understand the meaning of 'meaning,' we come to grips with the problem in its most fundamental and most essential formulation. What we discover are different levels or classes of "expression value," and we see the multi-dimensional nature of meaning. For her, there were three main levels of meaning: sense, meaning, and significance.

> (a) The first of these at the outset would naturally be associated with Sense in its most primitive reference; that is, with the organic response to environment, and with the essentially expressive element in all experience. We ostracize the senseless in speech, and also ask "in what sense" a word is used or a statement may be justified.
>
> (b) But "Sense" is not in itself purposive; whereas that is the main character of the word "Meaning" which is properly reserved for the specific sense which it is *intended to convey*.
>
> (c) As including sense and meaning but transcending them in range, and covering the far-reaching consequence, implication, ultimate result or outcome of some event or experience, the term "Significance" is usefully applied.[19]

These are not, of course, the only meanings of 'meaning.' "We have also signification, purport, import, bearing, reference, indication, application, denotation and connotation, the weight, the drift, the tenour, the lie, the trend, the range, the tendency of given statements."[20] And we must become sensitive to all of these and other variations that different situations and contexts demand. Critical attention to the different uses of meaning puts us on guard with respect to other equally important terms and points to the need for a systematic consideration of common, but often misleading, terms.

Lady Welby placed a high value on the triadic relationship between sense, meaning, and significance, and this relationship was obviously important to Peirce. Quite apart from his general agreement that philosophical method is directed toward the clarification of meaning, he was able to relate this triadic division of the levels of meaning to his own distinction between the three grades of the logical interpretant. And he saw similarities between sense, meaning, and significance and his categories of firstness, secondness, and thirdness.

In terms of her own analysis of meaning, Lady Welby did not go too far beyond her distinction between sense, meaning, and significance. Her work, particularly her book *What is Meaning?*, is full of examples which attempt to illustrate the nuance of meaning, particularly of words whose meanings are often taken for granted. There is a strong moral tone in her work, no doubt a carry-over from her early religious concern. There is an almost evangelical zeal, the suggestion of a moral obligation to seek clarity of understanding. But her work still lacked the logical rigor that characterizes Peirce's work.

Peirce seemed to have understood the tenor and the aim of her program, and he was tolerant of her limitations. Yet he was gracious enough to acknowledge her contributions. In the letter dated March 14, 1909, he commented:

> ... I had not realized, before reading it [her *Encyclopaedia Britannica* article], how fundamental your trichotomy of Sense, Meaning, and Significance really is. It is not to be expected that concepts of such importance should get perfectly defined for a long time. ... I now find that my division [of the three kinds of Interpretant] nearly coincides with yours, as it ought to do exactly, if both are correct.[21]

IV

Peirce's work in the theory of signs is much more complex and elaborate than the program of significs proposed by Lady Welby. It is difficult to discuss his theory of signs without touching on almost every aspect of his work. One needs some understanding of the metaphysical categories upon which his whole pragmatic philosophy is based; and one would have to understand how Peirce extended these categories into esthetics, ethics, logic, epistemology, and all the other traditional subdivisions of philosophy.

In this brief introduction, no attempt will be made to outline Peirce's theory of signs. For such an outline, the letters themselves offer perhaps the best starting point. The value of these letters, indeed, lies in their significance as a general introduction to this aspect of Peirce's work. In writing to Lady Welby, he took great pains to explain his work in the theory of signs and to relate it to his other work. The October 12, 1904 letter is of particular importance in this regard.[22]

For a more complete presentation of his theory of signs, one would be advised to study the *Collected Papers*, particularly Volume II, Book II.[23] An attempt has been made by Hartshorne and Weiss to present systematically Peirce's theory of signs and to show its relation to his logic. One would also be advised to consult the index to each volume of the *Collected Papers* for entries about signs and for the terms Icon, Index, and Symbol. It must be mentioned also that there are a considerable number of items in Peirce's unpublished papers related to signs. One should consult Robin's *Annotated Catalogue* for entries on signs to gain a better understanding of the importance Peirce placed on the study of signs in relation to his other work. As has already been noted, Peirce made numerous attempts to relate the study of signs to every aspect of his pragmatic philosophy. Peirce was a systematic thinker, and he tended to build his system by interweaving themes and ideas, constantly interrelating them, with the total design of his system in view.

This characteristic of Peirce's method can be seen in the letter of October 12, 1904. He begins the letter with a discussion of the division of all ideas into the classes of Firstness, Secondness, and Thirdness, and moves from that into his discussion of signs. Peirce considered this distinction to be one of his most important discoveries, and even though he tended, as he says in the letter, to "pooh-pooh" the notion of triads at first, triadic relations play an important role in almost every aspect of his philosophy. His initial suspicion of triadic relations stemmed from his dislike for Hegelian philosophy, but he found the use of these three classes of idea so extremely fruitful that he was "conquered" by the idea completely.

Equally important for an understanding of Peirce's interest in signs is the comment that "the highest grade of reality is only reached by signs. . . ."[24] The meaning of this comment can be understood only by carefully considering Peirce's account of Firstness, Secondness, and Thirdness. But one can grasp something of the significance of what he meant by noting the following comment:

> It appears to me that the essential function of a sign is to render inefficient relations efficient,—not to set them into action, but to establish a habit or general rule whereby they will act on occasion. According to the physical doctrine, nothing ever happens but the continued rectilinear velocities with the accelerations that accompany different relative positions of the particles. All other relations, of which we know so many, are inefficient. Knowledge in some way renders them efficient; and a sign is something by knowing which we know something more. With the exception of knowledge, in the present instant, of the contents of consciousness in that instant (the existence of which knowledge is open to doubt) all our thought & knowledge is by signs.[25]

Semiotic, then, or the general study of signs, is one of the most fundamental of all disciplines, and it is not surprising that Peirce gave it such an important place in his philosophy.

One can see from the quotation above that Peirce was interested in the epistemological implications of a theory of signs. This is contrary to the view, developed early in Peirce scholarship, that his theory of signs was primarily a classificatory system.[26] Although Peirce made several attempts to classify signs, it is not the case that this was his major concern.[27] His major concern was in showing that "a sign is something by knowing which we know something more."

It would be safe to say that very little had been done before the work of Peirce to bring to light the importance of a systematic study of the nature of signs.[28] Peirce's work in this regard was truly original. It is equally easy to see why Peirce had so much difficulty presenting his theory in a way acceptable both to himself and to his colleagues. In a draft of a letter to Lady Welby dated December 28, 1908, after having given a rather long account of his work, he remarked:

> Well, dear Lady Welby, you deserve this infliction, for having spoken of my having "always been kindly [!!!] interested in the work to which my life is devoted," when I have myself been entirely absorbed in the very same subject since 1863, without meeting, before I made your acquaintance, a single mind to whom it did not seem very like bosh.[29]

Peirce's interest in the study of signs was a natural outgrowth of the pragmatic conception of philosophy which he originated. Unlike James, Peirce did not see the pragmatic method as merely a way of settling disputes over difficult concepts. For Peirce, the pragmatic method was a way of achieving conceptual clarity. It was this idea, quite apart from his interest in signs, that established a link between his work and that of Lady Welby.

The task of philosophy, as Peirce saw it, was to render vague ideas of common experience more precise. This notion was deeply rooted in his early struggle with Kantian philosophy.[30] Making common experience more intelligible was an enterprise that took place at various levels of experience. It was a task that, according to Peirce, required not only new categories of interpretation but also a careful analysis of signs and their use. Peirce saw his own efforts to establish a viable study of semiotic as a move in this direction.

The analysis of signs and their uses requires a special kind of analysis, for which Peirce coined the word 'Ideoscopy.' "*Ideoscopy* consists in describing and classifying the ideas that belong to ordinary experience or that naturally arise in connection with ordinary life, without regard to their being valid or invalid or to their psychology."[31] This idea is in keeping with his pragmatic maxim which is a guide to achieving successive levels of clarity of meaning. The aim of philosophical inquiry is to render vague concepts precise. This is not, however, a linguistic enterprise. It involves a method of inquiry that brings to bear scientific method on a problematic situation.[32]

In an unpublished manuscript entitled "The Basis of Pragmaticism," Peirce makes this point clear.[33] He says, for example, "In one of the two usual acceptations of the term 'philosophy', that one in which the present writer is accustomed to employ it, as meaning cenoscopic, not synthetic or positive, philosophy, a philosophical explanation is as much a logical analysis as is a philosophical definition."[34] Research in the special sciences "either consists in, or springs out of, the discovery of novel phenomena." "But," he continues, "after one such phenomenon has been discovered and some conditions of its apparition have been ascertained, one's next step will naturally be to formulate its laws. . . ."[35]

The notion of discovery, as Peirce is discussing it here, is most often associated with the physical sciences. For Peirce, however, the method of the physical scientist is but a special case of a more pervasive activity called inquiry, the aim of which is to settle doubt and fix beliefs. The result of inquiry is the incorporation of novel experience into an established belief system. The fixation of belief can be accomplished in many ways. But for Peirce, the only desirable way is by a method which promotes what he called "concrete reasonableness." This involves an instinctive tendency toward a goal or aim that would render action rational. This involves, in turn, the establishment of habits of action that are controllable and predictable.

Pragmatism is a method, for Peirce, that capitalizes upon this instinctive tendency of human behavior and that attempts to superimpose upon an unconscious penchant for order a conscious attention to norms. The search for norms is not, however, arbitrary, nor does it involve mere subjective preferences. The ultimate aim of thought and behavior is concrete reasonableness, which, for Peirce, involved the discovery and recognition of habits that have the character of lawlikeness. In order to achieve this aim, the study of semiotic is vital, for if all thought is in signs, then it is important to determine how signs function.

Although Peirce's work in the theory of signs began as early as 1867, he devoted increasing attention to the subject in his later years. It is natural, of course, that Peirce tended to discuss this aspect of this work in the correspondence with Lady Welby, recognizing that this was a mutual interest. Again, this is why the letters are so valuable. One gets the impression that Peirce is dealing with semiotic from a fresh point of view.

From the brief account given here of Peirce's interest in semiotic, and from its relation to the previous discussion of Lady Welby's interest in significs, one can see why Peirce was so readily drawn to her work. Despite the many technical differences in their views, they were remarkably close at least in spirit. Lady Welby certainly lacked the secure understanding of technical philosophy that Peirce had readily at his disposal. But like Peirce she realized that a new starting point for achieving conceptual clarity was in order, whatever it was to be called—significs or semiotic.

There was enough common in their views, however, to allow a significant meeting of minds. With this understood, the importance of the correspondence can be seen. Peirce was at least convinced that Lady Welby understood what he was attempting to do, and even more impressed with having found, for the first time, someone who understood one of the most important discoveries of his long philosophical career.

V

One final aspect of the correspondence needs to be mentioned. It is now evident that Lady Welby played an important role in introducing Peirce's later work on the theory of signs to some important British philosophers. The extent to which her influence had a direct bearing on a serious acceptance of Peirce's work on signs is difficult to determine. But none the less, the link is there.[36]

Lady Welby was already familiar with pragmatic philosophy. She had corresponded with William James, with James's friend the British pragmatist F. C. S. Schiller, and with the Italian pragmatists Vailati and Calderoni. In a letter to James, she said:

> ... Indeed, I am really an aboriginal pragmatist, for, many years ago—long before the name came into use—I was seeing more and more clearly that 'intellectualism' was now feeding upon husks and turning upon itself, engendering nothing but fresh and abortive controversy; and also that words like 'make' (on the use of which most argument about truth turns) were terrible traps for the unwary. That has led to my plea for the recovery of what I am calling (for want of a better term) the primal sense, the inborn and generative alertness to danger and profit in mind which answer to that wariness which has enabled the race to survive the formidable dangers of early life; that 'fitness' is unerring response which has been 'selected'.[37]

During the time she was corresponding with Peirce (1903-1911) she was also corresponding with Bertrand Russell and J. Cook Wilson. She made copies of Peirce's letter of December 14, 1908, and sent them to both Russell and Cook Wilson. Cook Wilson was not, evidently, impressed by Peirce's letter, even though there were aspects of Peirce's Firstness,

Secondness, and Thirdness that corresponded with his notion of oneness, twoness, and threeness. Russell, however, was aware of Peirce's pragmatic philosophy and his contributions to logic, although he was not immediately impressed by the content of the letter.

Lady Welby thought it important to try to instigate an interchange of ideas among the three philosophers. She wrote to G. F. Stout, the editor of *Mind*, to whom she also sent a copy of Peirce's letter:

> I think that you would like to see the enclosed document from Dr. Peirce. ... You will see at the end that he suggests its being included in a second edition of my book! ... I sent a copy to Mr. Bertrand Russell, and enclose you his answer, which I have forwarded to Dr. Peirce, as I am delighted to be the means of conveying to the one the others's readiness for his criticism. Who knows but that a similar *rapprochement* might be effected in the case of Prof. Cook Wilson. I feel quite like a 'Hague Commission!'[38]

Russell's opinion was mixed. He was not much impressed with Peirce's division between Firstness, Secondness, and Thirdness. "I should also admit," he wrote in reply, "(and so, I fancy, would he) fourthness, etc. ..."[39] Russell went on to comment:

> I do not know where Whitehead or I have said that the need of Dr. Peirce's algebra of dyadic relations seldom occurs. I think myself that a symbolism based on Peano's is practically more convenient, but I hold it quite essential to have a method of expressing relations, and I have always thought very highly of Dr. Peirce for having introduced such a method. I should be interested to know what are the faults he finds with my book, as his criticism would probably be instructive.[40]

In Peirce's correspondence there is a draft of a letter to Lady Welby in which he defends his categories of Firstness, Secondness, and Thirdness against Russell's criticism, but evidently it was never sent.[41]

But if Russell and Cook Wilson were not overly impressed by Peirce's letter, Peirce did acquire a disciple in C. K. Ogden, who, while a student at Cambridge, was a protege of Lady Welby.[42] Ogden was enough impressed by Peirce's work to include a long excerpt from Peirce's correspondence with Lady Welby in the appendix of *The Meaning of Meaning*, a book he coauthored with I. A. Richards. These excerpts, along with a discussion of Peirce's "Prolegomena to an Apology for Pragmaticism," constitute one of the first serious considerations of Peirce's work in semiotic.

The British philosopher who was evidently most interested in Peirce's theory of signs at the time was F. P. Ramsey. Whether Ramsey knew of the letters to Lady Welby or whether he knew Ogden is not known. But it is apparent that he was very much interested in Peirce's theory of signs, and he incorporated it into his own logical works. When Ramsey reviewed Ogden and Richards' *The Meaning of Meaning* for *Mind* he noted that the "excellent appendix on C. S. Peirce deserves special mention."[43]

It is interesting to speculate about how much influence Ramsey may have had on Wittgenstein with regard to Ramsey's own interest in Peirce. He mentions Peirce's distinction between token and type, and acknowledges Peirce's writing in his review of the *Tractatus Logico-Philosophicus*. Ramsey was one of Wittgenstein's closest friends and was instrumental in getting him to return to England. But even though there are strong pragmatic aspects in Wittgenstein's later work, there is no mention of Peirce by Wittgenstein.[44]

It is difficult to determine how significant or how pervasive Lady Welby's influence was in introducing Peirce's work to these British philosophers. Though Russell, Cook Wilson, and Stout took note of it, none of them seemed interested enough to study Peirce's work in the theory of signs in greater detail. It was obviously Ogden, sharing a common interest in the study of meaning with both Lady Welby and Peirce, who was most instrumental in bringing this aspect of Peirce's work to the attention of others.

It is, however, very much to Lady Welby's credit that she was among the first to recognize the importance of Peirce's work in semiotic. Though she may not have fully understood the implications of his work, she did understand that Peirce, like herself, had put his finger on a new and emerging problem in philosophy—the study of meaning. And the history of twentieth-century philosophy has proven them both correct in their assessment of the importance of the problem.

NOTES

1. Paul Weiss, "Charles S. Peirce," *Dictionary of American Biography*, Vol. 14 (New York, 1934), p. 403.

2. C. S. Peirce, "A Syllabus of Certain Topics of Logic" (Boston, 1903).

3. C. S. Peirce, "What Pragmatism Is," *The Monist*, Vol. 15, pp. 161-181; "The Issues of Pragmaticism," Vol. 15, pp. 481-492; "Prolegomena to an Apology for Pragmaticism," Vol. 16, pp. 492-546.

4. C. S. Peirce, "A Neglected Argument for the Reality of God," *The Hibbert Journal*, Vol. 7, pp. 90-112.

5. J. M. Baldwin, ed., *Dictionary of Philosophy and Psychology* (New York, 1902).

6. See Appendix A.

7. There are three brief accounts of Lady Welby's life and works: Mrs. W. K. Clifford, "Victoria, Lady Welby," *The Hibbert Journal*, Vol. XXIII, No. 1 (October, 1924), pp. 101-106; William Macdonald, "Lady Welby," *The Sociological Review*, Vol. V., No. 2 (April, 1912), pp. 152-156; Charles Whibley, "Lady Welby," *Blackwoods*, Vol. 191 (May, 1912), pp. 706-710.

8. See Mrs. Henry Cust, *Wanderers: Episodes from the Travels of Lady Emmeline Stuart-Wortley and her daughter Victoria, 1849-1855* (London, 1928).

9. Cust, *Wanderers*, p. 19.

10. Charles Whibley, "Lady Welby," p. 707.

11. See, for example, D. C. Somerville, *English Thought in the Nineteenth Century* (London, 1964), pp. 99-122.

12. Victoria Lady Welby, *Echoes of Larger Life: A Selection from the Early Correspondence of Victoria Lady Welby*, edited by Mrs. Henry Cust (London, 1929), p. 18.

13. William Macdonald, "Lady Welby," p. 154.

14. Victoria Welby, *Witnesses to Ambiguity: A Collection* (Grantham, 1891).

15. *Ibid.*, p. 1.

16. Victoria Welby, "Meaning and Metaphor," *The Monist*, Vol. 3, No. 4, 1892, pp. 510-525.

17. V. Welby, "Sense, Meaning and Interpretation," *Mind*, Vol. V., Nos. 17 and 18, pp. 24-37, 186-202.

18. See her delightful essay, "A Royal Slave," *Fortnightly Review*, Vol. 68, No. 62 (September, 1897), pp. 432-434. She was perhaps inspired by an idea she quoted from Jowett in another of her articles: "The greatest lesson the philosophical analysis of language teaches us is, that we should be above language, making words our servants, and not allowing them to be our masters." (*Dialogues of Plato*, 2nd edn., Vol. 1, p. 285.)

19. V. Welby, "Significs," *Encyclopaedia Britannica*, 11th edn., Vol. XXV (New York, 1911), p. 79.

20. *Ibid.*, p. 79.

21. See below, p. 109.

22. See below, p. 22.

23. Although there are a number of works on Peirce's theory of signs, there are three which can be especially recommended: John J. Fitzgerald, *Peirce's Theory of Signs as Foundation for Pragmatism* (The Hague: Mouton and Company, 1966); Joseph Morton Ransdell, *Charles Peirce: The Idea of Representation*, unpublished dissertation (Columbia, 1966); and Douglas Greenlee, *Peirce's Concept of Sign*, "Approaches to Semiotics" (The Hague: Mouton and Company, 1973).

24. See below, p. 23.

25. See below, pp. 31-32.

26. See, for example, Paul Weiss and A. W. Burks, "Peirce's Sixty-Six Signs," *The Journal of Philosophy*, XLIII (1945), pp. 383-388. It would be wrong, of course, to say that Peirce was not interested in the classification of signs. There is ample evidence, as Weiss and Burks show, that Peirce did see the classification of signs as essential to an understanding of their function. An overconcern for classification, however, tends to de-emphasize the much more important epistemological significance of Peirce's theory of signs. To date, little has been done to emphasize the epistemological implications of Peirce's sign theory.

27. For an interesting analysis of Weiss and Burks, see Gary Sanders, "Peirce's Sixty-Six Signs?" *Transactions of the Charles S. Peirce Society*, Winter 1970, Vol. VI, No. 1, pp. 3-16.

28. Peirce considered his own work in the theory of signs to be unique with regard to the philosophy of his time. He did, however, acknowledge the pioneers in semiotics, particularly the medieval philosophers, whose work in this area had, for the most part, been neglected. For an interesting account of Peirce's work in relation to some important medieval philosophers, see: Ransdell, *Charles Peirce: The Idea of Representation*.

29. *Collected Papers* 8.376. This is a draft of a letter that was later sent to Lady Welby. For the final version of the letter see below, pp. 66-85. Note also that Peirce mentions the December 28 letter on p. 109 below.

30. For an interesting autobiographical account of Peirce's intellectual development, see the Preface to Vol. I of the *Collected Papers*, pp. vii-xi.

31. See below, p. 24.

32. Two essays which are extremely important for an understanding of Peirce's method are: "The Fixation of Belief," *Collected Papers* 5.358-387; and "How to Make Our Ideas Clear," *Collected Papers* 388-410.

33. "The Basis of Pragmaticism," Robin, Ms. number 280.

34. *Ibid.*, p. 1.

35. *Ibid.*

36. For an interesting account of Lady Welby's role in establishing the link between Peirce's work on the theory of signs and British analytical philosophy, see H. S. Thayer, *Meaning and Action* (New York, 1968), pp. 304-313.

37. Victoria Welby, *Other Dimensions: A Selection from the Later Correspondence of Victoria Welby*, ed. by Mrs. Henry Cust (London, 1931), p. 246.

38. *Ibid.*, p. 159.

39. *Ibid.*

40. *Ibid.*

41. A draft copy of this letter is in the Peirce Correspondence, Houghton Library, Harvard University.

42. See letter dated May 2, 1911.

43. F. P. Ramsey, "The Meaning of Meaning," *Mind*, N.S., Vol. 33, No. 129, pp. 108-109.

44. Again, see Thayer, *Meaning and Action*, pp. 311-313. Wittgenstein does mention pragmatism in *On Certainty* (Oxford: Basil Blackwell, 1969), a work particularly loaded with Peircean themes.

A Note on the Texts

In presenting the correspondence between Charles Peirce and Victoria Lady Welby, I have refrained from imposing a false consistency of style on the letters, preferring rather the accuracy of retaining the spellings and punctuation of the original material. Both Peirce and Lady Welby were of the habit of underlining words and phrases; where italicized words now appear in the printed text, they reflect underlining by Peirce or Lady Welby in the original letters, unless otherwise noted by editorial comment. Peirce also enclosed a number of comments in his letters in brackets; unless otherwise noted (or obvious, as with [*sic*]), the bracketed material in the printed text appeared in brackets in the original correspondence. Where obvious omissions or slips of the pen by Peirce or Lady Welby drastically change the sense of the text, I have so indicated in footnotes. Unless otherwise specified, the footnotes are mine.

The Correspondence between
Charles S. Peirce
and Victoria Lady Welby

November 1st 1898

Mr. Charles S. Peirce,
Milford, Penn.

My Dear Sir:—

We have selected a few men of prominence to whom we send copies of Lady Welby's pamphlet, which she has sent to us for private distribution.[1] She is a woman of high standing in the English aristocracy, having a place among the scientists of Old England, being honored with the personal friendship of such men as the late Romanes,[2] Professor C. Lloyd Morgan,[3] Oliver Lodge,[4] and many others.

If you are interested in the book, she will doubtless be pleased to receive a few lines in acknowledgement sent to her personally. Her address is The Hon. Lady Victoria Welby, Denton Manor, Grantham, Eng.

Very truly yours,
The Open Court Publishing Co.

---

1. V. Welby, *The Witness of Science to Linguistic Anarchy: A Collection of extracts chiefly from 'Nature,' 'Science,' and 'Natural Science,'* printed for private circulation, Grantham, England, 1898.

2. George John Romanes (1848-1894), author of *A Candid Examination of Theism* (1878), *Mental Evolution in Man: Origin of Human Faculty* (1888), *Mind, Motion and Monism* (1895), etc.

3. Conwy Lloyd Morgan (1852-1936), a pioneer in the study of animal psychology; author of *Instinct and Experience* (1912), *Emergent Evolution* (1923), etc.

4. Sir Oliver Lodge (1851-1940), Principal of the University of Birmingham; author of *The Ether of Space* (1909), *Advancing Science* (1931), etc.

Duneaves, Harrow, England
May 24th 1903

My dear Sir,

I have ventured to request Messrs. Mcmillan to send you a copy of my book 'What is Meaning?', because if you do me the honour to read it any comments from you will be of special value in my eyes. I do not pretend to be able to follow the course of your technical arguments, being quite untrained in that direction; but I have constantly come upon points in your writings which have for me a keen interest from my special point of view. This is markedly the case in your contributions to the Philosophical Dictionary.[1] Among these I would mention what you say about 'Laws of Thought'*, and especially about the 'contradictory' and the 'principle of contradiction'. Also about the lack of any definite meaning in philosophy of the word 'opposite'. Again, your criticism of the misunderstanding as to the proper meanings of 'axiom' and of 'postulate'.

But my book would show my reasons for warmly welcoming criticism of this kind, to which I am only too well aware that my own writings must be subject.

It is, unfortunately, one thing to see the needless traps of which language is full and quite another to succeed in avoiding them. In some cases indeed as you and others show, there is no commonly received alternative.

Yours faithfully
V. Welby

---

1. *Dictionary of Philosophy and Psychology*, ed. J. M. Baldwin (New York, 1902).

* (last page, Vol. I.) [Lady Welby's footnote, a reference to Peirce's article on Laws of Thought, Vol. I, pp. 641-644, appeared after her signature at the end of this letter.]

"Arisbe," Milford Pa.
1903 June 7

My dear Sir:

I thank you for your pleasant letter. I had already received your book from the London Macmillan firm and had looked it through with much interest, for I have often thought a book ought to be written on that subject.

As to my own writings on the subject, there were two in the *Revue Philosophique*. I think one was in volume VI and the other in vol VII. They were translated into English and printed in the Popular Science Monthly (Edited by E. L. Youmans) at the end of 1877 or beginning of 1878.[1]

To the doctrine there proposed I gave the name *pragmatism*, which is defined in Baldwin's Dictionary, and which has some adherents in Oxford—Schiller,[2] Sturt,[3] etc. But I do not subscribe to all their extensions.

I have just been delivering a course of lectures[4] on the subject in Harvard University, and these will be printed if I can find a publisher.

---

1. C. S. Peirce, "The Fixation of Belief," *Popular Science Monthly*, Vol. 12 (November 1877), pp. 1-15, and "How to Make Our Ideas Clear," *Popular Science Monthly*, Vol. 12 (January 1878), pp. 286-302. See also *Collected Papers*, 5.358-387 and 5.388-410 respectively; and item G-1878-7 in Arthur Burks, "Bibliography of the Works of Charles Sanders Peirce," *Collected Papers*, Vol. 8.

2. Ferdinand Canning Scott Schiller (1864-1937), senior tutor of Corpus Christi College, Oxford; author of *Humanism* (1903), *Our Human Truths* (1939), *Studies in Humanism* (1907), etc.

3. Henry Cecil Sturt (1863-?), British philosopher; author of *Idola Theatri* (1906), *Human Value* (1923), *The Idea of a Free Church* (1909), and editor of *Personal Idealism* (1902).

4. The Lowell Institute Lectures of 1903.

There was also a review by me of the first three chapters of Pearson's Grammar of Science in the Popular Science Monthly of Jan. 1901 or thereabouts.[5]

When I get time I shall read your book consecutively and will call attention to it in the *Nation*, if the editor will insert a short note for that purpose. I know the columns of that journal to be so crowded that is it difficult to get anything into it.

Yours very truly
C. S. Peirce

---

5. C. S. Peirce, "Pearson's Grammar of Science," *Popular Science Monthly*, Vol. 58 (January 1901), pp. 296-306.

Milford, Pa.
1903 Nov. 5

My dear Lady Victoria Welby:

I mail you herewith a copy of my notice of "What is Meaning?"[1] You understand that I could not in a notice say how warmly I am with your purposes; for the writer of a book-notice has simply to try to make his readers know what *they* would think of the book, & keep his own sentiments to himself. I hope soon to be able to get something of importance printed about logic[2] and if I do, I shall feel that you would like to see it & will send it to you. I mostly write stuff of no interest; but in order to express my thanks for your volume, I will enclose some Nations containing some bits I have been writing about British science. It was *à propos* of Lockyer's B.A. address, whom I used to know very well in

---

1. C. S. Peirce's review of *What is Meaning?*, *The Nation*, 77 (15 Oct 1903), 308-309. Appended to this collection of letters as Appendix A.

2. C. S. Peirce, "A Syllabus of Certain Topics of Logic," a pamphlet published by Alfred Mudge & Sons, Boston, 1903. For a more complete account of the material Peirce intended to include in the Syllabus, see Robin, Ms. 478. Also, items G-1903-2b and G-1903-2c in Arthur W. Burks, "Bibliography of the Works of Charles Sanders Peirce," *Collected Papers*, Vol. 8.

bygone years; and I think the quality of his reasoning often very high, notwithstanding his book on the orientation of temples.[3] I remain

with very high respect
C. S. Peirce

The pieces are on pages 308, 229, (265), 263, 320.[4]

---

3. Sir Norman Lockyer, *The Dawn of Astronomy*, Macmillan Company, New York, 1894. For Peirce's review of this work see *The Nation*, 58 (29 March 1894), 234-236.

4. These page numbers from Vol. 77 of *The Nation* are in reference to the following: 308-the review of Russell's *The Principles of Mathematics* and Lady Welby's *What is Meaning?* (see Appendix A); 229-untitled note on Sir Norman Lockyer; 265-"The Decline of Mathematics in England," a letter to the editor signed "H. T."; 263-"British and American Science," an article by Peirce; 320-"Practical Application of the Theory of Functions," a letter to the editor signed "James McMahon" with an editorial reply from Peirce following.

Duneaves, Harrow
November 18th. 1903

My dear Dr. Peirce

I have been much hindered lately but have now been able to read not only your generously appreciative Notice[1] of my little book, but the other contributions to "The Nation" which you have so kindly sent me; and can but express my warm gratitude. I shall look forward much to the work in preparation, of which you speak.[2] I wonder if that is to be in the form of Harvard Lectures as earlier mentioned?

I have a special excuse for a feeling of pride in your coupling my humble work and B. Russell's together as 'two really important works on logic' in spite of their being so 'utterly disparate' that in every sense but one such a comparison is grotesque. For as it happens, whereas I have never supposed it possible for me to master the very elements of

---

1. See Appendix A.
2. Peirce's "Syllabus."

mathematics, I am now engaged in reading through for the fourth time and as far as possible analysing from my own point of view, his amazing 'Principles of Mathematics'. Though naturally it is not possible at my age for the first time to follow adequately such highly elaborated trains of reasoning, still I can see enough to recognize in this, for me, impossibly technical form, many of the very ideas which for long years I have vainly tried convincingly or even intelligibly, to express.

I am now making a set of special indexes of the book for my own purposes, and with their aid propose to write some Notes on those parts or passages which more especially concern my work and aims. This I shall hope to send to him, and also to Prof. G. Vailati,[3] who shares your view of the importance of that—may I call it, practical extension?—of the office and field of Logic proper, which I have called Significs. For the latter seems to see as I do that the acceptance of such an extension will bring a time when no one with any sense will any longer say 'Oh, I don't care for (or, am incapable of) the study of Logic. That isn't my line.' For that would be to announce indifference not merely to rational order, but also to the very attribute which may be said to give its human value to life,—that is (1) its 'Sense' and sense-power in every sense from the biological to the logical, (2) its intention, conscious and increasingly definite and rational, which we call 'Meaning' and (profess to) use language to express, (3) its Significance, its bearing upon, its place among, its interpretation of, all other cosmical facts. To be thus indifferent, indeed, would be to stultify not only every word they said but all the activities of their life. And then, in our expressive English idiom, nothing to them would signify at all, and they would not signify either!

You have observed that I have made no attempt at formal definition of the 'triad of signification'. It seemed better to state it vaguely in as many ways as possible first (as e.g. the

---

3. Giovanni Vailati (1863-1909), Italian mathematician, logician, and pragmatic philosopher.

above) in order that the very inconsistencies, apparent or real, between them, may be suggestive of the need of systematic study, and the rewards that this must bring.

With regard to the relation between the triad I suggest and that of Hegel (also that of Comte) I may say that long before I knew anything about Hegel, I was asking myself why my thinking, when I tried to make it clear, fell naturally into triads. Then I looked round and found more or less the same tendency everywhere. At first therefore I was inclined to think that Hegel had got what the French call 'le mot de l'énigme'. But the more I studied all that could be read of his in English, and the comments of his followers, the deeper was my disappointment.

I must not inflict more upon you and will only just say, therefore, that I fully realize "how deep the knife would have to go into the body of speech to make it really scientific". And that is why I urge that a new generation must be trained from the first to focus its attention on the point of the cardinal importance of Sense, Meaning and Significance, and of classifying and verifying what we broadly call analogy. It may be then that we shall find the needed advances silently, unconsciously, naturally coming about; and that our descendants will only realize the greatness of their gain by comparison with our present welter of inexpressiveness and our really shameful content with, if not creation of, linguistic pitfalls.

May I send you also a typed copy, when finished, of my Note on Mr. Russell's work? It would indicate some aspects of my own subject which I have not been able to bring forward. Meanwhile I venture to enclose a Note which was suggested to me by one of the newest of the physical triads.

You will I know excuse its defects in view of the great difficulty, in such cases, of choosing irreproachable and unambiguous language.

With renewed and respectful thanks

> I am yours most faithfully
> Victoria Welby

Since writing this I have been reading an article on 'The revelations of radium' in the Edinburgh Review[4] for October. There I find the triad of rays described as 1. atomic, 2. cathodic 3. etherial–this almost strangely corresponds with my own primitive triadic ideas.

---

4. *Edinburgh Review*, Vol. 198, October, 1903.

[Postcard, postmarked Milford, Pa., Nov 29 7PM 1903.]

I was so afraid of extending unduly my already long letter that I left out something I now venture to add. As I am now preparing for a second edition of 'W. is M.?' May I ask if you would add to your kindness by indicating (even on a post-card) those parts of the book which you would consider especially weak?

I might in some cases at least be able either to suppress or to strengthen them.

I am especially glad of your endorsement of my view of the 'primitive mind'.[1]

V. Welby

Harrow–England
Nov 20 1903

---

1. See Appendix A.

6 Prescott Hall, Cambridge, Mass.
1903 Dec. 1

My dear Lady Victoria:

I receive this morning your deeply interesting letter of Nov. 18, being here delivering some lectures of which I enclose a list.[1] As soon as I get back to Pike County whither I intend

---

1. Peirce had prepared an eight-part outline for his Lowell Lectures (see Robin, Ms. 470). The titles of the eight lectures given were: I. What Makes a Reasoning Sound?; II. A System of Diagrams for Studying Logical Relations; III. The Three Universal Categories and their Utility; IV. Exposition of the System of Diagrams Completed; V. The Doctrine of Multitude, Infinity and Continuity; VI. What is Chance?; VII. Induction as Doing, not mere Cogitation; VIII. How to Theorize. See Burks, "Bibliography," G-1903-2.

to start on the night of Dec. 17 (though I may be detained) I mean to hunt up a solitary copy which I think I possess of my original paper on the three categories published in the Proceedings of the American Academy of Arts and Sciences (Boston) for 1867 May 14;[2] for I perceive that it will interest you. So you shall have the last copy. I will also get a part of what I said at my lecture last night on the subject type-written & send that. I mean also to load you with a Syllabus of some parts of logic which I am now getting printed. For all these relate to triads, & I am confident they will interest you.

As to Bertrand Russell's book,[3] I have as yet made but a slight examination of it; but it is sufficient to show me that whatever merit it may have as a digest of what others have done, it is pretentious & pedantic,—attributing to its author merit that cannot be accorded to him. Your ladyship perhaps did not notice that I hinted at this in the *Nation*, in saying your book was such a contrast to his. *The* man is Dr. Georg Cantor.[4] Besides his strictly mathematical presentations, there is an interesting set of letters by him to philosophers in the Zeitschrift für Phil. u. phil. Kritik for 1890.[5] I am myself working on the doctrine of multitude & that is one reason why I have not read what Whitehead & Russell have written. I dont want my own train of thought shunted for the present.

You may remark that not only do triads turn up in abundance in all sorts of *true* doctrines, but they are even more abundant in *false* ones, so that we must always suspect a triad to be of subjective provenance until it can show positive credentials.

It seems to me that the objections that have been made to my word 'pragmatism' are very trifling. It is the doctrine that

---

2. C. S. Peirce, "On A New List of Categories," *Proceedings of the American Academy of Arts and Sciences*, Vol. 7 (May 1867), pp. 287-289. Reprinted in *Collected Papers*, 1.545-567.

3. See Appendix A.

4. Georg Cantor (1845-1918), mathematician, logician, and founder of set theory.

5. Published in *Zeitschrift für Philosophie und philosophische Kritik* for 1887 and 1888 as "Mitteilungen zur Lehre von Transfiniten."

truth consists in future serviceableness for our ends. 'Pragmatism' seems to me to express this. I might have called it 'practism', or 'practicism' πρακτικός being rather more classical than πραγματικός, but pragmatism is more sonorous.

My heart always warms toward the very few who do not think themselves deeply aggrieved by my notices of their books; but I have a much more deeply-seated sympathy with your ladyship & with your ideas.

Believe me

very faithfully yours
C. S. Peirce

6 Prescott Hall Cambridge Mass.
1903 Dec. 1

My dear Lady Victoria:

Since I wrote this morning your post-card comes. No letter from you, I beg you to believe, could be too long, especially if it has in view the more forcible presentation of your recommendations. But at this moment I have not your volume at hand & besides am driven by these lectures twice a week. Therefore, I can only be vague now. But if you could delay for a few weeks, I would gladly make some suggestions as to mitigating your insistence on some points; and besides, I should not wonder if you could get some positive suggestions from the Syllabus I am printing. If so, I beg you will appropriate whatever may be useful, & a general acknowledgment of aid will be more than sufficient. I shouldn't want you to do even that unless you were decidedly moved to do so.

I did not say that any parts of your book were weak, but only that some minds might think them so. What I meant was this. The greatest analyst of thought that ever lived might spend an indefinite amount of time in endeavoring to express his ideas with perfect accuracy. Expression and thought are one. It would be time & energy spent in making his thoughts themselves perfectly distinct. But he never would perfectly succeed. He would only make his thoughts so involved that they would not be apprehended. I think your extreme insistence on accuracy of metaphor,—say about the expression "coining a word,"—might well be tempered, without really yielding any point. I fully and heartily agree that the study of what we mean ought to be the—how shall I express it so as not to offend your fastidious requirements?—ought to be [the] general purpose of a liberal education, as distinguished from special education,—of that education which should be required of everybody with whose society & conversation we are expected to be content. But, then, perfect accuracy of thought is unattainable,—*theoretically unattainable*. And undue striving for it is worse than time wasted. It positively renders thought unclear. This very summer I rejected over a hundred consecutive pages of my MS., most painfully & slowly made, simply because it was too elaborated. After all we want to get our thought expressed in short metre somehow. But I will write you further as soon as I can be more definite. I am glad you liked what I said about your view of the primitive mind. I noticed your ladyship had omitted all reference to that in your letter, & thought perhaps you were not satisfied with what I said. It seems to me, as I said, a good introduction to *you.*

> very faithfully
> C. S. Peirce

I brought along with me an old number of The Monist in order to read an article of yours that it contains.[1] I haven't yet had the time. I don't believe I shall ever cross the water again, & shall not have the pleasure of seeing you; but it would be a great delight to me if I could have a photograph of your ladyship.

I am going to send a type-written bit of my last night's lecture as soon as I can get it done. We say "type-written"

---

1. V. Welby, "Meaning and Metaphor," *The Monist*, Vol. 3 ns, No. 4 (July 1893), pp. 510-525.

here; but your "typed" is better. Ours sounds like a German word. There is too much German influence in this country, in every way. Their subjectivism is detestable & antipragmatical.

6 Prescott Hall, Cambridge, Mass.
1903 Dec. 4

My dear Lady Victoria:

I enclose you a piece of the Syllabus, of which I wrote you. There will be a good deal more of it, if I can raise the money to pay the printer. It has been written hurriedly at different times, and the bits sent to the printer without my retaining any copy or receiving any proof. Hence there are several misprints and two or three formal inconsistencies of statement. I send it, however, believing that a part of it, at least, may interest your ladyship. I remain

very truly yours
C. S. Peirce

[Postcard]

I have three kind letters to thank you for but have been rather severely ill and even now cannot write more than this—

Your last letter (Dec 4) had *no* Syllabus in it, so I am still hoping for it as doubtless it was accidentally omitted.

I will write as soon as I can. Excuse this.

V. Welby

Harrow. England
Dec 17 1903

I send this to Milford as your Lectures[1] will be over. Their titles on the Ticket sound most interesting to me, especially the three last.[2]

---

1. The Lowell Lectures.
2. These three topics were to be: What is Chance?; Induction as Doing, not mere Cognition; How to Theorize.

Duneaves, Harrow
December 22nd. 1903

My dear Dr. Peirce

Since sending off my last postcard (while still severely unwell) I have safely received your interesting Syllabus, though not the other documents you kindly promised. I must again express my gratitude for your generous appreciation and the trouble you have taken to help and encourage one somewhat burdened by the sense of the generally ignored importance of her thesis and of her personal unfitness to raise such a question as the need for 'Significs'.

Before I say more, may I confess that in signing my book 'V. Welby' I hoped to get rid as far as possible of the irrelevant associations of my unlucky title? I am called 'V. Lady Welby' merely to distinguish me from my son's wife, now Lady Welby; which is a custom of ours. Thus I have no right to be called Lady Victoria Welby. I explained this to Prof. Baldwin[1] but like many others he forgot to correct the name. You will understand my desire to be known as simply as possible though I cannot altogether ignore the 'Hon.' conferred upon me as Maid of Honour to the late Queen. But the only honour I value is that of being treated by workers as a serious worker.

As I am now speaking personally I may perhaps mention that I never had any education whatever in the conventional sense of the term. Instead of that I travelled with my mother over a great part of the world under circumstances of difficulty and even hardship. The present facilities did not then exist! This I think accounts in some degree for my seeing things in a somewhat independent way. But the absence of any systematic mental training must be allowed for of course in any estimate of work done. These peculiar circumstances have suggested to me very strongly that the average ability of

---

1. James Mark Baldwin (1861-1934), American psychologist, founder of *Psychological Review* and editor of *Dictionary of Philosophy and Psychology*.

man in early childhood is higher than we suppose; and that the problem before us is how to preserve the freshness and penetration of the child's mind while supplying the—mainly logical—training, the lack of which is so great a disadvantage. But I only allude to the unusual conditions of my childhood in order partly to account for my way of looking at and putting things: and my very point is that any value in it is impersonal. It suggests an ignored heritage, an unexplored mine. This I have tried to indicate in 'What is Meaning?'

With regard to Mr. Russell of course my interest in any such work simply arises from its presentation in non-technical form of those points in advanced modern mathematics which affect philosophical thinking and supply a translation into logical language (as much of your writing seems to do) of some of my own vague ideas. Thus I ignore any pretentiousness, pedantry, claiming of merit, &c. I could see e.g. through all that, what the eminence of Dr. Cantor must be. How I wish I could read his letters to philosophers!

With regard to the triads, I am quite aware that error may take a triadic form and thus indeed put on a specious value. That seems to me an additional reason why the subject should be brought forward. I have hesitated long whether to send you enclosed proof of a sadly incoherent attempt to deal with triadism, and to use it as a mode of expression or as an expressive order. You will however easily gather its general sense. I wish some competent mind would take up the subject on a really broad basis. For apparently the same tendency to a triadic order is found objectively in physical and biological phenomena. I have been much struck with this in my rather extensive scientific reading and was surprised to find that no one seemed to notice it.

I welcome with gratitude your 'profession of faith' on the ethics of terminology[2] —a sadly neglected subject. It will be of the greatest value to me and I hope I may use it in a second edition of 'What is Meaning?'

---

2. From Peirce's "Syllabus." Also reprinted in *Collected Papers*, 2.219-2.226.

May I say in conclusion that I see strongly how much we have lost and are losing by the barrier which we set up between emotion and intellect, between feeling and reasoning. Distinction must of course remain. I am the last person to wish this blurred. But I should like to put it thus: The difference e.g. between our highest standards of love and the animal's is that they imply knowledge in logical order. We know *that, what, how* and above all, *why* we love. Thus the logic is bound up in that very feeling which we contrast with it. But while in our eyes logic is merely 'formal', merely structural, merely question of argument, 'cold and hard', we need a word which shall express the combination of 'logic and love'. And this I have tried to supply in 'Significs'.

I have much more to say but am able to do very little just now and besides must not overtax your patience. Some day I will ask you to look at a suggestion of mine regarding the status of *time*[3] which has apparently never yet been made. Dr. Stout[4] and others find the point interesting and important, but I am afraid of not doing it justice. You may know of some student who could take up this apparently 'dropped thread'. I shall venture also presently to offer some notes on a work ('The Teaching of Elementary Mathematics' by D. Eugene Smith)[5] which has just been recommended to me and has greatly interested me.

But now, with all good wishes of the season I must end what I fear is a rambling letter.

Yours most truly
Victoria Welby

------

3. Formalized by Lady Welby as "Time As Derivative," *Mind*, Vol. XVI, 1907, pp. 383-400. See also a note: V. Welby, "Mr. McTaggart on the Unreality of Time," *Mind*, Vol. XVIII ns, 1909, pp. 326-328.

4. George Frederick Stout (1860-1944), British philosopher and psychologist; author of *Analytic Psychology* (1896), *Manual of Psychology* (1898), and *Studies in Philosophy and Psychology* (1930). Editor of *Mind* (1891-1920).

5. For Peirce's review of David Eugene Smith's *The Teaching of Elementary Mathematics* see *The Nation*, 70 (22 March 1900), 230.

I must just add that of course there is no question of publishing the slip I send at least in its present form. It was only printed then for private comment, a good many years ago.

March 20th 1904
Duneaves, Harrow

Dear Mr. Peirce—(you have never told me whether I ought or ought not call you Dr.?)—

In your last kind letters (of Dec 1. & 4 1903) you allowed me to hope that I would hear again from you and perhaps receive a further instalment of your very interesting Syllabus of lectures on logic.

I hope your silence is not caused by illness. I must not trouble you further till I know this, but I am now anxious to know whether I have your permission to quote from the section called 'Ethics of Terminology' as it seems to me of great value. I am proposing to include it in an Essay on Sociological Significs, one of a series now being arranged for. Parts of this may I hope be of some interest to you as I have endeavoured to put my position with increased clearness.

Hoping to see more of your work and to hear that you are well, I am yours most truly

Victoria Welby

Milford Pa.
1904 April 10

My dear Lady Welby:

I received your ladyship's photograph last night & put it on my study mantelpiece among the very small number of those friends whose faces I love to look at, and I am sure there will be none that will do me more solid good than your bright & good face. The reason I have not written for so long is that my dear wife has been very ill & for five weeks I hardly left her bedside & even now that she is up, I am continually worried about her too great energy, besides being myself in a state of nervous fatigue with it all. It was the most terrible winter & great floods in the autumn & spring carried away all our bridges & then the ferries that were substituted (with the loss of a number of lives of acquaintances) & we had no way of getting coal. So that this house which has always been delightful in winter as well as in summer had to be heated by wood burnt in open fireplaces.

I *very often* wished to write to you during my wife's illness; but I was unwilling to do so without explaining my exceptional dependence upon her & in order to do that I should have had to tell the whole story of my life, which I had no time for, nor have I now. But I will mention that she is much younger than I, is a Frenchwoman, (knew no English when we were married) and is a person whom all men reverence & all women love & of whom it is impossible to tire. If I were to lose her, as I feared I should, & am not yet quite reassured, it would be the end of me. If we can only sell this place, I will take her travelling for a year.

I beg you will make any use you can of anything I have written or can write for you. I shall be greatly pleased. The reason I did not send more of my syllabus was that after a few very dry pages the money suddenly gave out quite unexpectedly to me & I did not think the rest worth sending. I will enclose something I wrote about the Metric System[1] & something about the French Academy of Sciences,[2] the latter printed from a MS I had not intended for printers copy & without my having an opportunity to correct the proofs so that it is full of misprints.

very faithfully
C. S. Peirce

---

1. "The Metric Fallacy," a review by Peirce of *The Metric Fallacy*, by Frederick A. Halsey, and *The Metric Failure in the Textile Industry*, by Samuel S. Dale, *The Nation*, 78 (17 March 1904), 215-216.

2. C. S. Peirce, "French Academy of Science," *New York Evening Post*, 5 March 1904.

April 22, 1904

My dear Mr. Peirce[1]

I must write at once to tell you how glad I was to hear from you again, as I had rather feared that illness might be one cause for silence. And now you must let me offer you an experienced sympathy with your present anxiety. I can enter into all you say so well and only wish there were hope of my knowing Mrs Peirce as well as yourself. Your description reminds me somewhat of my dear friend Mrs Tyndall of whom indeed the professor used to speak, as well he might, in those terms. I can only say I hope that all will now go well and your anxiety be relieved.

Many thanks also for the two interesting Papers. I cannot of course express any opinions on the technical side of the 'weights and measures' question. But you will understand that my interest would naturally lie on the side of a universal system of symbol in commerce, like that in mathematics. Also I should be inclined to favor anything that tended in the direction of 'interconversion,' an excellent word I had not seen before and which expresses part of my aim better than 'intertranslation.'

Also I have long seen that our retention of *ten* is pure conservatism. It has been clear to me that 'we virtually put to the balance a series of questions answerable by yes and no,' so that it is important to be able to bisect all the possibilities, whereas at present we are tolerating a harmful loss of time and energy. And I am afraid to think that an endeavour to rectify this radical blunder is only 'sheer insanity' because we assume much more rectification to be impossible. I believe that if even one generation were brought up from the first in the assurance that no desirable and really progressive reform was impossible or even unduly difficult to a trained and fully developed social will, the result in utilizing the latent poten-

---

1. This letter was not in Peirce's correspondence. An edited version of the letter was published in *Other Dimensions*. A complete draft of the letter is, however, in Lady Welby's correspondence.

cies of man would be amazing and seem at first miraculous. I do not know if you have considered this matter from the physiological and psychological side? I will not say more today but will wait till things brighten for you.

Yours most faithfully
V. Welby

P.O. Milford Pa.
1904 May 7

My dear Lady Welby:

Thank you for your sympathetic & considerate note. My wife is better & my *immediate* anxiety is relieved; but she remains weak, & without her indomitable energy would be crawling about an invalid; while the trial has aged me,—for the time being, at any rate,—and I am able to accomplish little.

Nevertheless, I have actually written your ladyship a letter that weighs 5 oz. But I shall not bore you with it, but will just say that your note developes this difference between us, that you are a rationalistic radical, while I am a conservative on rationalistic & experiential grounds.

In the first place, I insist, before favoring any extensive change, upon evaluating, as well as I can, the cost of it, on the one hand, and the *present value* (as we speak of the present value of an annuity) of all the good it would do, on the other.[1]

Moreover, it is necessary to take into consideration the fact that we never can foresee all the consequences of a great change, and that some of its consequences are sure to be corrupting. (I may note that Americans are mostly great conservatives.) Reason blunders so very frequently that in practical matters we must rely on instinct & subconscious operations of the mind, as much as possible, in order to succeed. Thus, in my logic there is a great gulf between the methods proper to practical and to theoretical question, in

---

1. See *Collected Papers*, 1.122-125.

which latter I will not allow instinct, "natural" reason, etc. to have any voice at all.[2]

Besides all these considerations which apply to all reforms, in regard to proposals for changing modes of expression it has to be remembered that the past cannot be reformed; and consequently, its memory and records subsisting still, no prevalent mode of expression can be annihilated. The most you can do is to introduce an *additional* way of expressing the same meaning. Now the multiplication of equivalent modes of expression is itself a burden. You speak as if the abandonment of decimal numerations were a reasonable object of endeavor. Well, the only way to get rid of it would be to persuade the human race to set a day when we should all commit suicide & so leave room for the evolution of a new race of rational animals who might adopt some other base of numeration, & might not. There are some evils that, once embraced, had better be adhered to.

very very faithfully
C. S. Peirce

----

2. See *Collected Papers*, 1.616-677.

June 29th 1904
Duneaves, Harrow

My dear Mr Peirce

I did not want to answer your last kind and interesting letter until I could do so after full consideration of its contents. And this, from exceptional pressure of work (connected with the founding of a Sociological Society which I hope will eventually join forces with the American one) has hitherto been impossible. Indeed even now I can not write you a worthy answer. I am very sorry that you did not send me that other letter that weighs 5 oz.! It would have been fully appreciated. May I not still hope for it? I can't help a little regretting that such a thinker as you should describe a difference between you and me as consisting of my being a rationalist or radical while you are conservative on rationalistic & experiential grounds. For while in a narrow or conventional sense I am neither the one nor the other, in a deeper and more ultimate sense I am both. Meanwhile if there be a leaning rather to one than to the other, the racial motherhood in me as in every woman ensures its being the conservative. Only the question remains, Conservative of what? Of the antiquated, the obsolete, the effete? Of the once fitting, now misfitting? Of the once congruous, now incongruous? Of the once workable, now unworkable? Of that which once promoted growth and development and now stunts, backens, withers it?

I venture to enclose a brief and closely compressed Paper which I was asked to contribute to the discussion on Mr Galton's momentous Lecture on Eugenics[1] (well reviewed I am glad to see in the 'Nation'). You will there see my interpretation of your statement that "reason blunders so very frequently that in practical matters we must rely on instinct and subconscious operations of the mind as much as possible, in order to succeed." But in *my* logic (if you will allow me any!) I see no great gulf, but only a useful distinction between methods proper to practical and theoretical questions. So then 'Never confound, and never divide' is in these matters my motto. And I had gathered, I hope not quite mistakenly, that you also saw the disastrous result of digging gulfs to *separate* when it was really a question of *distinction*,—as sharp and clear as you like. I am glad to have received a warm welcome for my poor little Paper from those who are the deepest students of biology, heredity, and the psychology of sex. For it gives me fresh hope that when the subject finds itself in more competent hands than mine can be, we shall gain fresh light from making a fresh start in a fresh direction, and thus instead of flinging over or ignoring the 'past' become

1. Sir Francis Galton, *Hereditary Genius: An Inquiry into Its Laws and Consequences*, Macmillan & Co., 1892. This work is reviewed in *The Nation*, 56 (6 April 1893), 260.

better able to interpret inherited treasures of racial wisdom common to us all.

I cannot resist enclosing an extract from a letter received only this morning from Prof. Poulton,[2] who is much more than an entomologist and would certainly tolerate no utterance which was not true to such knowledge as we have of the history of the race.

I hope both you and Mrs Peirce are feeling better than when you last wrote. You will I hope be enjoying a thorough change in this beautiful summer time; it is many years since I have seen so perfect a spring and early summer in this country.

But I hope that this will be forwarded, and that sometime I may hear from you again.

Believe me yours most truly
Victoria Welby

------

2. Sir Edward Bagnall Poulton (1856-1943), British zoologist and professor at Oxford; author of *The Colours of Animals* (1890), *Charles Darwin and the Theory of Natural Selection* (1896), and *Essays on Evolution* (1908).

P.O. Milford Pa.
1904 Oct. 12

My dear Lady Welby:

Not a day has passed since I received your last letter that I have not lamented the circumstances that prevented me from writing that very day the letter that I was intent upon writing to you, nor without my promising myself that it should soon be done. But living in the country on this side of the Atlantic, unless one is a multimillionaire is attended with great friction. Though it is done more of late years, it is not yet a usual thing, and in this country one is expected to be just like everybody else. I will venture to say that your imagination could not compass the picture of the sort of domestic servant that an American girl makes. Then too an inconsiderate contract I entered into to get certain definitions for a supplement to the Century Dictionary ready by a certain time drives me like the furies. To be sure I might have scribbled a line to explain myself; but I was always telling myself that in a very few days I should get time to write as I desired, until now my idea of what it was I wanted to write is blurred. I hope, however, that you will have had faith to know that only an impossibility could have prevented my writing; for from one who lives in the country one may hope for more of that sort of faith than from a *citadin*.

For one thing, I wanted to express my surprise at finding you rather repelled the designation of a "rationalist," and said that as a woman you were naturally conservative. Of course, the lady of the house is usually the minister of foreign affairs (barring those of money and law) and as an accomplished diplomat is careful and conservative. But when a woman takes up an idea my experience is that she does so with a singleness of heart that distinguishes her. Some of my very best friends have been very radical women. I do not know that I dont think your recommending a serious consideration of changing the base of numeration is a bit radical.

But I wanted to write to you about signs, which in your opinion and mine are matters of so much concern. More in mine, I think, than in yours. For in mine, the highest grade of reality is only reached by signs; that is by such ideas as those of Truth and Right and the rest.[1] It sounds paradoxical; but when I have devolved to you my whole theory of signs, it will seem less so. I think that I will today explain the outlines of my classification of signs.

You know that I particularly approve of inventing new words for new ideas. I do not know that the study I call *Ideoscopy*[2] can be called a new idea, but the word *Phenom-*

---

1. See *Collected Papers*, 5.283-309.
2. Elsewhere called by Peirce "phenomenology." Not to be confused with Idioscopy. See *Collected Papers*, 1.183-202. For the chronology of names for phenomenology see Herbert Spiegelberg, "Husserl's and Peirce's Phenomenologies: Coincidence or Interaction," *Philosophy and Phenomenological Research*, Vol. 17 (1956), pp. 164-185.

enology is used in a different sense. *Ideoscopy* consists in describing and classifying the ideas that belong to ordinary experience or that naturally arise in connection with ordinary life, without regard to their being valid or invalid or to their psychology.[3] In pursuing this study I was long ago (1867) led, after only three or four years' study, to throw all ideas into the three classes of Firstness, of Secondness, and of Thirdness.[4] This sort of notion is as distasteful to me as to anybody; and for years, I endeavored to pooh-pooh and refute it; but it long ago conquered me completely. Disagreeable as it is to attribute such meaning to numbers, & to a triad above all, it is as true as it is disagreeable. The ideas of Firstness, Secondness, and Thirdness are simple enough. Giving to being the broadest possible sense, to include ideas as well as things, and ideas that we fancy we have just as much as ideas as we do have, I should define Firstness, Secondness, and Thirdness thus:

Firstness is the mode of being of that which is such as it is, positively and without reference to anything else.

Secondness is the mode of being of that which is such as it is, with respect to a second but regardless of any third.

Thirdness is the mode of being of that which is such as it is, in bringing a second and third into relation to each other.

I call these three ideas the cenopythagorean categories.[5]

The typical ideas of firstness are qualities of feeling, or mere appearances. The scarlet of your royal liveries, the quality itself, independently of its being perceived or remembered, is an example, by which I do not mean that you are to imagine that you *do not* perceive or remember it, but that you are to drop out of account that which may be attached to it in perceiving or in remembering, but which does not belong to the quality. For example, when you remember it, your idea is said to be *dim* and when it is before your eyes, it

---

3. See *Collected Papers*, 1.284.
4. See *Collected Papers*, 1.545-567.
5. For a comprehensive analysis of these categories, see *Collected Papers*, 1.141-353.

is *vivid*. But dimness or vividness do not belong to your idea of the quality. They *might* no doubt, if considered simply as a feeling; but when you think of vividness, you do not consider it from that point of view. You think of it as a degree of disturbance of your consciousness. The quality of red is not thought of as belonging to you, or as attached to liveries. It is simply a peculiar positive possibility regardless of anything else. If you ask a mineralogist what hardness is, he will say that it is what one predicates of a body that one cannot scratch with a knife. But a simple person will think of hardness as a simple positive possibility the *realization* of which causes a body to be like flint. That idea of hardness is an idea of Firstness. The unanalyzed total impression made by any manifold not thought of as actual fact, but simply as a quality, as simple positive possibility of appearance is an idea of Firstness. Notice the *naïveté* of Firstness. The cenopythagorean categories are doubtless another attempt to characterize what Hegel sought to characterize as his three stages of thought. They correspond to the three categories of each of the four triads of Kant's table. But the fact that these different attempts were independent of one another (the resemblance of these Categories to Hegel's stages was not remarked for many years after the list had been under study, owing to my antipathy to Hegel) only goes to show that there really are three such elements. The idea of the present instant, which, whether it exists or not, is naturally thought as a point of time in which no thought can take place or any detail be separated, is an idea of Firstness.

The type of an idea of Secondness is the experience of effort, prescinded from the idea of a purpose. It may be said that there is no such experience, that a purpose is always in view as long as the effort is cognized. This may be open to doubt; for in sustained effort we soon let the purpose drop out of view. However, I abstain from psychology which has nothing to do with ideoscopy. The existence of the word *effort* is sufficient proof that people think they have such an idea; and that is enough. The experience of effort cannot exist without the experience of resistence. Effort only is effort by virtue of its being opposed; and no third element enters. Note that I speak of the *experience*, not of the *feeling*, of effort. Imagine yourself to be seated alone at night in the basket of a balloon, far above earth, calmly enjoying the absolute calm and stillness. Suddenly the piercing shriek of a steam-whistle breaks upon you, and continues for a good while. The impression of stillness was an idea of Firstness, a quality of feeling. The piercing whistle does not allow you to think or do anything but suffer. So that too is absolutely simple. Another Firstness. But the breaking of the silence by the noise was an experience. The person in his inertness identifies himself with the precedent state of feeling, and the new feeling which comes in spite of him is the non-ego. He has a two sided consciousness of an ego and a non-ego. That consciousness of the action of a new feeling in destroying the old feeling is what I call an experience. Experience generally is what the course of life has *compelled* me to think. Second-ness is either *genuine* or *degenerate*. There are many degrees of genuineness. Generally speaking genuine secondness consists in one thing acting upon another,—brute action. I say brute, because so far as the idea of any *law* or *reason* comes in, Thirdness comes in. When a stone falls to the ground, the law of gravitation does not act to make it fall. The law of gravitation is the judge upon the bench who may pronounce the law till doomsday, but unless the strong arm of the law, the brutal sheriff, gives effect to the law, it amounts to nothing. True, the judge can create a sheriff if need be; but he must have one. The stone's actually falling is purely the affair of the stone and the earth at the time. This is a case of *reaction*. So is *existence* which is the mode of being of that which reacts with other things. But there is also action with-out reaction. *Such is the action of the previous upon the subsequent.*[6] It is a difficult question whether the idea of this

---

6. The italicized sentence is, in manuscript, underlined in pencil. Perhaps it was underlined by Lady Welby, yet it was not her habit to annotate Peirce's letters.

one-sided determination is a pure idea of secondness or whether it involves thirdness. At present, the former view seems to me correct. I suppose that when Kant made Time a form of the internal sense alone, he was influenced by some such considerations as the following. The relation between the previous and the subsequent consists in the previous being determinate and fixed for the subsequent, and the subsequent being indeterminate for the previous. But indeterminacy belongs only to ideas; the existent is determinate in every respect; and this is just what the law of causation consists in. Accordingly, the relation of time concerns only ideas. It may also be argued that, according to the law of the conservation of energy, there is nothing in the physical universe corresponding to our idea that the previous determines the subsequent in any way in which the subsequent does not determine the previous. For, according to that law, all that happens in the physical universe consists in the exchange of just so much *vis viva* $\frac{1}{2}m \left(\frac{ds}{dt}\right)^2$ for so much displacement. Now the square of a negative quantity being positive, it follows that if all the velocities were reversed at any instant, everything would go on just the same, only time going backward as it were. Everything that had happened would happen again in reverse order. These seem to me to be strong arguments to prove that temporal causation (a very different thing from physical dynamic action) is an action upon ideas and not upon existents. But since our idea of the past is precisely the idea of that which is absolutely determinate, fixed, *fait accompli*, and dead, as against the future which is living, plastic, and determinable, it appears to me that the idea of one sided action, in so far as it concerns the being of the determinate, is a pure idea of Secondness; and I think that great errors of metaphysics are due to looking at the future as something that will have been past. I cannot admit that the idea of the future can be so translated into the Secundal ideas of the past. To say that a given kind of event never will happen is to deny that there is any date at which its happening will be past; but it is not equivalent to any affirmation about a past relative to any assignable date. When we pass from the idea of an event to saying that it never will happen, or will happen in endless repetition, or introduce in any way the idea of endless repetition, I will say the idea is *mellonized* (μέλλων, about to be, do, or suffer). When I conceive a fact as acting but not capable of being acted upon, I will say that it is *parelélythose* (παρεληλυθώς, past) and the mode of being which consists in such action I will call *parelelythosiné* (-ine= εἶναι, being) I regard the former as an idea of Thirdness, the latter as an idea of Secondness. I consider the idea of any dyadic relation not involving any third as an idea of Secondness; and I should not call any completely degenerate except the relation of identity. But similarity which is the only possible identity of Firsts is very near to that. Dyadic relations have been classified by me in a great variety of ways; but the most important are first with regard to the nature of the Second in itself and second with regard to the nature of its first.[7] The Second, or *Relate*[8] is, in itself, either a *Referate* if it is intrinsically a possibility, such as a quality or it is a *Rerelate* if it is of its own nature an Existent. In respect to its first, the Second is divisible either in regard to the dynamic first or to the immediate first. In regard to its dynamic first, a Second is determined either by virtue of its own intrinsic nature, or by virtue of a real relation to that second (an action). Its immediate second is either a Quality or an Existent.

I now come to Thirdness. To me, who have for forty years considered the matter from every point of view that I could discover, the inadequacy of Secondness to cover all that is in our minds is so evident that I scarce know how to begin to persuade any person of it who is not already convinced of it. Yet I see a great many thinkers who are trying to construct a system without putting any thirdness into it. Among them are some of my best friends who acknowledge themselves indebted to me for ideas but have never learned the principal

7. See *Collected Papers*, 3.571-608.
8. 'Relate', in manuscript, is underlined in pencil, hence perhaps by Lady Welby.

lesson. Very well. It is highly proper that Secondness should be searched to its very bottom. Thus only can the indispensibleness and irreducibility of thirdness be made out, although for him who has the mind to grasp it, it is sufficient to say that no branching of a line can result from putting one line on the end of another.[9] My friend Schröder fell in love with my algebra of dyadic relations. The few pages I gave to it in my Note B in the 'Studies in Logic by Members of the Johns Hopkins University' were proportionate to its importance.[10] His book[11] is profound, but its profundity only makes it more clear that Secondness cannot compass Thirdness (He is careful to avoid ever saying that it can, but he does go so far as to say that Secondness is the more important. So it is, considering that Thirdness cannot be understood without Secondness. But as to its applications, it is so inferior to Thirdness as to be in that aspect quite in a different world.) Even in the most degenerate form of Thirdness, and thirdness has two grades of degeneracy, something may be detected which is not mere secondness. If you take any ordinary triadic relation, you will always find a *mental* element in it. Brute action is secondness, any mentality involves thirdness. Analyze for instance the relation involved in 'A gives B to C'. Now what is giving? It does not consist in A's putting B away from him and C's subsequently taking B up. It is not necessary that any material transfer should take place. It consists in A's making C the possessor according to *Law*. There must be some kind of law before there can be any kind of giving,—be it but the law of the strongest. But now suppose that giving *did* consist merely in A's laying down the B which C subse-

---

9. See *Collected Papers*, 1.346-349.

10. *Johns Hopkins Studies in Logic*, ed. C. S. Peirce, Little, Brown, & Co., Boston, 1883. Peirce's "Note B" is on pp. 187-203. Reprinted as *Collected Papers*, 3.571-608.

11. Ernst Schröder, *Vorlesungen über die Algebra der Logik*, B. G. Teubner, Leipzig, 1890. For Peirce's reviews of this work see *The Nation* 53 (13 Aug. 1891), 129; 62 (23 April 1896), 330-332; and *The Monist*: "The Regenerated Logic," Vol. 7 (1896), pp. 19-40; "The Logic of Relatives," Vol. 7 (1897), pp. 161-217. *The Monist* reviews are reprinted in *Collected Papers*, 3.425-552.

quently picks up. That would be a degenerate form of Thirdness in which the thirdness is externally appended. In A's
putting away B, there is no thirdness. In C's taking B, there is
no thirdness. But if you say that these two acts constitute a
single operation by virtue of the identity of the B, you
transcend the mere brute fact, you introduce a mental element. As to my algebra of dyadic relations, Russell in his
book[12] which is superficial to nauseating me, has some silly
remarks, about my "relative addition" etc. which are mere
nonsense.[13] He says, or Whitehead says, that the need for it
seldom occurs. The need for it *never* occurs if you bring in
the same mode of connection in another way. It is part of a
system which does not bring in that mode of connection in
any other way. In that system, it is indispensible. But let us
leave Russell and Whitehead to work out their own salvation.
The criticism which I make on that algebra of dyadic relations, with which I am by no means in love, though I think it
is a pretty thing, is that the very triadic relations which it
does not recognize it does itself employ. For every combination of relatives to make a new relative is a triadic relation
irreducible to dyadic relations. Its *inadequacy* is shown in
other ways, but in this way it is in a conflict with itself *if it
be regarded*, as I never did regard it, *as sufficient for the
expression of all relations*. My universal algebra of relations,
with the subjacent indices and Σ and Π is susceptible of being
enlarged so as to comprise everything and so, still better,
though not to ideal perfection, is the system of *existential
graphs*.[14] I have not sufficiently applied myself to the study

---

12. Bertrand Russell, *The Principles of Mathematics*. See Appendix A.

13. The passage referred to, from page 24 of Russell's book, is as
follows: "Peirce and Schröder have realized the great importance of the
subject, but unfortunately their methods, being based, not on Peano,
but on the older Symbolic Logic derived (with modifications) from
Boole, are so cumbrous and difficult that most of the applications which
ought to be made are practically not feasible."

14. See *Collected Papers*, 4.347-584. For a recent study of Peirce's
existential graphs see Don D. Roberts, *The Existential Graphs of Charles
S. Peirce* (The Hague: Mouton, 1973).

of the degenerate forms of Thirdness, though I think I see that it has two distinct grades of degeneracy. In its genuine form, Thirdness is the triadic relation existing between a sign, its object, and the interpreting thought, itself a sign, considered as constituting the mode of being a sign. A sign mediates between the *interpretant* sign and its object. Taking sign in its broadest sense, its interpretant is not necessarily a sign. Any concept is a sign, of course. Ockham, Hobbes, and Leibniz have sufficiently said that. But we may take a sign in so broad a sense that the interpretant of it is not a thought, but an action or experience, or we may even so enlarge the meaning of sign that its interpretant is a mere quality of feeling. A *Third* is something which brings a First into relation to a Second. A sign is a sort of Third. How shall we characterize it? Shall we say that a Sign brings a Second, its Object, into *cognitive* relation to a Third? That a Sign brings a Second into the same relation to a first in which it stands itself to that First? If we insist on *consciousness,* we must say what we mean by consciousness of an object. Shall we say we mean Feeling? Shall we say we mean association, or Habit? These are, on the face of them, psychological distinctions, which I am particular to avoid. What is the essential difference between a sign that is communicated to a mind, and one that is not so communicated? If the question were simply what we *do* mean by a sign, it might soon be resolved. But that is not the point. We are in the situation of a zoölogist who wants to know what ought to be the meaning of "fish" in order to make fishes one of the great classes of vertebrates. It appears to me that the essential function of a sign is to render inefficient relations efficient,—not to set them into action, but to establish a habit or general rule whereby they will act on occasion. According to the physical doctrine, nothing ever happens but the continued rectilinear velocities with the accelerations that accompany different relative positions of the particles. All other relations, of which we know so many, are inefficient. Knowledge in some way renders them efficient; and a sign is something by knowing which we know something more. With the exception of knowledge, in the present instant, of the contents of consciousness in that instant (the existence of which knowledge is open to doubt) all our thought & knowledge is by signs. A sign therefore is an object which is in relation to its object on the one hand and to an interpretant on the other in such a way as to bring the interpretant into a relation to the object corresponding to its own relation to the object. I might say 'similar to its own' for a correspondence consists in a similarity; but perhaps correspondence is narrower.

I am now prepared to give my division of signs, as soon as I have pointed out that a sign has two objects, its object as it is represented and its object in itself. It has also three interpretants, its interpretant as represented or meant to be understood, its interpretant as it is produced, and its interpretant in itself. Now signs may be divided as to their own material nature, as to their relations to their objects, and as to their relation to their interpretants.[15]

As it is in itself, a sign is either of the nature of an appearance, when I call it a *qualisign*; or secondly, it is an individual object or event, when I call it a *sinsign* (the syllable *sin* being the first sillable [*sic*] of *sem*el, *sim*ul, *sin*gular, etc); or thirdly, it is of the nature of a general type, when I call it a *legisign*.[16] As we use the term 'word' in most cases, saying that 'the' is one 'word' and 'an' is a second 'word', a 'word' is a legisign. But when we say of a page in a book, that it has 250 'words' upon it, of which twenty are 'the's, the 'word' is a sinsign. A sinsign so embodying a legisign, I term a 'replica' of the legisign.[17] The difference between a legisign and a qualisign, neither of which is an individual thing, is that a legisign has a definite identity, though usually admitting a great variety of appearances. Thus, &, *and*, and the sound are all one word. The qualisign, on the other hand, has no

---

15. See Appendix B.

16. See *Collected Papers*, 2.243-246.

17. Peirce's usual term is 'sinsign.' Instead of 'replica' he sometimes uses 'token.'

identity. It is the mere quality of an appearance & is not exactly the same throughout a second. Instead of identity, it has *great similarity*, & cannot differ much without being called quite another qualisign.

In respect to their relations to their dynamic objects, I divide signs into Icons, Indices, and Symbols (a division I gave in 1867.)[18] I define an Icon as a sign which is determined by its dynamic object by virtue of its own internal nature. Such is any qualisign, like a vision,—or the sentiment excited by a piece of music considered as representing what the composer intended. Such may be a sinsign, like an individual diagram; say a curve of the distribution of errors. I define an Index as a sign determined by its dynamic object by virtue of being in a real relation to it. Such is a Proper Name (a legisign); such is the occurrence of a symptom of a disease (the symptom itself is a legisign, a general type of a definite character. The occurrence in a particular case is a sinsign). I define a Symbol as a sign which is determined by its dynamic object only in the sense that it will be so interpreted. It thus depends either upon a convention, a habit, or a natural disposition of its interpretant, or of the field of its interpretant (that of which the interpretant is a determination). Every symbol is necessarily a legisign; for it is inaccurate to call a replica of a legisign a symbol.

In respect to its immediate object a sign may either be a sign of a quality, of an existent, or of a law.[19]

In regard to its relation to its signified interpretant, a sign is either a Rheme, a Dicent, or an Argument.[20] This corresponds to the old division Term, Proposition, & Argument, modified so as to be applicable to signs generally. A *Term* is simply a class-name or proper-name. I do not regard the common noun as an essentially necessary part of speech. Indeed, it is only fully developed as a separate part of speech in the Aryan languages & the Basque,—possibly in some other

18. See *Collected Papers*, 2.247ff, and 1.558.
19. In his letter dated December 23, 1908, Peirce provides a trichotomy *for* the immediate object. Also, see Appendix B.
20. See *Collected Papers*, 2.250-254.

out of the way tongues. In the Shemitic languages it is generally in form a verbal affair, & usually is so in substance too. As well as I can make out, such it is in most languages. In my universal algebra of logic there is no common noun. A rheme is any sign that is not true nor false, like almost any single word except 'yes' and 'no', which are almost peculiar to modern languages. A *proposition* as I use that term, is a dicent symbol. A dicent is not an assertion, but is a sign *capable* of being asserted. But an assertion is a dicent. According to my present view (I may see more light in future) the act of assertion is not a pure act of signification. It is an exhibition of fact that one subjects oneself to the penalties visited on a liar if the proposition asserted is not true. An act of judgment is the self-recognition of a belief; and a belief consists in the acceptance of a proposition as a basis of conduct deliberately. But I think this position is open to doubt. It is simply a question of which view gives the simplest view of the nature of the proposition. Holding, then, that a Dicent does not assert, I naturally hold that an Argument need not actually be submitted or urged. I therefore define an argument as a sign which is represented in its signified interpretant not as a Sign of the interpretant (the conclusion) [for that would be to urge or submit it] but *as if* it were a Sign of the Interpretant or perhaps as if it were a Sign of the state of the universe to which it refers, in which the premisses are taken for granted. I define a dicent as a sign represented in its signified interpretant *as if it were* in a Real Relation to its Object. (Or as being so, if it is asserted). A rheme is defined as a sign which is represented in its signified interpretant as *if it were* a character or mark. (or as being so).

According to my present view, a sign may appeal to its dynamic interpretant in three ways:

1st, an argument only may be *submitted* to its interpretant, as something the reasonableness of which will be acknowledged.

2nd an argument or dicent may be *urged* upon the interpretant by an act of *insistence.*

3rd Argument or dicent may be and a rheme can only be, presented to the interpretant for *contemplation.*[21]

Finally, in its relation to its immediate interpretant, I would divide signs into three classes as follows:

> 1st, those which are interpretable in thoughts or other signs of the same kind in infinite series,
>
> 2nd those which are interpretable in actual experiences,
>
> 3rd those which are interpretable in qualities of feelings or appearances.[22]

Now if you think on the whole (as I do) that there is much valuable truth in all this, I should be gratified if you cared to append it to the next edition of your book, after editing it & of course cutting out personalities of a disagreeable kind *especially if accompanied by one or more* (running or other) *close criticisms*; for I haven't a doubt there is more or less error involved.

My wife tells me I should try to persuade you to come over and make us a visit here. I wish with all my heart you would, though I am not sure that we shall not sell out & go to France.

I have a feeling of deep guilt in inflicting your ladyship with such a dissertation.

> very truly
> C. S. Peirce

P.S. On the whole, then, I should say there were ten principal classes of signs

1. Qualisigns
2. Iconic sinsigns
3. Iconic legisigns
4. *Vestiges,* or Rhematic Indexical Sinsigns
5. *Proper names,* or Rhematic Indexical Legisigns

---

21. Names for the items in this trichotomy are provided by Peirce in his letter dated December 23, 1908.

22. This trichotomy is modified by Peirce in his December 23, 1908 letter. The order in these two trichotomies is unusual for Peirce. If '3rd' and '1st' were interchanged, Peirce's usual order of enumeration would be restored.

6. Rhematic Symbols
7. Dicent sinsigns (as a portrait with a legend)
8. Dicent Indexical Legisigns
9. *Propositions*, or Dicent symbols
X. Arguments.[2][3]

---

23. Although in the body of his letter Peirce provides conceptions for ten trichotomies, and hence sixty-six classes of signs, he enumerates here only the ten classes of signs that derive from three of his trichotomous divisions: (1) a sign considered in itself, (2) the connection between a sign and its dynamoid object, and (3) a sign as a representation for a final or significant interpretant. See Appendix B.

November 2nd 1904
Duneaves, Harrow

Dear Mr Peirce

Your letter was very gratefully received and was of the deepest interest to me. I had fully hoped to be able to answer it at length before this. I have however been inevitably hindered from doing so. And even now, I can do little more than just thank you for it, as Prof. Höffding[1] is staying here, and plans for enabling him to see those he wishes to meet, &c, still further restrict my time. I will therefore only repeat that your letter has the greatest possible value for me. This is all the more the case, because I have been for some time in correspondence with Prof Cook Wilson[2] of Oxford, who has been raising a question akin to yours about Firstness Secondness and Thirdness; only he presents it as oneness, twoness, and threeness, and shows that we have constantly overlooked here a distinction of the greatest importance.

I am hoping therefore to send him a part of your letter and send you corresponding certain extracts from an article by Prof. Cook Wilson in the Classical Review[3] dealing with

---

1. Harald Höffding (1843-1931), Danish philosophical historian and positivist.

2. John Cook Wilson (1849-1915), British realistic philosopher and classical scholar.

3. John Cook Wilson, "On the Platonist Doctrine of the ἀσύμβλη-τοί ἀρίθμοί," *The Classical Review*, Vol. XVIII, 1904, pp. 247-260.

Plato's theory of the non-addible numbers. But this would require certain explanations and applications with reference to my own work—in its very humble sphere—and this must perforce be put aside for the present.

Yes, from all I have heard (and from very early experiences in the U.S.A.) I can well imagine the difficulties of life in the country in America. I cannot help hoping that you may really decide on moving to France! I believe the domestic difficulty is less there than anywhere on account of the mutual consideration and goodwill generally shown.

Even in England, when one has done one's best to make a servant comfortable and happy it will only 'spoil' some of them. But I must not write another word to-day; I shall hope to do so next week.

Yours most truly
Victoria Welby

November 20th. 1904
Duneaves, Harrow

Dear Mr. Peirce,

Your letter of October 12th., leads one so far in its wonderful mastery of the question of Signs that I have not yet really begun to frame a comment upon it from my own embryonic point of view.

Just lately I have been endeavouring to make improvements in the statement of a view of the origin and nature of 'time' which I have never seen advanced. It is still in tentative form and I fear full of oversights and stupidities.* But your own argument about time beginning from the question of action without reaction—that of the previous upon the subsequent— has thus a special interest for me, so perhaps I may first say something about that.

---

* I hope I am not wrong in sending a copy of the first draft of my 'Time' paper. [Lady Welby's note originally appeared after her signature at the end of this letter.]

You maintain that the action of the previous upon the subsequent is action without reaction. Here I think my invariable reservation 'in some sense' and my invariable question 'In what sense?' come in. For there are other, and pressing aspects of the action of the previous upon the subsequent. You go on: "The relation between the previous and the subsequent consists in the previous being determinate and fixed for the subsequent, and the subsequent being indeterminate for the previous. But indeterminacy belongs only to ideas; the existent is determinate in every respect; and this is just what the law of causation consists in. Accordingly, the relation of time concerns only ideas."

I am tempted to say that indeterminacy belongs only, not to ideas but to ignorance.[1] Because of the mist I am to-day ignorant of the railway-making movements in the valley below; they are so far to me indeterminate, although hearing and even smell (worse luck!) may bring me hints and justify conjectures. Because of the curve of the earth the movements of ships beyond a narrow horizon are indeterminate unless we get news through wire or etherwaves!

What we want [are] answers to the completeness of the sense-witness. Where this fails us there is doubt, like the doubt of what the 'future' will bring, doubt as to our own best 'course'. The difficulty is to show, supposing our knowledge of the 'future'—the yet to come[2]—were as precise and complete as that of the 'past'—the passed, the left behind,—we should not be shut up in a fatal round of blind 'necessity'. Sooner than this, let all be uncertain,—even our memory!

---

1. This and the following notes are marginal comments made by Peirce at various places in the letter: "When I said that indeterminacy belongs to 'ideas' I meant to ideas collectively,—to the world of ideas, & neither to existence nor to feelings. Ignorance belongs to the world of ideas. By the world of ideas I meant the world of Thirdness."

2. "But to suppose our knowledge of the yet to come were to [?] determinate is to suppose its mode of being not the mode of Thirdness. There lurks a subtle contradiction in the hypothesis. It is out of the 'nature of things,' by which we mean the 'nature of ideas' in themselves." (Peirce.)

But we are all clear as to the effect of the past upon the present (the presented) and, to speak of the effect of the future on the present seems for the reason you give, paradoxical. But to me the secret here lies (though most difficult to express) in the difference between Firstness, Secondness and Thirdness as you expound them. (Mr. Russell asks for Fourthness but that in the end only gives Twicetwoness; are not the even numbers just multiples?)

'Time' as we conceive or experience it is only a line and that irreversible. When it acquires surface and volume then we get its secondness and thirdness. But as I see it, we are just as 'free' as before: the distinction between life and not-life still applies, there are still the modes of growth—the accretive and the inherent.

I have had much talk with Prof. Höffding about this just now. (He was sorry not to see you in America). He does not so much accuse me of moral fatalism (the usual irrelevancy) as complain that logically any comparison of the future to visual distance in space (the comparison already made in the case of the *passed*) deprives the cosmos of the hope of the *new*, which would shut us into a deadly imprisoning circle. That is the last thing *I* could tolerate! For I start from and in and with and as Motion. For me, in the 'spiritual' as well as the physical world, there is of course no Rest as the ultimate goal or as the antithesis of Motion. The changeless is less than the dead, it is the non-existent. The secret here again for me lies in the unexplored conception of Order.[3] Have you ever written on the idea of order as part of that of 'freedom', and conversely? What *is* Order? (asked by Mr. Russell) is to me a twin question to What *is* Meaning? Certainly it applies to the dynamic as to the static, and a disorderly spontaneity, the reign of Chance, would be the worst the most grinding of tyrannies. Your Thirdness comes in here. I often say that I

---

3. "What you call Order I conceive not to be mere serial arrangement. What you mean is Law looked upon from the point of view of its effects. So understood, it is as you say, precisely parallel to the question What is meaning." (Peirce.)

am determined to be free and free to be determined. Why?
Because of the unnamed Third yet lying in the womb of
Motion, to which both the determinate and the indeterminate
have reference. All this however sounds perilously like nonsense, and there is probably confusion somewhere.[4] But 'é pur
si muove' is my motto. To me the ideas of the new, the
young, the fresh, the possible, are of deeper than any time-
import, and are indeterminate only in a special sense.[5] Of
course I know the Position you take on 'necessity'. But I own
that even if I am right and not the victim of some undetected
fallacy, *language here fails*. It insists on keeping us in the toils
of Secondness—either this *or* that: your money or your life!
Now the either-or is an admirable servant but an impossible
master. So is language. We have e.g. to pay a heavy price for
having exalted time to a categorical co-equality with Space.
The best I can do is to say, I wish instead of the Future we
could begin to talk of the Unreached as the Yet distant! We
do already talk of the near or distant future; and 'future'
itself like *all* the time-words is non-temporal. It is just the
Beyond now; and the now is essentially the here. This gives
the transcendent a new legitimacy. What we transcend is a
garden-hedge or a horizon; and you may go on transcending
till you are back again at your own back-door! But meanwhile
the round world has moved on and dragged you, the trans-
cendentalist, with it, on a freshly transcendent expedition.

Now may I say that I think it makes a great difference
whether you are speaking out of the racial mother-experience
(including the father-experience) or out of one complete and
ending in itself. In the latter case, of course the present, like
the individual, is all-important. The past is its obsequious
servant or its despotic master—you may put it either way—but
it is independent of the 'future', which as non-existent in any
sense is to it 'no concern of mine'.

---

4. "It may *sound* like nonsense because it is insufficiently defined;
but it corresponds to the truth." (Peirce.)
5. "That is what I came near calling Firstness,—Freshness." (Peirce.)

But in the former case the whole weight of reference, the whole trend of interest, the whole demand for knowledge is transferred to the 'future'. The mother lives for and in her 'child' as possibly innumerable generations 'potentially' existent, and, circumstances being favorable, inevitably accruing. Her 'child' is only the Race to come: it comes towards her from a distance as real as that in the dim past whence she also, as in her true 'child', has arrived. To the race-motherhood there is and can be no difference in existential reality between the past and the future any more than between a mile just left behind and a mile just entered upon.

Thus I should say (may I say?) the relation of time concerns only our as yet but partially developed ideas. It is a pregnant reflection that we are in a state of discontent precisely from the intolerable misfit between our ideals and our scientific and mathematical view of that reality we call the universe. Thus the very idea that the status of 'time' is inferior to that of space as being merely derivative, accords with the fact that "there is nothing in the physical universe corresponding to our idea that the previous determines the subsequent in any way in which the subsequent does not determine the previous". Reverse the velocities and "everything would go on just the same" except that poor time would have to perform an awkward somersault or stand on its head or 'take a back seat'. I fear *I* think it 'high time' (whatever that may be) that it did!

Thus, as you say, according to our present and as *I* see it radically defective valuation of 'time', it involves a pure idea of Secondness: but the "looking to the future as something which will have been past", seems, while as you say metaphysically the source of error, also due to an obscure instinct that there *is* somewhere a promise of Thirdness in time as really a partial translation of the space-idea. I wonder what you will say to this? Please say your worst without any softening!

I agree with all my heart of course with the "inadequacy of Secondness to cover all that is in our minds" and with you am amazed at the way in which so many thinkers "are trying to construct a system without putting any Thirdness into it". But also I agree that Secondness must be exhaustively examined, although—an admirable illustration—"no branching of a line can result from putting one line on the end of another". And 'time after time' (really *in case after case*) I see that the very triadic relations not recognized by dyadism (?) "this does itself employ".

Your analysis of the idea of Sign is so profound and far-reaching that [at] present anyhow I can only thank you for it. I hope to use it widely.

At present there is no question of a second edition of 'What is Meaning?' and if there were, this Paper is far too important to appear thus! I wish you would offer it to 'Mind'. Meanwhile I am showing it to Prof. Stout for whom I am sure it will have much interest.

Now I have a confession to make. You see, from Mr. Russell's toleration of my audacities I suspected that he was not quite so impervious to criticism as people seem to think. I am afraid the Russell heredity, intensified by his father's unusual training of his children, is responsible for much that 'riles' you and others. Anyhow as he had given my ideas a sympathetic reception, even where they took a critical form, I sent him a copy of your letter, a duplicate of the one which I now send separately to you. You will see that personalities are deleted! I enclose a copy of his answer. Surely there are signs of grace therein? Do take him at his word.

I am in the midst of an engrossing correspondence with Prof. Cook Wilson whom doubtless you know of, a man who does himself injustice by never publishing; for all to whom he is known—even those who differ from him—agree in a very high estimate of his abilities. I am adding to the general exhortations of his many friends and hope that he is at last bringing something out. But he is at present a more implacable adversary of Mr. Russell's than you are for he denounces the whole post-Euclidean geometry. Yet he encourages me to write, although I was always a naive and intuitional 'neo-geometrician'. And it is remarkable that he has been working on the subject of 'Oneness, Twoness, Three-ness', not with reference to triadism or triadic relations, or with reference to the nature of sign, but in connection with one of the elementary confusions of which I am always complaining. He is emphatic on the need of examining and revising presuppositions, and thus encourages my primitive and instinctive treatment of these questions. Being equally strong on the classical, philosophical, logical and mathematical sides (as Oxford understands these things) his criticisms, like yours, have a wide range.

So I am sending a copy of your letter to him.

With repeated thanks for your kindness in sending me so valuable a letter, & hopes that you may still come to Europe I am yours most truly

Victoria Welby

Arisbe, Milford Pa.
1904 Dec. 2

My dear Lady Welby:

I am dangerously fatigued from overwork. A man of 65 ought not to work through two consecutive nights & three days as I have done; but the work was pressing. I say this to show why I can only acknowledge your big package,—the bigger the better,—which has this minute come to hand. I will only say that Mr. Russell's idea that there is a *fourthness*, etc is natural; but I prove absolutely that all systems of more than three elements are reducible to compounds of triads;[1] and he will see that it is so on reflection. The point is that triads evidently cannot be so reduced since the very relation of a whole to two parts is a triadic relation.

I have determined "in principle," as they say in diplomacy, to accept a small consulate that has been offered to me in Ceylon, & to sell out this place. Many reasons urge me to

---

1. See *Collected Papers*, 1.363-368.

this, & for one thing, small as the consul's pay is, I need it. I should like very much to take England on my way & carry away the memory of having passed some hour or two with you, as well as to see those Oxford men of the new movements. Much of my work never will be published. If I can, before I die, get so much made accessible as others may have a difficulty in discovering, I shall feel that I can be excused from more. My aversion to publishing anything has not been due to want of interest in others but to the thought that after all a philosophy can only be passed from mouth to mouth, where there is opportunity to object & cross-question & that printing is not publishing unless the matter be pretty frivolous.

very faithfully
C. S. Peirce

December 13th 1904
Duneaves, Harrow

Dear Mr Peirce

I hope my cablegram—the first I ever sent—arrived all right and was clear. Also I hope that you will make your plans in accordance with it. It would be more than a mere pleasure to me if you could and would, and I should do my best to make your stay pleasant and useful to you both. While the air here is very good except in one happily rare wind which brings the London smoke, we shall be before long more conveniently accessible to intellectual London than in many parts of the city itself. We are also practically on the way to Oxford now. If you could arrange a stay of some weeks, making your headquarters here, you could easily see anyone you liked and at the same time enjoy leisure and quiet impossible in London itself. I should give up the Library to you as I did last year in a similar case. And I should much look forward to making friends with Mrs Peirce.

What you say about publishing almost exactly expresses my own feeling, although the two cases are widely different! The great bulk of my own humble 'mother' work is done in conversations here or private correspondence. A very able young Oxford man is here at this moment for 'long talks'.

I can't help hoping that before long something not quite so remote as a Ceylon consulship may turn up. But in any case do let me look forward to receiving you both here.

Yours most faithfully
V. Welby

Milford Pa.
1904 Dec. 16

My dear Lady Welby:

I must first explain why I have allowed several days to pass without answering your most kind Cable. In the first place it did not reach me for three days; for the telegraph operator in Milford has directions to mail telegrams unless they seem urgent. Now my mail is brought by a neighbor, my next neighbor but a mile & more away, to his house & I do not every day seek it. It happened that the day after the cable came, I saw my wife sitting in my study and toasting her feet at the steam radiator although there was a fire in the fire place. So when she was called out of the room a few minutes I hurriedly slipped out of the house to get a log of wood for the fire (we still burn great logs here) knowing she would remonstrate if she saw me do so. In my hurry, I slipped on the waxed floor. Now it has been a nervous peculiarity of late years that when I fall, I become stiff & cannot put out a hand or do anything to fall in an easy way. So down I went, hit my forehead over my eye & cut it open & had a slight concussion of the brain. This letter is the first I have done with pen & ink since. I had not long before stumbled over a steam pipe in the dark cellar & bruised the shoulder of my writing hand so that I have by no means recovered from that yet.

Certainly dear Lady Welby we must accept your ladyship's kind hospitality; and it is an immense pleasure to do so,—

would be so, even if I could not accept. But it is by no means an easy thing to sell this place & that I must do; for I could not be worried with it. I am very sorry to do so, too; because the house is a work of art of my wife's decoration. We planned it, together. I was my own builder, hiring the workmen direct & buying the materials that I could not have procured easily. My wife is a true artist in decoration. Everything is exquisitely soft without the faintest suggestion of ambition. The house is entirely unlike any other & breathes a spirit of deep peace. I am sorry to lose it. But to be away and worry about it would be far worse. So, though we are putting the price very low indeed,—needlessly, perhaps,—still one cannot sell a place so out of the social world, so out of the world that is afraid to be alone, in a day, or a week. Besides, I haven't received my appointment yet. I am a friend of Roosevelt's of many years. My brother[1] is Assistant Secretary of Foreign Affairs (of "State," as we call it) and has all matters connected with consuls under his special charge. All appointments are made by the President, ordinarily at my brothers recommendation, and have to be confirmed by the Senate, this last step being by no means a mere matter of form. One of the most powerful senators Cabot Lodge of Massachusetts is a cousin of mine and his wife is a specially intimate cousin of mine, too; and in the Senate, "courtesy" is a very great consideration. Besides all that, I have personal claims to some rewards or recognition. Therefore, I do not *think* there will be any difficulty in my getting the consulate,—a minor one,—which is to be vacated; but it is impossible to be sure, for I have powerful enemies. It would be an immense advantage to all I have at heart to see you and the Oxford thinkers. I hope it may be possible.

Your ladyship's essay on Time was probably sent to me because I mentioned having been at work on that subject. But

---

1. Herbert Henry Davis Peirce (1849-1916), diplomat; third assistant secretary of state under John Hay (1894-1911). He held the office 1901-1906.

the directions of your work and mine are as different as they well could be. Although you do not explicitly state whether the dependence of Time on Space for which you contend is a logical, metaphysical, epistemological, psychological, or ethno-logical-anthropological dependence, yet from the account you make of the usages of speech I infer that it is of the last kind mainly. It appears to me that the method of designating temporal relations by their analogies with spatial relations must date from the very beginnings of speech. For language can have had very little development when it was not yet settled how one was to express temporal relations. I therefore imagine the method took rise between two persons who met and endeavored to communicate partly by words and partly by signs. These persons would be together with a common spatial environment, which was visible, and in which special parts could be pointed out by gesture. It would therefore be particularly easy to form a terminology for spatial relations. On the other hand, they would probably have no great variety of common memories, and the few they had could not be indicated by gesture, without their analogies to spatial rela-tions. Hence, if you do not assume a dependence of Time on Space to be otherwise independently proved, it appears to me that circumstances would nevertheless infallibly drive those two persons to the expression of temporal relations through their analogy with spatial relations; and I see nothing in these circumstances to prove any dependence of Time on Space except in the matter of expression in speech. There is much else that is suggestive in the essay, but somehow my mind fails to apprehend it very sharply.

This I have little doubt is my fault. For I must tell you that my philosophical studies have a very narrow range,— except in reading. Bred in an atmosphere of mathematics and of the severest branches of physics, all my studies, excepting some ancillary inquiries, have been directed toward proving points that I thought could be put beyond all intelligent doubt. I have studied philosophy only in so far as it is an exact science, not according to the childish notions of proof of the metaphysicians but according to the logic of science. Hence it has seemed to me that the first thing to be done was to define accurately the relations of time as common-sense assumes them, before entering upon the questions of whether or how far or in what respect these conceptions are valid and still less into any psychological questions about them & still less yet into attempt to make a history of the conceptions. This first humble labor of defining the temporal and spatial relations had never been rightly done. For I can absolutely refute the notions of the mathematicians on the matter. I need not say that at the outset of the inquiry I asked myself by what tests I should know that my definitions when I got them were correct, nor that I provided myself with several independent tests. One of these was as follows. There is one of the main branches of geometry, Topics, which alone occupies itself with properties of Space itself, namely, with the order of connection of its parts. This has been little studied, and no regular method of treating it is known. But if I obtain the proper definitions of temporal relations, little more will be required to furnish me with definitions of the Spatial relations, and if this is rightly done, it must throw a strong light on Topics, while if it is not rightly done it will do nothing for topics.

I first commenced tracing out the doctrine of Topics when my definition of continuity was faulty; and therefore made little progress. Still, I worked out the beginnings of a system. Then I fell in with a great paper of J. B. Listing (not John Baptist by the way but Johann Benedict) in the Göttingen Abhandlungen.[2] This set me right on many points while my previous studies set the paper right. For many years I have not seen the paper, & am now as completely unable to say what is mine and what is Listing's as any third party could be, although I know that certain things are Listing's and that

---

2. Johann Benedict Listing, "Der Census raumlicher Complexe," published in the *Abhandlungen der Gesellschaft der Wissenschaft zu Göttingen.*

certain things are mine. I know that the four Listing numbers, and *some* enunciation of the census-theorem with a scheme

$$+N_0^0$$

$$+N_1^1 \quad -N_1^0$$

$$+N_2^2 \quad -N_2^1 \quad +N_2^0$$

$$+N_3^3 \quad -N_3^2 \quad +N_3^1 \quad -N_3^0$$

and I know that all exact definitions and the whole doctrine of singularities is mine, and the discovery that there are several different census theorems, together with other relations between Listing numbers. I assume that you know nothing of this out of the way subject and since it is a fascinating subject & very easy when one once knows how to handle it, though inscrutable until one knows how, I must try to draw up a little sketch of it for your Ladyship. When I see you, however, I can make it clear in a trice. I cannot put that into this letter; but I will give spare minutes to it.

Since I have been ill with my accidents, a generalization has occurred to me which seems to me both novel, surprisingly wide, obvious, and useful. The proposition is that when the store of any quantity is in process of increase, actions are facilitated that would draw upon that store, while actions that would add to the store are hindered.

Let a man be growing rich and he will be more likely to go into operations involving the expenditure of money than if he were growing poor, and less active in going into operations to bring in immediate money.

Let heat be pouring into an agglomeration of substances, and reactions between them that involve using up heat will be facilitated while reactions that evolve heat will be retarded.

Increase the pressure upon the agglomeration and actions involving contraction (and consequent action of pressure) will be facilitated, while actions involving expansion & consequent increase of pressure will be hindered.

The principle, you will understand, only undertakes to say in which of two opposite directions a change will take place. Namely, it will always take place so as to retard the changing condition. The man getting rich will be led into operations retarding his getting rich rather than into operations *immediately* bringing in funds.

If any change induces an electrical current, the direction of the current will be such as to retard that change.

An increasing supply of any commodity will cause such a change in the price as will discourage the production of it.

Perhaps the generalization has already been made; but I never met with it. It might be called the economic law.

Mrs. Peirce wanted to add something in her hand to this letter. But writing occasions her so much pain, not merely while she writes, but for a long time after, that I would not permit her to do it. She is one of those persons whose energy far exceeds their strength, and is really in a most precarious condition, the reflection of which poisons my life.

very faithfully
C. S. Peirce

January 7, 1905

Dear Mr. Peirce[1]

Your kind letter had the greatest interest for me. I am doubly sorry to hear of your accident since I can give the sympathy of a fellow-sufferer, having got scalded and otherwise hurt just lately. Also we have had the most appalling fog which brought by a S.E. wind from London hung round this hill and nearly choked us. That is happily a rare experience here; but if London continues to grow without consuming its own smoke I am afraid that we shall oftener suffer this way.

I am very glad that if you come to England I may look forward to seeing you and Mrs. Peirce here. I can enter well

---

1. This letter was not in the Peirce correspondence. It has been reconstructed from an edited version of the letter published in *Other Dimensions* and a draft in Lady Welby's correspondence.

into the wrench that it may be to leave the home which you and she have in fact created. And your account of her health makes me rather dread the break for her.

With regard to the rest of your letter, I have ever since repented having sent you the essay on *Time*, as I have much additional material which if properly embodied ought I think to make it more convincing, and I have now a prospect of collaboration in doing this. As to the point of view from which I approach it, I suppose, as you surmise, the ethno-anthropological comes nearest to it, for, after all, all the more formal or abstract treatments of the subject must begin in, and issue from, the original fountain of race experience.

I am interested by your saying that the 'first humble labour of defining the temporal and spatial relations had never been rightly done.' Also that you can 'absolutely refute the notions of the mathematicians on the matter.' I would like to add one word about the relative originality and centrality in ex-perience of space and time. What you say about the inevitable reason for an initial spatial terminology is of course and obviously true. But I think that in all other cases we find that though man may have had to begin with a vocabulary bor-rowed from his original experience, he has soon dropped it, as his mental powers grew, in favor of a specialized one. The case of number itself is surely one in point. You had finger 1, then finger-finger 11. But you soon had to evolve a number-notation. The same is apparently true of all the other cate-gories except time, and, as I venture to suggest, for the best of reasons: that time is a product of space + motion—is in fact a kind of space and not an independent category at all—whereas space could never from any point of view be called a kind of time, or reckoned as dependent upon it. But I am not offering this as an adequate rejoinder to your criticism. You have in fact confirmed my view of the all-coercive nature of space + motion, which gives me hopes that my case may find a more worthy exponent than I can be.

As to your doctrines of topics and singularities, I shall look forward with great interest to hearing your explanations of them, and should meanwhile greatly appreciate the sketch you speak of if you could make one. With regard to the generalizations of which you speak, that is, the proposition 'that when the store of any quantity is in process of increase, actions are facilitated that would draw upon that store, while actions that would add to the store are hindered,' it is to me of great interest, because, when translated into certain forms of experience about which I have thought a good deal, I also have seen its extreme importance.

I have pleasure in enclosing an extract from Mr. Russell's last letter to me by which you will again see how glad he would be to profit by your ideas and researches. On every side there seems now to be a rising tendency to transfigure and humanize mathematics and logic: to put an end to their hermit life in what to the rest of us is an inaccessible desert, to give them a wider appeal.

Many thanks for your kind card: my best wishes in return for you both.

V. Welby

"Arisbe" near Milford Pa.
1905 Apr 16
Palm Sunday

My dear Lady Welby
Early in February I was suddenly collapsed with nervous prostration. After more than two full months I find myself able to do half a day's work, but all my engagements are thrown back, a great printing establishment is put to inconvenience & I am in a *panting* condition of effort that brings little fruit. And besides that the *res domi* begins to be uncomfortable. My wife too went to Cambridge for a visit to Mrs. Wm. James and was there struck with the Boston east wind. That is one of the few houses where it does not penetrate the heart (as it does in the Peirce house, between you & me.) When she got back as far as New York it was terribly rainy (all this time the weather was summery here in Pike County)

and she took another cold on top of the other & for a fortnight has been confined to her room,—I in my study struggling to get work done, she lonely. You no doubt got a marked copy of the Monist with my article.[1] A platoon of philosophers from Eastport Maine to San Diego Cal. has me under fire at the moment. Today I am starting for Washington for a meeting of the Natl. Academy of Sciences where I have nothing myself to present owing to the above circumstances. My next Monist article[2] will have something to say about Meaning & anything stimulating, especially anything antagonistic, that may occur to you to say would be a help to me.

My dear Lady Welby, I constantly have you in mind, so far as I can be said to have any mind left. But you see how it is.

always faithfully yours
C. S. Peirce

---

1. C. S. Peirce, "What Pragmatism Is," *The Monist*, Vol. 15, No. 2 (April 1905), pp. 161-181. Reprinted in *Collected Papers*, 5.411-437.

2. Charles S. Peirce, "The Issues of Pragmaticism," *The Monist*, Vol. 15 (October 1905), pp. 481-492. Reprinted in *Collected Papers*, 5.438-463.

May 4th 1905
Duneaves, Harrow.

Dear Mr Peirce

Your letter of April 16 reached me while in my old home, to which I have gone for a little rest. This turned out so much needed, that I had to put aside all my letters. I cannot however delay longer thanking you for yours and telling you how much your account of your own breakdown troubled me. I am afraid that it hardly surprises me after your previous account of your overdraft on the nervous system. Children ought to be brought up to consider any waste of vitality like that as immoral as the opposite waste of idle and selfish neglect! I am very sorry too to hear that Mrs Peirce has also been laid up by that wicked East wind. But I thought with you it blew over the sea and was thus robbed of its malice; which the west wind became treacherous, as blowing over that vast continent. I must thank you much for the copy of the Monist with your article in it. I had already read that as I take in the Monist.

I am not able to offer now such humble remarks as may occur to my elementary mind, though I have noted the passages which I found most suggestive of 'significs'. But as you do me the real honour to ask for them I shall hope to forward some before long.

I have just lately been occupied in preparing a list of 'Overlooked Points' to which I greatly want to direct attention. The first—our inconsistent use of the idea of 'Nature'—is the only one as yet in the form of a Paper.

But I must not write more today except to tell you that I hope before long a book will appear in America in which I am interested, since it is written by a very able friend of mine, one who has a touch of the sacred fire. The subject is Benjamin Franklin in whom I hope you feel an interest! My friend's view is so far as I know original.

He is now helping me—out of his knowledge both of reviewing and of editing—to make my work less enigmatic to the general reader; so I hope before long to be better understood. I can give you more particulars presently but you will soon hear I think of a book which I think will make a deep impression.

Once more thank you for your kind and friendly words, and wishing we could meet I am yours most truly

V. Welby

Milford Pa.
1905 May 14

My dear Lady Welby:

I will not let a steamer go without writing to you to say that in consequence of information we have received during the last few days, we have pretty much given up all expectation of selling the place this year, and therefore shall be unable to avail ourselves of your ladyship's hospitality.

There are parties buying up "options" i.e. agreements to sell real estate, covering the whole valley. Pipe-wells are being sunk to a great depth, there is much mystery, and unless we receive a very tempting positive offer, we had better wait developments before parting with the only really good residence in the valley.

I received a letter from Mr. Schiller and at once wrote him as amiable a reply as I could—moved in part by his being a friend of yours,—but then I shouldn't & indeed couldn't answer otherwise than I did. Garrison[1] had sent me for review "Personal Idealism" & I was much struck, of course, by "Axioms as Postulates."[2] But Garrison never sends me anything to review without saying 'Don't be heavy, and don't discuss philosophy.' His readers wont stand it & he himself detests it. So my notice was light & almost bantering.[3] After it was written, I reflected that sharp wits are generally excessively sensitive to the least pleasantry & I submitted my notice separately to two of Schiller's most closest friends in this country. Both assured me it was all right & I sent it to Garrison. But further consideration made me feel that it was not all right & that it was really not a proper notice & I wrote to Garrison to send it back. But he replied that I wrote nonsense, that the article was right & that the kind I wanted to substitute would not be acceptable and to close the discussion he printed it. [All that is said from memory. There may very likely be some slight inaccuracies; but that is right as far as I can now recall.]

1. Wendell Phillips Garrison (1840-1907), editor of *The Nation* from 1865 until 1906.

2. *Personal Idealism: Essays by Eight Members of the University of Oxford,* ed. Henry Cecil Sturt, Macmillan, 1902. The second of these essays is "Axioms as Postulates" by F. C. S. Schiller.

3. For Peirce's review see *The Nation* 76 (4 June 1903), 462-463. Also see Frederich J. Down Scott, "Peirce and Schiller and Their Correspondence," *Journal of the History of Philosophy*, Vol. XI, No. 3 (July 1973), pp. 363-386.

I heard afterward that Schiller had protested, & his Humanism[4] was sent to James to notice, I suppose. I noticed that it contained a remark about my work that nobody but an angry man could think veracious.[5] In my April paper[6] it was stated that what he had said was not true, with mentioning him. I also had a sentence which to those who knew his comic *Mind* would convey my opinion of that. And both together amounted to saying, what I think, that he introduces his personal passions into philosophy in a reprehensible way. In another passage I alluded to him by name as one that a school of philosophy could be proud to include,—or something to that effect. There was another remark alluding to something I had read but had but a vague recollection of. It may possibly have been by him.

Anyway his letter, which I received yesterday morning contained an attempt to put upon Baldwin & James the responsibility of what he had said about me without directly stating his object. I politely showed him that it was impossible that Baldwin could have said anything more than my printed article would justify.

As for James I must admit that in his desire to bring out his meaning he is sometimes unconsciously one-sided; but Schiller being such a great friend of James, I ventured on telling him that I had remonstrated with James about some statement, I could not yesterday think what. But I now remember. It was on the first and second pages of his article 'Humanism and Truth' in *Mind* No 52,[7] where he conveys the idea that I do not insist that the truth of any statement

---

4. F. C. S. Schiller, *Humanism*, Macmillan and Co., London, 1903.

5. In *Humanism* Schiller remarks that James gave pragmatism its name. To the remark he appends this note: "Strictly speaking, I am reminded, it was Mr. C. S. Peirce, but it would seem to follow from pragmatist principles that a doctrine belongs to him who makes an effective use of it."

6. Peirce, "What Pragmatism Is." For specific references to Schiller by Peirce, see *Collected Papers*, 5.414, 416.

7. William James, "Humanism and Truth," *Mind*, Vol. 13 ns, No. 52 (October 1904), pp. 457-475.

consists in what flows from the proposition [But note James's illogic. He speaks of this as a *broader* doctrine than his own.] I am entirely with Schiller on that point & so I told James. He seemed surprised that I should care for so very slight a misrepresentation, another proof of his inability to understand my thought.

I thought it proper that I should inform you, dear Lady Welby, how the matter is in my mind. I hope Schiller will let it rest. I shall do so. I do not doubt he is a very lovable man as James is; and of the two perhaps Schiller is stronger in philosophy. But I have not a very high admiration for the philosophical calibre of pluralists.

I have a terrible pile of letters to answer & urgent work to do; and this uninteresting letter had better be closed.

very faithfully
C. S. Peirce

Milford Pa.
1905 Sep 28

Dear Lady Welby:

The photo I am sending is of our house and surroundings.[1]

very faithfully
C. S. Peirce

_____

1. The photograph is not included in Lady Welby's letter file.

Duneaves, Harrow, England
February 23 1906

My dear Mr. Peirce

I now have to thank you for the kind thought of sending me the number of the Monist with your remarks on Mr. Peterson's 'Discussion'[1] and also your review of Mr. Gosse on Sir Thomas Browne[2] in which I found much interest. I am

1. C. S. Peirce, "Mr. Peterson's Proposed Discussion," *The Monist*, Vol. XVI (January 1906), pp. 147-151. Also *Collected Papers*, 5.610-614.

2. "Gosse's Sir Thomas Browne," *The Nation*, 81 (14 Dec 1905), 486-488.

sending you by this post a copy of the recently started 'University Review' which is finding a considerable circulation; as you will see that it contains some humble verses of mine.

I scarcely can write in verse, and don't claim the poetic gift but these lines came in very insistent fashion one morning in the Highlands.

Three days afterward a leading article in the Times, dealing with Prof. G. Darwin's[3] Presidential Address to the British Association in S. Africa, took precisely the same line. But that is a kind of coincidence which frequently happens! I felt very unwilling to allow this to be published but was overruled.

I wonder if you would care to see an article by Professor G. Vailati, now of Florence on the Metaphors of Logic?

He takes my ground and points out that the images of 'support' 'dependence' etc have a more dangerous effect on the ordinary mind than is usually realized.

I hope you have been well in the lovely Home of which you kindly sent me such an attractive photograph.

People ask me if you are not interested in publishing a book representative of some part of your life's work?

As for me I am mainly content with typing short notes & Papers to send to friends.

With thanks and good wishes I remain

> Yours most truly
> V. Welby

---

3. George Howard Darwin (1845-1912), British astronomer and mathematician; son of Charles Darwin.

> Milford Pa.
> *1906 Oct. 21*

My dear Lady Welby:

I do not know how many months ago it was that as I was writing the twenty-somethingth page of a letter to you about your poem and about Meanings, I was called away by something relative to my wife's health, which does not improve, & my own is much weakened in consequence.

I do not know what you have thought of me, or whether you have deigned to think anything under the circumstances. I only know that I have been made of late to feel very severely my own limitations. I cannot reconcile all my duties.

I am sending you a Monist article by me.[1] I had the misfortune to offend the foreman of Carus's[2] printing office by Carus's letting him see, or telling him, of some remark of mine about Proof Readers in general. That it was, and that aggravated by my desiring that my numerous capitals be allowed to stand as capitals. So you will see what a lesson I have been made to learn.

I am also venturing to send you a photograph by a farmer's boy of Mrs. Peirce,—my wife, I beg your pardon,— and of myself. I have that eternal look of preaching which, as I find it in all my photographs almost, I conclude must really be a *trait* of mine, though nobody can detest it more than I.[3]

I would like so much to hear something of you, of your health, and whether we are to have something more from you about Meaning. I shall have a great deal to say upon the subject and upon the whole structure of signs, when I can appease that foreman & be encouraged to write it. I suppose there is no journal in England that would be open to me. I think Carus thinks that would be the simplest way to straighten out the snarl.

I will also enclose a copy of a wholly unimportant notice by me that the *Nation* refused to print (about Carveth Read.[4])

---

1. C. S. Peirce, "Prolegomena To An Apology for Pragmaticism," *The Monist*, Vol. 16 (October 1906), pp. 492-546. Reprinted in *Collected Papers*, 4.530-572.

2. Paul Carus (1852-1919), editor and author; *The Ethical Problem* (1899), *Primer of Philosophy* (1893), *The Foundations of Mathematics* (1908); editor of *The Open Court* and *The Monist*.

3. The photograph is not in Lady Welby's letter file.

4. Carveth Read (1848-1931), Professor of Philosophy and Comparative Psychology, University of London; author of *A Theory of Logic* (1878), *The Metaphysics of Nature* (1905), *The Origin of Man and of His Superstitions* (1920), etc.

We are in the midst of unspeakable "politics" here.[5] A
friend of mine, Albert Stickney,[6] has written a little book in
a good oral style. But to me it seems strange that any man of
sense could think that any device could cure our condition of
public health. The fatal thing with us, as with most peoples, is
the dreadful *légèreté* of the people in regard to public affairs.
I have a remedy for that. It is to start a certain movement
which would of itself have a natural & inevitable power of
growth. But I haven't space left on my sheet, nor time left, to
tell you what it is. Besides, why should you particularly care
for it?

We have been making up to some delightful English people
in Milford. He is a man of my age or older, born in Lan-
cashire, apparently close to the Usk or one of those streams,
& she is Welsh of French intermixture & they have lived long
in Virginia and have that delightful Virginian flavor. And then
there has been a delightful old sister of his who lives in
Jamaica where she has founded some institution for sailors,
and is delightfully simple and old-fashioned.

Very faithfully
C. S. Peirce

Nous n'écoutons d'instincts que ceux qui sont les nôtres, Et
ne croyons le mal que quand il est venu.

---

5. Regular congressional elections were held in 1906.

6. Albert Stickney (1839-1908), lawyer; author of *A True Republic*
(1879), *The Political Problem* (1890), *Organized Democracy* (1906), etc.
Organized Democracy was reviewed by Peirce in the *Nation*, 85 (12
September 1907), 229.

November 8, 1906

My dear Mr. Peirce,[1]

It was indeed a pleasure to receive a letter from you again (though I consider myself defrauded of the twenty something pages not received of which you speak!) with so delightful an enclosure as the photograph of yourself and Mrs. Peirce.

I don't see any 'preachiness' in yours, only a sense of what are fine and deep things married to a sense of fun. What more can one want? And now I feel to know Mrs. Peirce too. I wish you had been able to carry out your European plan and could have called here on your way! But no doubt that was wisely given up.

(By the way the notice of Carveth Read was not enclosed.)

I am afraid I know of no journal here which admits the sort of article you speak of anyhow yet! But there are signs of a change at last; and of the approaching recognition at least as a subject for discussion of SIGNIFICS.

You are indeed "on the other side" in a tremendous political tangle. I began by admiring your President's indomitable knight-errantry; but I am not sure that he will not prove in the end to have served the dragon's turn. To judge by his photograph Hearst is a thorough Cat in the bad sense of the word, and will know how to meet all frontal attacks with a dangerous feline slyness. If I am wrong I beg his pardon!

I should be interested some day to hear something about the remedy for public apathy or levity on state matters which you would suggest.

You kindly ask about my own work. It has been developing a good deal lately though still as ever on private lines. You will see that we are getting on when I say that a young medical man of some eminence, also a rising psychologist has given up his practice and come to live near here

---

1. This letter has been reconstructed from a draft in Lady Welby's correspondence. As is the case with many drafts in Lady Welby's correspondence, it is partially in a typewritten "shorthand." Brackets have been added to indicate words omitted.

to write a book to be called by some title like The Study of
Significs, for which I propose to supply him with materials.
Also a noted schoolmaster [who is] a contributor of Science
Notes to our premier Evening Paper (you will understand why
at present [I] withhold names) and Editor of a mathematical
Gazette (complete stranger to me) is proposing to introduce
Significs at some length to his scientific readers. [I] begin
[to] think [I] have perhaps carried [a] horror of publishing
and 'booming' and [a] desire for personal effacement to
undue lengths so that [the] work which [I] hold dearer than
life (since [it] makes for something better than we call that)
has never yet come to its flower and fruit. So [I] am anyhow
feeling that by all means matters must now be pressed on
while my brain is still in healthy work. . . . But [I] had [the]
other day [a] sharp reminder that time is daily more precious; and the worst is that as one ages one tires sooner.
Presuming on your generous kindness [I am] forwarding (with
copies) two or three recent short Papers. [I] find I am typing
the wrong letters so only add eager response of [my] grand-
son to ideas still unmeaning because [I] don't know what Sign
is? Real comfort. He at least sees that coming from the racial
mother-sense they come closely home to us all at all times
and in all places.

> Good wishes,
> Yours cordially
> [V. Welby]

[I] find [I] never thanked you for [the] *Monist*. [I] had
already read [it]; technically somewhat beyond me. Have you
any young disciple who 'signifies' in my sense?

December 4. 1908[1]
Duneaves, Harrow

My dear Mr Peirce

I have been reading with great interest and admiration your Article in the October 'Hibbert'.[2] May I greatly venture to ask for light on some points there raised? You start as we all ought to start by defining not terms but your intended use of them.

In the case of 'brute' I am tempted to plead that the word may be reserved for a perversion, morally evil in man because out of harmony with the 'pitch' of his nature; and that conversely we should gain some other term with less shameful associations than brute, for the non-conscious forces, things, facts. We instinctively reproach an animal with being a brute when it shows 'vice'. And 'beastie' is a pet name, while brutie is never used! It seems to answer to *crooked* in contrast to *curve.*

But passing that, I come to what is my business though in a much more elementary sense that it is yours. I mean the essential value of Sign; "so to speak, the Sign's Soul". For that, as you know, under the term Significs and the phrase *what things signify*, is my special interest. You concede the truth that "religion, were it but proved, would be a good outweighing all others". Now here we have one of the words used in senses so widely apart that we are always employing them in peril of confusion. Do you here mean that religion

---

1. The gap in the correspondence between November 8, 1906 and December 4, 1908 is unexplainable. There are no drafts in either Lady Welby's or Peirce's correspondence to indicate that letters were sent during this period. A large number of draft pages in Peirce's correspondence dated December 1908 (see Appendix F, item 9) indicate Peirce's effort to respond to Lady Welby's letter of December 4, 1908 with a more detailed account of his theory of signs, but there is nothing to indicate correspondence between Peirce and Lady Welby for the period between November 1906 and December 1908.

2. C. S. Peirce, "A Neglected Argument for the Reality of God," *The Hibbert Journal*, Vol. 7 (1908-1909), pp. 90-112. Reprinted in *Collected Papers*, 6.452-493.

must be thoroughly *tested*, and as it were the chemical result perfectly isolated and thus 'pure'; or do you mean *logically proved*; given this, that must follow?

Of course we know that the Scriptural "Prove all things" is to be taken in the former sense. My own position, as you know, is that religion will never be proved in either sense until we learn to *signify*, to attribute consequence or effect in a far more mordant and unquestionable sense than we do yet. Then it will be, as I understand you to mean, that which reveals by coordinating not by sundering the human race or indeed life on this or any world. "Full of nutrition" it must be for any conceivable 'highest growth'. The completing element of your triad is the "active power to establish connections between different objects"—and surely between different ideas and acts also? As to our use of the phrase 'belief in God' I suspect that it betrays an unconscious lack of *faith*, for which belief is indeed a poor substitute. For 'belief' may be mistaken, may both begin and end in error and waste. But faith in the Perfection on all planes of which 'God' is our present symbol, is our central need. When indeed we realize the many despicable associations of the term 'God' (our 'god' may be Self or our stomach!) we long for some purer symbol for the Better than the Best we know . . . . As for Argumentation it is becoming more and more a plague of futility, as any Critical Journal witnesses. And Play too; which we so often connect, not with the Play of cosmical forces or of controlled impetus, but with the mere random wandering, a sign of mental disease, which no true Play can be.

I wish we could learn in our deadening use of the 'founding' and 'building' image, to apply the concept of growth as you do (p. 97).[3] But may I plead for the substitution of revealing or suggestive image, for "attractive fancy"? For we are not "stirred to the depths" of our nature by the beauty of a merely attractive fancy. And our love and adora-

---

3. Peirce, "A Neglected Argument . . .," p. 97. See *Collected Papers*, 6.465.

tion are due, surely to a more than *hypo*-thetical, rather a *proto*thetical Supremacy. (I borrow from Ostwald[4] here).

Your term Retroduction seems to me much needed. In my humble way I claim to be a Muser, though I see that entrance into the world of Musement needs—for at least—an ungrudging study of the conditions of a healthy exploration. I may also claim to be conscious of the unique value of Sign (and Icon) in all its forms, including Indices and Symbols; and of the necessity of the 'corrolarial'. Of course (p. 108) "all thinking is performed in signs"[5] and a concept is intentional,—has meaning.

What you say on p. 105[6] of the proof that Man's mind is presumably (the presumption being unavoidable unless reality is a worse than chaos?) "attuned to the truth of things in order to discover what he has discovered", is indeed to me more than a bedrock; rather the controlling sun, fostering and illuminating, of the loyal planet of logical truth.

But I must not venture further except to note your reminder that too often forgotten but most significant fact that "scientific belief is always provisional." This is our model for all belief. Faith, on the other hand, is a moral quality: one which even if its object fails us has unfailingly ennobled our character and life. Faith is never afraid of knowledge; fresh knowledge only calls it to deeper triumphs by a frank acceptance of new light in which to envisage old ideas. For it is always true that, even if intellectually ignorant or mistaken, loyalty—fidelity through life and death—to the Supreme Reality, or even to a loved one on earth, must always transfigure as it consecrates humanity.

You have always been kindly interested in the work to which my life is devoted. I am glad to be able to say that at last it is coming nearer to recognition by representatives of

---

4. Wilhelm Ostwald (1853-1932), German physicist and philosopher.
5. Peirce, "A Neglected Argument . . .," p. 108. See *Collected Papers*, 6.481.
6. Peirce, "A Neglected Argument . . .," p. 105. See *Collected Papers*, 6.476.

work and thought. I have been asked for and have written an article on Significs for the next edition (1910) of the Encyclopaedia Britannica. This is an encouraging symptom (especially as I know none of the editorial staff), since it is an obviously exceptional case. An Encyclopaedia exists to summarise subjects already recognised by the educated world and demands a bibliography. Significs is still unknown except to very few and has practically no bibliography. I wonder whether you would care to see the proof of the article? I much hope that this letter will find you and Mrs. Peirce in good health; you both have my best wishes for the new year. I have had a good deal of illness myself but am thankful to be able to work nearly as hard as ever.

Milford, Pa.
1908 Dec 14

My dear Lady Welby:

Please Excuse my writing on this paper, as I find to my surprise that I have run out of everything else except such as is still less fit for writing to you; and it is 3½ A. M. and I am 5 or 6 miles from a stationer's.

I cannot tell you how delighted I was on Saturday last to see your hand-writing on the envelope; and my delight was enhanced by finding you gave your opinion of some points of my Hibbert article.[1] For I am particularly interested in knowing what different people think of it; though unfortunately those who think it all bosh only let me guess their opinion from their silence. I am particularly curious to know what sensible women think of it; for I think they are less likely to be influenced by theories of logic, and that their instincts in such matters are better than men's.

As to the adjective "brute," I cannot quite agree with you. The adjective the noun, and the two derived adjectives "brutal" and "brutish" have very different implications. All

---

1. "A Neglected Argument for the Reality of God."

your arguments seem to refer to the noun. In classical latin my impression is that its commonest use is in such phrases as Cicero's *bruta fortuna*, and the common *bruta fulmina et vana*. When Horace speaks of *bruta tellus et vaga fulmina,* meaning apparently immovable, I think he is stretching the word. It seems to be connected with βαρύς *heavy* & βριθος *weight*, etc. In English, I think *brute force, brute matter*, and the like are the most familiar applications of the adjective. Recent events have caused me to read anew some of Milton's verse, and I don't think that Dagon,

> Who mourn'd in earnest, when the captive ark
> Maim'd his *brute* image, head and hands lopt off
> In his own temple, on the grunsel edge,
> Where he fell flat, and sham'd his worshippers

—I do not think, I say, that he or his image was insulted when the latter was called 'brute'; and when the Lady in Comus says to the latter

> Thou art not fit to hear thyself convinced;
> Yet should I try, the uncontrolled worth
> Of this pure cause would kindle my rapt spirits
> To such a flame of sacred vehemence
> That dumb things would be mov'd to sympathize,
> And the *brute* earth would lend her nerves, and shake
> Till all thy magic structures rear'd so high
> Were shatter'd into heaps o'er thy false head,

the application is better English than Horace's (from which Milton's is pedantically copied) is good Latin. You will observe that the word "brute" is primarily an adjective, not a substantive; and that when the lower animals are called "brute," the meaning is that they are irrational, that is to say, are *incapable of self-control*, which is relatively the case. So that, far from any *blame* being implied in the epithet, their being *brute* is a valid excuse for any conduct whatever. I am not far from using the adjective in this same sense when I speak of *brute force*, meaning force *in no measure derived from reason*, like the muscular force of the policeman's or *huissier's* (bailiff's?) arm, even if it obeys reason; just as a dog is none the less brute for obeying a master who taught him by force of habit, if not by bruter means. My own impression is that if but half the peculiar expressions to which I am driven were but as apt as that of Brute force, I should be a far happier writer than I can flatter myself that I am. It seems to me decidedly expressive.

You ask whether, when I speak of religion being "proved" I mean "tested" or "logically proved." I reply that the question of the truth of religion being a question of what *is* true, and not of what *would be* true under an arbitrary hypothesis, such as those of pure mathematics, the only logical proof possible is the testing. If, for example, the question be whether the Koh-in-Noor diamond if thrown up *in vacuo* will describe a parabola with a vertical axis, it is no proof to say that the Kohinoor is a body having weight and all bodies having weight so move *in vacuo*, but the whole question is the question of fact whether it has weight or not, that is, the *same* weight at all heights and at all times, and this can only be known by testing; and the sufficient testing is to give a glance at the thing. For it is known already, as a fact, that everything but an optical image or illusion that is visible does have weight. For if, to prove a given experiential proposition, a mixture of testing and mathematical reasoning be required, the latter does not count at all in characterizing the proof, since mathematical reasoning is well understood to be a necessary ingredient of all testing. I object strongly, however, to making mathematical demonstration the sole "logical proof." On the contrary, I maintain that "testing" is the sole logical proof of any question concerning Real objects.[2] Mathematical demonstration only shows that one arbitrary hypothesis involves another;[3] and such reasoning can only concern real

----

2. See *Collected Papers*, 6.327.
3. See *Collected Papers*, 4.233.

matter of fact because, since it appears by testing that an arbitrary hypothesis is approximately fulfilled, we presume that its mathematical consequences will be approximately fulfilled. But this is not proved until it is tested.

You ask me whether, when I said the mind is characterized by its "active power to establish relations between objects," I would extend this to establishing relations between ideas and acts, *also*. In answer, I must explain that, according to my note on the Ethics of Terminology,[4] which I must have sent you, but will now send another copy, I use the term "object" in the sense in which obiectum was first made a substantive early in the XIIIth century; and when I use the word without adding "*of*" what I am speaking of the object, I mean anything that comes before thought or the mind in any usual sense. Stout and Baldwin use the term in the same sense, though not upon the same principle. I will add, while I am about it, that I do not make any contrast between Subject and Object*, far less talk about "subjective and objective" in any of the varieties of German senses, which I think have led to a lot of bad philosophy, but I use "subject" as the correlative of "predicate," and speak only of the "subjects" of those signs which have a part which separately indicates what the object of the sign is. A subject of such a sign is that kind of object of the sign which is so separately indicated, or would be if the sign were uttered in more detail.[5] [By "uttered," I mean put forth in speech, on paper, or otherwise.] Of course, your question is already answered, at least, it is so as to ideas; what you mean by establishing relations between *acts*, as distinguished from ideas of acts, is not clear to me. But I will go on to say something more about subjects, since the study of significs must, I should think, involve a good deal of fine logical analysis, i.e. definition. Now what I

---

4. See *Collected Papers*, 2.219-226.

* And Burgersdicius, who is excellent authority upon such points, says: (Inst. Log I. xix. 11) "Obiectum & Subiectum in disciplinis fere sine discrimine usurpantur," etc. [This note was added by Peirce.]

5. See *Collected Papers*, 2.328-331.

have to say about subjects is particularly relevant to the doctrine of logical analysis. The subject of a pure symbolic proposition, i.e. one in which no diagram is involved, but only conventional signs, such as words, might be defined as that with which some collateral acquaintance is requisite to the interpretation (the understanding,) of the proposition. Thus the statement, "Cain killed Abel" cannot be fully understood by a person who has no further acquaintance with Cain and Abel than that which the proposition itself gives. Of course, Abel is as much a subject as Cain. But further, the statement cannot be understood by a person who has no collateral acquaintance with killing. Therefore, Cain, Abel, and the relation of killing are the subjects of this proposition. Of course, an Icon would be necessary to explain what was the relation of Cain to Abel, in so far as this relation was *imaginable* or imageable. To give the necessary acquaintance with any single thing an Index would be required. To convey the idea of causing death in general, according to the operation of a general law, a general sign would be requisite; that is a *Symbol*. For symbols are founded either upon habits, which are, of course general, or upon conventions or agreements, which are equally general.[6] Here I may remark that *brute* compulsion differs from rational necessitation founded on law, in that one can have an idea of it,—a sense of it,—in the single case, quite regardless of any law. A law of nature, which I insist, is a reality, and not, as Karl Pearson[7] tries to show, a creature of our minds, an *ens rationis*, I am fond of comparing with a legislative enactment, in that it exercises no compulsion of itself, but only because the people *will* obey it. The judge who passes sentence on a criminal, applies the statutes to an individual case; but his sentence exercises no more force *per se* than the general law. But what the sentence does effect is to bring the execution of it into the field of

6. For Peirce's detailed analysis of Icons, Indices, and Symbols, see *Collected Papers*, 2.274-308.

7. Karl Pearson (1857-1936), mathematician and biologist; author of *The Grammar of Science* (1892).

purpose of the sheriff, whose brute muscles,—or those of
bailiff or hangman under him, exercise the actual compulsion.[8] Thus the Icon represents the sort of thing that may
appear and sometimes does appear; the Index points to the
very thing or event that is met with,—and I mean by an
Occurrence such a single thing or state of things; and finally,
the Symbol represents that which may be observed under
certain general conditions and is essentially general. When we
have analyzed a proposition so as to throw into the subject
everything that can be removed from the predicate, all that it
remains for the predicate to represent is the form of connection between the different subjects as expressed in the
propositional *form*. What I mean by "everything that can be
removed from the predicate" is best explained by giving an
example of something not so removable. But first take something removable. "Cain kills Abel." Here the predicate appears
as "_____ kills _____." But we can remove killing from the
predicate and make the latter "_____ stands in the relation
_____ to _____." Suppose we attempt to remove more from
the predicate and put the last into the form "_____ exercizes
the function of relate of the relation _____ to _____" and
then putting the function of relate to the relation into
another subject leave as predicate "_____ exercizes _____ in
respect to _____ to _____." But this "exercizes" expresses
"exercizes the function." Nay more, it expresses "exercizes
the function of relate," so that we find that though we may
put this into a separate subject, it continues in the predicate
just the same. Stating this in another form, to say that 'A is
in the relation R to B' is to say that A is in a certain relation
to R. Let us separate this out thus: "A is in the relation R^1
(where R^1 is the relation of a relate to the relation of which
it is the relate,) to R to B." But A is here said to be in a
certain relation to the relation R^1. So that we can express the
same fact by saying "A is in the relation R^1 to the relation

---

8. Peirce's account of the reality of law is given in *Collected Papers*,
5.93-119.

R^1 to the relation R to B," and so on *ad infinitum*. A predicate which can thus be analyzed into parts all homogeneous with the whole I call a *continuous predicate*. It is very important in logical analysis, because a continuous predicate obviously cannot be a *compound* except of continuous predicates, and thus when we have carried analysis so far as to leave only a continuous predicate, we have carried it to its ultimate elements. I wont lengthen this letter by easily furnished examples of the great utility of this rule.[9] But I proceed to the next point of your letter.

By *belief*, I mean merely holding for true,—real, genuine, practical holding for true,—whether that which is believed be the atomic theory, or the fact that this is Monday, or the fact that this ink is pretty black, or what you will. You well say that Belief may be mistaken. Yet the nearest certain of anything is for example, that this paper is white or whitish,— or *appears* so. Yet it is easy to show that this belief may be mistaken. For the judgment can never relate to the appearance at the instant of the judgment, because the subject of any judgment must have been known by *collateral* acquaintance. There can be no judgment of the very judgment itself. The old *Insolubilia*, such as "this proposition is false" are examples of this. If it be false, since this is all that it asserts, it must be true; and if it be true, since it denies this, it must be false.[10] Belief that could not be false would be infallible belief and Infallibility is an Attribute of Godhead. The fruit of the tree of knowledge which Satan told Adam and Eve was to make them equal with God was precisely the doctrine that there is some kind of Infallible belief. This must be so; for after this was rendered still more blasphemous by asserting that the kind of belief that was to be Infallible was belief about God, the most utterly inscrutable of any subject, it became the means of corrupting christianity until the religion of Love was confounded with the Odium theologicum.

----

9. See *Collected Papers*, 4.438.
10. A different treatment of the *insolubilia* is given in *Collected Papers*, 3.446.

1908 Dec. 23

Dear Lady Welby, for the past week all my time and all my energy have been taken up with what we Yankees (i.e. the stock of those who came over to Massachusetts before 1645—I forget the exact date,) call "chores." I believe that in standard English the word is lost. It means the menial offices of every day in a household, especially, a primitive household,—the hewing of wood and the drawing of water and the like.

I now return to the expression of my abhorrence of the doctrine that any proposition whatever is infallibly true.[11] Unless truth be recognized as *public*,—as that of which *any* person would come to be convinced if he carried his inquiry, his sincere search for immovable belief, far enough,—then there will be nothing to prevent each one of us from adopting an utterly futile belief of his own which all the rest will disbelieve. Each one will set himself up as a little prophet; that is, a little "crank," a half-witted victim of his own narrowness.

But if Truth be something public, it must mean that to the acceptance of which as a basis of conduct any person you please would ultimately come if he pursued his inquiries far enough;—yes, every rational being, however prejudiced he might be at the outset. For Truth has that compulsive nature which Pope well expressed:

> The eternal years of God are her's.

But, you will say, I am setting up this very proposition as infallible truth. Not at all; it is a mere definition. I do not say that it is infallibly true that there is any belief to which a person would come if he were to carry his inquiries far enough. I only say that that alone is what I call Truth. I cannot infallibly know that there is any Truth.[12]

---

11. For a statement of Peirce's fallibilism see *Collected Papers*, 1.141-175.

12. See *Collected Papers*, 5.549-604.

You say there is a certain "Faith" the object of which is absolutely "certain." Will you have the goodness to tell me what you mean by "certain"? Does it mean anything more than that you personally are obstinately resolved upon sticking to the proposition, *ruat caelum*? It reminds me of an anecdote that was told me in 1859 by a southern darky. "You know," says he, "massa, that General Washington and General Jackson was great friends, dey was [the fact being that the latter was an irreconcileable [*sic*] opponent of the former, but did not become a figure in national politics until after Washington had retired from public life.] Well, one day Gen'l. Washington, he said to Gen'l. Jackson, "Gen'l, how tall should you think that horse of mine was?" "I don't know, General," says General Jackson, "how tall is he, General Washington?" "Why," says General Washington, "he is sixteen feet high." "Feet, General Washington," say Gen'ral Jackson, "feet, General Washington? You means *hands*, Gen'ral!" "Did I say *feet*, General Jackson," said General Washington. "Do you mean to say that I said my horse was sixteen *feet* high?" "You certainly said so, General Washington." "Very well, then, Gen'ral Jackson, if I *said* feet, *if* I said feet, then I sticks to it!" Is your "sublime faith" any more "sublime" than that? How?

Now I will tell you the meaning that *I* would, in my turn, attach to the word faith. The New Testament word is πίστις, which means, in its most proper sense, *trust;* i.e. belief in something not as having any knowledge or approach to knowledge about the matter of belief, but "implicit belief," as the catholics say, i.e. belief in it derived from one's belief that a witness who testifies to it would not so testify if it were not so. Hence, the latest writers of classical Greek, such as Plato and Isocrates, and the earliest writers of common Greek, such as Aristotle, use it for any mediate belief, any belief well founded on another belief. That is, these writers apply πίςις [*sic*] to an assured belief. They also apply it to an *assurance* of any belief. But the English word "faith" could not be used so without great violence to usage which would be entirely unwarranted by any need. I think that what the word is needed to express, and what it might be restricted to express without too great violence to usage is *that belief which the believer does not himself recognize*, or rather (since that cannot properly be called belief,[)] that which he is prepared to conform his conduct to, without recognizing what it is to which he is conforming his conduct. For example, if I do not know what Liddell & Scott say is the meaning of πίστις but am convinced that whatever they may say is its meaning really is so, I have a *faith* that it is so. A person who says "Oh, I could not believe that this life is our only life; for if I did I should be so miserable that I should suicide forthwith," I say that he has a *Faith* that things are not intolerably bad for any individual or at any rate are not so for *him*. Every true man of science, i.e. every man belonging to a social group all the members of which sacrifice all the ordinary motives of life to their desire to make their beliefs concerning one subject conform to verified judgments of perception together with sound reasoning, and who therefore really believes the universe to be governed by reason, or in other words by God,—but who does not explicitly recognize that he believes in God,—has Faith in God, according to my use of the term Faith. For example, I knew a scientific man who devoted his last years to reading theology in hopes of coming to a belief in God, but who never could in the least degree come to a consciousness of having the least belief of the sort, yet passionately pursued that very mistaken means of attaining his heart's supreme desire. He, according to me, was a shining example of Faith in God. For to believe in reasoning about phenomena is to believe that they are governed by reason, that is, by God. That to my mind is a high and wholesome belief. One is often in a situation in which one is obliged to assume, i.e. to go upon, a proposition which one ought to recognize as extremely doubtful. But in order to conduct oneself with vigorous consistency one must dismiss doubts on the matter from consideration. There is a vast difference between *that* and any holding of the proposi-

tion for certain. To hold a proposition to be certain is to puff
oneself up with the vanity of perfect knowledge. It leaves no
room for Faith. It is not absolutely certain that twice two is
four. It is humanly certain that no conception of God can be
free from all error. I once made a careful study of Dr.
Schaff's[13] three solid volumes on "The Creeds of Christendom." I found not one that said one word about the principle
of love, although that seems to be the leading element of
christian faith. In order to find out, if I could, the reason for
this passing strange omission, I made a study of the circumstances which determined the formulation of each Symbolum,
and ascertained that, with the possible exception of what we
erroneously call "The Apostle's Creed," concerning whose
origin we have no definite information, but which is no
exception as regards the information in question, and certainly does not breathe the spirit of such early documents as the
Διδαχή, every one sprang from the *odium theologicum* and
the desire to have some certain person excommunicated, with
the evident wish that he might be damned. Theology arises
from discontent with religious Faith,—which implies a lack of
such Faith, and with a desire to substitute for that a scientific
anatomy and physiology of God, which, rightly considered, is
blasphemous and antireligious. It is also in most striking
disaccord with the spirit of the son of Mary.

Your pleading that I should not use such a phrase as
"attractive fancy" and I suppose you might feel so about the
phrase "strictly hypothetical God" seems to show that I quite
failed to convey my own sense of the value of the Neglected
Argument, in that it does not lead to any theology at all, but
only to what *I* mean by a purely religious *Faith*, which will
have already taken deep root before the subject of it thinks
of it at all as a belief.[14] Writing this is like having to explain
a joke.

---

13. Philip Schaff (1819-1893), theologian and professor; author of
The Creeds of Christendom, Harper & Brothers, New York, 1877.
14. See *Collected Papers*, 6.452-493.

As to the word "play," the first book of philosophy I ever read (except Whately's Logic,[15] which I devoured at the age of 12 or 13,) was Schiller's *Aesthetische Briefe,*[16] where he has so much to say about the Spiel-Trieb; and it made so much impression upon me as to have thoroughly soaked my notion of "play," to this day.

I have never seen Ostwald's book.

A comical slip in spelling occurs in your letter. The spelling is corrolarial, and the odd thing about it is that there really was a medieval verb rolare, whence French *rouler,*—and ultimately (I suppose) our "roll;"—although Hatzfeld and Darmstetter are so little aware of it that they even prefix an asterisk to the much commoner form *rotulare (where I give their erroneous asterisk.) Thus, "corrolary" might mean *involved* in the theorem. I dare say you are aware of the true origin of *corollary*. But still, you may like to see it restated.

Euclid's "Elements" (which some persons erroneously call "Elements of Geometry,") although it contains 414 theorems and 51 problems, 132 definitions (with 9 axioms, 5 postulates, and 2 remarks) only has 23 or perhaps 24 ποξίσματα, which we translate "corollaries." His various editors inserted a vast host of others, which are merely such consequents of the propositions as Euclid deemed too obvious to require statement. The editors, however, regarded them as glorious discoveries; and since the editors rightly required additions to be marked in the margin, they chose for this mark a little wreath of victory, or corolla. In editions of the great Scriptum Oxoniense of Duns Scotus, additions to the text are accompanied by the mark or in the margin, which is more modest. I am myself *constantly* falling into such absurd misspellings; yet I think an advocate of reformed spelling is a person who airs his lack of common sense.

---

15. Richard Whately, *Elements of Logic*, B. Fellow, London, 1831.
16. Johann Christoph Friedrich von Schiller, *The Aesthetic Letters of Schiller*, trans. by John Weiss, C. C. Little and J. Brown, Boston, 1845.

By the way, when I was speaking of creeds, I might have mentioned (it occurs to me now as of a piece with my adherance [*sic*] to late eighteenth century spellings,—except when they are too puzzling: for I cut the Gordian Knot by spelling -ize in almost every case,) that I say the creed in church with the rest. By doing so I only signify, as I presume the majority do,—I hope they do;—my willingness to put aside, most heartily, anything that tends to separate me from my fellow christians. For the very ground of my criticism of creeds is that every one of them was originally designed to produce such a separation, contrary to the notions of him who said "He that is not against me is for me." By the way, I have been reading, with much study, the book of W. B. Smith entitled *Der vorchristliche Jesus,*[17] which I have little doubt is sound in the main; and I think probably christianity was a higher development out of Buddhism, modified by Jewish belief in a living god.

Being a convinced Pragmaticist in Semeiotic, naturally and necessarily nothing can appear to me sillier than rationalism; and folly in politics cannot go further than English liberalism. The people ought to be enslaved; only the slaveholders ought to practice the virtues that alone can maintain their rule. England will discover too late that it has sapped the foundations of culture. The most perfect language that ever was spoken was classical Greek; and it is obvious that no people could have spoken it who were not provided with plenty of intelligent slaves. As to us Americans, who had, at first, so much political sense, we always showed a disposition to support such aristocracy as we had; and we have constantly experienced, and felt but too keenly, the ruinous effects of universal suffrage and weakly exercized government. Here are the labor-organizations, into whose hands we are delivering the government, clamouring today for the "right" to persecute and kill people as they please. We are making them a

---

17. William Benjamin Smith, *Der vorchristliche Jesus*, E. Diedrich, Jena, 1906.

ruling class; and England is going to do the same thing. It will be a healthful revolution; for when the lowest class insists on enslaving the upper class, as they are insisting, and that is just what their intention is, and the upper class is so devoid of manhood as to permit it, clearly that will be a revolution by the grace of God; and I only hope that when they get the power they wont be so weak as to let it slip from their hands. Of course, it will mean going back relatively to the dark ages, and working out a new civilization, this time with some hopes that the governing class will use common-sense to maintain their rule. The rationalists thought their phrases meant the satisfaction of certain feelings. They were under the hedonist delusion. They will find they spell revolution of the most degrading kind.

The publishers of the Britannica have given an earnest of their determination to maintain the eminence of their Encyclopaedia in electing editors who would ask you to give a compend of the exact science of "significs."[18]

In a paper of 1867 May 14 (Proc. Am. Acad. Arts & Sci. [Boston] VII 295), I defined logic as the doctrine of the formal conditions of the truth of symbols; i.e. of the reference of symbols to their objects.[19] Later, when I had recognized that science consists in *inquiry*, not in "doctrine," (the *history* of words, not their *etymology*, being the key to their meanings, especially for a word so saturated with the idea of progress as science is,) and when I accordingly recognized that, in order that the lines of demarcation between what we call "sciences" should be real, in view of the rapid growth of sciences and the impossibility of allowing for future discoveries, those lines of demarcation can only represent the separations between the different groups of men who devote

---

18. For Lady Welby's article entitled "Significs," published in the tenth and eleventh editions of the *Encyclopedia Britannica*, see Appendix C.

19. C. S. Peirce, "On a New List of Categories," published in the *Proceedings of the American Academy of Arts and Sciences*, Vol. 7, May 1867, pp. 287-298. Reprinted in *Collected Papers*, 1.545-559.

their lives to the advance of different studies, I saw that for a long time those who devoted themselves to discovering the truth about the general reference of symbols to their objects would be obliged to make researches into the reference to their interpretants, too, as well as into other characters of symbols, and not *of symbols alone* but of all sorts of signs. So that, for the present, the man who makes researches into the reference of symbols to their objects will be forced to make original studies into all branches of the general theory of signs; and so I should certainly give the logic-book that I am writing the title "Logic, considered as Semeiotic," if it were not that I foresee that everybody would suppose *that* to be a translation of "Logik, als Semeiotik dargestellt," which would not comport with my disagreement (bordering closely upon contempt) from German logic.[20]

"Significs" would appear, from its name, to be that part of Semeiotic which inquires into the relation of signs to their Interpretants (for which, as limited to symbols, I proposed in 1867 the name Universal Rhetoric,) for I am sure you recognize that no usage of language is better established among students of semeiotic than that distinction to which the elegant writer and accurate thinker John of Salisbury in the XIIth century referred as "quod fere in omnium ore celebre est, aliud scilicet esse quod appellatiua significant, et aliud esse quod nominant. Nominantur singularia, sed universalia significantur." (*Metalogicus*. Book II. Cap. xx. Edition of 1620, p. 111.) But, assuming this to be your meaning, I should hardly think it possible, in the present state of the subject, to make much headway in a truly scientific investigation of significs in general without devoting a very large share of one's work to inquiries into other questions of semeiotic.

It is clearly indispensible to start with an accurate and broad analysis of the nature of a Sign. I define a Sign as anything which is so determined by something else, called its Object, and so determines an effect upon a person, which

---

20. The book was never completed.

effect I call its Interpretant, that the latter is thereby mediately determined by the former. My insertion of "upon a person" is a sop to Cerberus, because I despair of making my own broader conception understood. I recognize three Universes, which are distinguished by three Modalities of Being.[21]

One of these Universes embraces whatever has its Being in itself alone, except that whatever is in this Universe must be present to one consciousness, or be capable of being so present in its entire Being. It follows that a member of this universe need not be subject to any law, not even to the principle of contradiction. I denominate the objects of this Universe *Ideas*, or *Possibles*, although the latter designation does not imply capability of actualization. On the contrary as a general rule, if not a universal one, an Idea is incapable of perfect actualization on account of its essential vagueness if for no other reason. For that which is not subject to the principle of contradiction is essentially vague.[22] For example, geometrical figures belong to this Universe; now since every such figure involves lines which can only be *supposed* to exist as boundaries where three bodies come together, or to be the place common to three bodies, and since the boundary of a solid or liquid is merely the place at which its forces of cohesion are neither very great nor very small, which is essentially vague, it is plain that the idea is essentially vague or indefinite. Moreover, suppose the three bodies that come together at a line are wood, water, and air, then a whole space including this line is at every point either wood, water, or air; and neither wood and water, nor wood and air, nor water and air can together occupy any place. Then plainly the principle of contradiction, were it applicable, would be violated in the idea of a place where wood, water, & air come together. Similar antinomies affect all Ideas. We can only reason about them in respects which the antinomies do not

---

21. See Peirce's statement on the cenopythagorean categories in the letter dated October 12, 1904.
22. See *Collected Papers*, 5.450.

affect, and often by arbitrarily assuming what upon closer examination is found to be absurd. There is this much truth in Hegel's doctrine, although he is frequently in error in applying the principle.

Another Universe is that of, 1st, Objects whose Being consists in their Brute reactions, and of, 2nd, the Facts (reactions, events, qualities, etc) concerning those Objects, all of which facts, in the last analysis, consist in their reactions. I call the Objects, Things, or more unambiguously, *Existents*, and the facts about them I call Facts. Every member of this Universe is either a Single Object subject, alike to the Principles of Contradiction and to that of Excluded Middle, or it is expressible by a proposition having such a singular subject.

The third Universe consists of the co-being of whatever is in its Nature *necessitant*, that is, is a Habit, a law, or something expressible in a universal proposition. Especially, *continua* are of this nature. I call objects of this universe *Necessitants*. It includes whatever we can know by logically valid reasoning. I note that the question you put on the first page of your letter as to whether a certain proposition is "thoroughly tested" and supports the test, or whether it is "logically proved," seems to indicate that you are in some danger of enlisting in that army of "cranks," who insist on calling a kind of reasoning "logical" which leads from true premises to false conclusions, thus putting themselves outside the pale of sanity. People, for example, who maintain that the reasoning of the "Achilles" [and the tortoise] is "logical," though they cannot state it in any sound syllogistic or other form acknowledged by sane reasoners.[2][3] I knew a gentleman who had mind enough to be a crack chess-player, but who insisted that it was "logical" to reason

> It either rains or it doesn't rain,
> Now it rains;
> ∴ It doesn't rain.

---

23. See Peirce's remark on the paradox in *Collected Papers*, 6.177.

This is on a perfect level with saying that contemptible Achilles catch is "Logical." The truth is that an inference is "logical," if, and only if, it is governed by a habit that would in the long run lead to the truth. I am confident you will assent to this. Then I trust you do not mean to lend any countenance to notions of logic that conflict with this. It is a part of our duty to frown sternly upon immoral *principles*; and logic is only an application of morality. Is it not?[24]

A Sign may *itself* have a "possible" Mode of Being. E.g. A hexagon inscribed in or circumscribed about a conic. It is a Sign, in that the collinearity of the intersections of opposite sides shows the curve to be a conic, if the hexagon is inscribed; but if it be circumscribed the copunctuality of its three diameters (joining opposite vertices.) Its Mode of Being may be Actuality: as with any barometer. Or Necessitant: as the word "the" or any other in the dictionary. For a "possible" Sign I have no better designation than a *Tone*, though I am considering replacing this by "Mark."[25] Can you suggest a really good name? An Actual sign I call a *Token;*[26] a Necessitant Sign a *Type.*[27]

It is usual and proper to distinguish two Objects of a Sign, the Mediate without, and the Immediate within the Sign. Its Interpretant is all that the Sign conveys: acquaintance with its Object must be gained by collateral experience. The Mediate Object is the Object outside of the Sign; I call it the *Dynamoid* Object. The Sign must indicate it by a hint; and this hint, or its substance, is the *Immediate* Object. Each of these two Objects may be said to be capable of either of the three Modalities, though in the case of the Immediate Object, this is not quite literally true. Accordingly, the Dynamoid Object may be a Possible; when I term the Sign an *Abstractive*; such as the word Beauty; and it will be none the less an Abstractive if I speak of "the Beautiful," since it is the ultimate

---

24. See *Collected Papers*, 1.616-648.
25. Peirce's usual term for such a sign is 'qualisign'.
26. Peirce's usual term is 'sinsign'.
27. Peirce's usual term is 'legisign'.

reference, and not the grammatical form, that makes the sign
An *Abstractive*. When the Dynamoid Object is an Occurrence
(Existent thing or Actual fact of past or future,) I term the
Sign a *Concretive*; any one barometer is an example; and so is
a written narrative of any series of events. For a *Sign* whose
Dynamoid Object is a Necessitant, I have at present no better
designation than a "*Collective*," which is not quite so bad a
name as it sounds to be until one studies the matter: but for a
person, like me, who thinks in quite a different system of
symbols to words, it is so awkward and often puzzling to
translate one's thought into words! If the Immediate Object is
a "Possible," that is, if the Dynamoid Object is indicated
(always more or less vaguely) by means of its Qualities,[28]
etc., I call the Sign a *Descriptive*; if the Immediate [Object] is
an Occurrence, I call the Sign a *Designative*; and if the
Immediate Object is a Necessitant, I call the sign a *Copulant*;
for in that case the Object has to be so identified by the
Interpreter that the Sign may represent a necessitation. My
name is certainly a temporary expedient.

It is evident that a possible can determine nothing but a
Possible, it is equally so that a Necessitant can be determined
by nothing but a Necessitant. Hence it follows from the
Definition of a Sign that since the Dynamoid Object determines the Immediate Object,

Which determines the Sign itself,

which determines the Destinate Interpretant

which determines the Effective Interpretant

which determines the Explicit Interpretant

the six trichotomies, instead of determining 729 classes of
signs, as they would if they were independent, only yield 28
classes;[29] and if, as I strongly opine (not to say almost prove)
there are four other trichotomies of signs of the same order
of importance, instead of making 59049 classes, these will
only come to 66. The additional 4 trichotomies are un-
doubtedly 1st,

---

28. This word stands as "Quatities" in manuscript.

29. See Appendix B.

Icons (or Simulacra   Indices   Symbols
     Aristotle's ὁμοιώμητα)[30]

and then 3 referring to the Interpretants. One of these I am pretty confident is into: *Suggestives, Imperatives, Indicatives,* where the Imperatives include Interrogatives. Of the other two I *think* that one must be into Sign assuring their Interpretants by

       Instinct   Experience   Form

The other I suppose to be what, in my Monist exposition of Existential Graphs, I called

       Semes   Phemes   Delomes.[31]

You, with your life-long study of "significs" must surely have important teachings about the three Interpretants for me, whose studies have been diluted through the whole subject of semeiotic; and what I have succeeded in assuring myself of in significs has chiefly concerned Critic of Arguments, upon which the question you propound on the first page of your letter makes me think you are not at your best. But I smiled at your speaking of my having been "*kindly* interested" in your work, as if it were a divergence—I should say a *deviation*, from my ordinary line of attention. Know that from the day when at the age of 12 or 13 I took up, in my elder brother's room a copy of Whately's "*Logic*," and asked him what Logic was, and getting some simple answer, flung myself on the floor and buried myself in it, it has never been in my power to study anything,—mathematics, ethics, metaphysics, gravitation, thermodynamics, optics, chemistry, comparative anatomy, astronomy, psychology, phonetics, economic, the history of science, whist, men and women,

---

30. ". . . caught from Plato, who I guess took it from the Mathematical school of logic, for it earliest appears in the Phaedrus which marks the beginning of Plato's being decisively influenced by that school. Lutoslawski* is right in saying that the Phaedrus is later than the Republic but his date 379 B.C. is about 8 years too early." [Marginal comment by Peirce.]

*Wincenty Lutoslawski, *The Origin and Growth of Plato's Logic*, Longman, Green, & Co., London, 1897.

31. See Appendix B.

wine, metrology, except as a study of semeiotic; and how rarely I have been able to feel a thoroughly sympathetic interest in the studies of other men of science (how far *more* than rarely have met any care to understand my own studies,) I need not tell you, though fortunately I am of an ardently sympathetic nature,—I mean fortunately for my scientific development, under chilling circumstances.

I wish you would study my Existential Graphs; for in my opinion it quite wonderfully opens up the true nature and method of logical analysis;—that is to say, of definition; though *how* it does so is not easy to make out, until I shall have written my exposition of that art.

I am now working desperately to get written before I die a book on Logic that shall attract some good minds through whom I may do some real good, & may after all hear those wonderful words that will be better by far than any kind of Heaven I ever heard of.[32] Unless there is going to be work to do,—useful work,—I cannot conceive of another life as very desirable. I wish you with all my heart & soul a successful year! Don't forget your implied promise about the proof of the Britannica article. My dear wife constantly though slowly loses ground; & her disposition not to spare herself is most distressing. Very faithfully

C. S. Peirce[33]

---

32. Those wonderful words: Well done, good and faithful servant: thou hast been faithful over a few things, I will set thee over many things: enter thou into the joy of the lord.

33. Drafts of a letter bearing the dates 24, 25 and 28 December 1908 are in the Peirce Correspondence. These have been reprinted in *Collected Papers*, 8.342-379.

January 21st 1909
Duneaves, Harrow.

My dear Professor Peirce—

I cannot thank you enough for your comprehensive and *living* answer to my letter, a better term, I think, than 'kind', since usage now ignores the racial reference of 'kind' and thus misses the clue to a richer identity and the august prerogative of a 'free pass' to the treasurers of Man-kind.

I will take your points in order, only reminding you that I always write 'in pauper (why not pauperate?) form' since I claim nothing but what I would describe as the conscious Primal Sense or reaction to the gist or essential point of things. I could cite curious instances (which of course in your case would be 'taking coal to Newcastle') of how *formal* logicians themselves betray a lack of this. As to 'brute' therefore—I am speaking only of the use of the term by the average 'Hibbert Journal' reader or the 'educated man'—if any one says of a married couple "He is brutal and she is brutish", does he mean it in the classical Latin sense of 'brute'? Would the plea be admitted in Court? I suppose the case is not unlike the French abusive exclamation 'Animal!' though all the time the speaker is 'animé' with the noblest sentiments, and is also respectful to the *anima* except probably in its theological use. Thus of course I agree with you. It is a question of *sense*, and many a tragedy, many a collapse has depended on what at present are the caprices or inconsistencies or technicalities of Sense. The French *sens* means here *direction*, and it seems a pity we cannot adopt that expressive French idiom and ask, "In what direction are you thinking?"

In the present state of language, inconclusive argument is facilitated and fostered. I am far from denying that the endless discussion and abortive controversy thus raised is profitable to the race within limits and in one direction, that of exercise and of analysis. I would only venture to suggest that there ought to be an available alternative, that of consistent and consentient usage, in which all were trained from early childhood; and that each generation should be encouraged to make their means of expression clearer, more delicate, simpler, more richly adequate. Consistent usage and context, the adoption at all costs of the most illuminating forms of language, and the cultivation in education of a keen sense of fitness and freedom which is inborn (in various degrees) in every child, that is our crying need. In the direction of beauty, grace, dignity, some of us at least have it; we must have it also as the very condition of our awareness of these gifts in the direction of significance immeasurably more pene-trative, teeming and commanding than that with which all but men of rare genius have to be content. And even such men are constantly balked by the poor grasp of their fellows on the far reaches and fine meshes of their thinking, and by the failure of an Expression which at present makes them least clear in the clearest heavens of their sight. Our sense both of fitness and of consequence—not merely what *follows* but what *leads*, is more maimed than we know by the present lack betrayed by our helpless toleration of the unrecognized con-fusion of imposed usage in which the conventions of ex-pression for most of us remain. As to proof, of course I agree with all you say; but I have looked in vain among good writers for appreciation of the difference in this case between testing *process* and *result*. With most of us proof is either an unanswerable catena of reasoning, or the *result* of exhaustive test, or the actual production of an object of which the existence had been denied. I am amused at the example of present usage in this case, on the first page of the current 'Monist'.[1] It has many times been shown that an exception 'proves' nothing:[2] it neither probes nor tests, nor does it demonstrate or place beyond doubt. We could only say that it *implied* or *pre-supposed* a rule.

I am greatly interested by your treatment of the subject and object, and regret that I did not refer to your Ethics of Terminology in the 'Syllabus'. I should be very greatful for a

---

1. Edwin Tausch, "William James, The Pragmatist—A Psychological Analysis," *The Monist*, Vol. XIX (January 1909), pp. 1-26.

2. The passage referred to is as follows: "On the one hand I searched in vain for a single philosopher who was counted among the great systembuilders of international renown. Of course H. Spencer at first glance seems quite an exception to the rule; but I am not sure whether he is after all an exception. Anyway the exception proves the rule."

second copy of the Pamphlet, as mine, written over by my own notes, is rather spoilt by irrelevant comment from a friend. I have tried in my stumbling fashion to study all the sections, but only succeed in realising afresh what a consummate significian you are, and how very humble my own rôle must comparatively be.

It is of course true that the study of Significs implies the sense of order; but then all sane speech implies that, just as the study of music implies a musical ear for right progression. As to "fine logical analysis" I would rather say that Significs 'admits of' it than 'involves' it. For educational significs means first the general prevalence of limpid simplicity, fitness, adequacy, in expression, one partly comparable to the most notable triumphs of delicate 'machinery', where the very complication subserves simplicity in action; but still more comparable to the result of organic development.

Your illustration of 'Cain killed Abel', with its wealth of implication, applies here. And the rule you suggest, though it belongs to a complicative world beyond my limit, is obviously of great interest.

Your definition of belief—holding for true—and your criticism of 'infallible belief in GOD' (as we have it in magic and witchcraft of the grossest kind), I entirely accept. My valuation of the ennobling activity of Faith—that of which your own letter and its spirit are full—may be put thus: There is no truer believer than a traitor. He thoroughly believes that a certain person or cause is worth betraying, that he will gain by betrayal. The faithful man is the man not merely of belief but of unfailing honour, and devotion if need be to the death. Even manifest unworthiness does not necessarily touch that loyalty. The consecration of faithfulness which we may see even in a dog giving its life for a master, reacts upon and enriches the faithful nature. Its misdirection is so to speak accidental, its nobility essential. It is centrally related to the Real, however badly we may as yet translate and misread that Reality. All faith—not all belief—finds its way to the racial treasury. No throb of its self-gift can be lost; the motive

transfigures it. I am certain I have your sympathy here.
Indeed your last words affirm it.

But this is one of the cases where current language is too
in-significant to serve us, though it is full of possible service if
we will but determine to make it what it was to the Greeks,
and more so! So you see that for belief, raised as it were to
the power of Certainty, I would *substitute* loyalty to the Best
we know or can conceive; a Best which, whatever our short-
coming or mistake, must, as motive, make the best of us; a
Best always rising to the Better of which as yet we are
perhaps not worthy. Thus of course I share your view of the
scientific man's quest, and your protest against a dogmatic
'certainty'. Faith which uplifts, purifies, energizes, has nothing
to do with creed, as we curiously admit (how often thus in
language we convict ourselves!) by our contemptuous use of
credulous. Theology does indeed imply a lack of faith. It
satisfies a baser craving, for belief. So you see we think
together on this.

All I meant by deprecating in a certain context the phrase
'attractive fancy', was that it was apt to suggest the wayward-
ness of roving caprice or the call of deceptive fascination. But
of course it has also a quite innocent reference. One thing
puzzles me. I never thought of saying, for I do not think,
that "there is a certain Faith the object of which is absolutely
'certain'." The first use of the term in this passage is to me
the main one "A *certain* man had two sons" I err here, if at
all, in the direction of too open a mind and perfect readiness
to use the word in a conditional sense only.

The stupid hand-slip in 'corollarial' both amused and an-
noyed me! The worst of it is that in an automatic reversal
like that, one persists, even in revision, in reading it right; and
alas, there is another misprint in the next line; 'in' for 'is.' I
apologise; and I am pleased to hear about 'rolare'!

It seems to me that we can have no working 'politics' and
indeed no effective sociology until we have raised the level of
expression to that of coherent consistency, and really (theoretically and practically) know what we do and don't mean. So

on this account (rather, perhaps, you are thinking, on account of my ignorance!) I preserve a respectful and sympathetic silence.

Your page 14[3] stirs me very much and gives me the touch of shame that I should be entirely ignorant of Latin and Greek, which compels me to repeat the confession that I speak 'as a child' only. Of course I am fully aware that Semeiotic may be considered the scientific and philosophic form of that study which I hope may become generally known as Significs. Though I don't think you need despair of the acceptance of your own more abstract, logically abstruse, philosophically profound conception of Semeiotic. Of course I assent to your definition of a logical inference, and agree that Logic is in fact an application of morality in the largest and highest sense of the word. That is entirely consonant with the witness of Primal Sense. Alas, there is no word (except religion) more dangerously taken in vain than morality.

Your exposition of the 'possible' Sign is profoundly interesting; but I am not equal to the effort of discussing it beyond saying that I should prefer *tone* to *mark* for the homely reason that we often have occasion to say "I do not object to his words, but to his *tone*." Could the word *Suggestant* be used for Possible Sign?

Your 18th and 19th pages appeal strongly to me in an inarticulate way. I am conscious of the greatness of the issues raised, and of your power to deal with them. And I feel that here I am constrained to make a confession not of faith (for I hope *good faith* needs no confession, still less recitation!) but of position and attitude. I did my poor best to study your Existential Graphs in the 'Monist' of October 1906,[4] and am doing so again now. I could indeed from the first see that they were wonderful, and that when you have written your exposi-

---

3. "On Semeiotic, with a Latin passage at the end." [Marginal comment by Welby.]

4. C. S. Peirce, "Prolegomena To An Apology For Pragmaticism," *The Monist*, Vol. XVI, October 1906, pp. 492-546.

tion, all brains with any degree of your mastery of Logic must find them easy to make out.

I was reminded of one or two of your diagrams—especially Fig. 22, p. 543—this morning (5.30 A.M.) by one in Hans Driesch's Gifford Lectures[5] of what he calls an "Harmonious-equipotential system", though probably there is no real link between them.

I myself have done some thinking in diagram (always of course of a primitive kind) and your 'scroll' especially appeals to me. My attempts have been mainly on the physio-psychological ascent. Though with some misgiving I venture to enclose two out of a number of diagrams by which I tried to make clear to my mind the view of cosmical ascent suggested by modern science and by the 'givens' of experience. I am also enclosing one or two out of a mass of writings involving or implying what I see as religion in the sense of our central interest and our universal link. But here again, *Faith*—not belief, or a creed, or a theory—which may be delusive and fanatical—but the quality of steadfast loyalty to the best, the purest, the truest and the highest we can conceive and act upon: Faith as invulnerable as that which the facts and the order of nature and of our sane response to them, inspire and even urge upon us: Faith which never deserts, never garbles or suppresses or shirks: Faith which never betrays and thus,—be ignorance what it may—must ennoble and greaten that humanity which after all is cosmical: *that* Faith is not merely the highest emotional and moral, but even the highest logical gift of humanity: as I think your work illustrates. Certainty, except in the logical form or the actual sensation, is beyond us: faithfulness to the consecrating influence which can sway us: faith in the sense above defined is always within our reach.

---

5. Hans Adolph Driesch (1867-1941), German zoologist and philosopher. Delivered the Gifford Lectures before the University of Aberdeen for the years 1907-1908. The lectures were entitled "The Science and Philosophy of the Organism."

Meanwhile may I venture to suggest that Logic in graphic form as you give it is as it were an Immuniser, an enemy and destructive absorbent of rational *toxins*, and also that it weds the pictorial and the abstract.

I will brood upon the matter of your three Interpretants and see if anything emerges that I could venture to send. In any case it could only be from my natural standpoint which is that, as I cannot repeat too often, of the nursery of the world wherein the infant mind grows and learns to see all things as signals of boundless significance. In this I am compelled to be content with my A.B.C. We have, it may be, become too exclusively devoted to our X.Y.Z. and they are turning upon us and refusing to work until we have recognized the spiral course of the mental alphabet, and recovered *on a higher sweep* our touch with our A.B.C.

So you see you must not smile when I call your interest kind! It is as you confess the outcome of an ardently sympathetic nature; and for that and your patience with my inevitable crudities you must let me thank you. It is difficult indeed to express my sense of the honour done me and the service rendered to my work in such generous recognition as you have given.

I am afraid indeed that you have done it at some cost to your comfort. 'Chores' is still a word we quote from village usage; and in the north it is constantly used. But there is nothing sadder than the way in which the base lingo of the elementary school replaces the fine sounding and consistently significant speech of the 'folk'. Only a few years ago every countryman spoke of his self and their selves while we adopt the absurd himself and themselves!

Now let me return from my heart your kind good wishes. Your letter came at a time of great depression in which I could see *only* defect in that fleeting self which we so strangely confound with its Owner, You or Me. It has helped to revive courage.

I am grieved to hear of your anxiety. May I send my love to your wife and my earnest and warm good wishes to you that you may be able to do all the work that is in you before you go, and see that the world and man are the better for it in the fullest sense.

Yours ever
Victoria Welby

I am enclosing the Encyclopaedia article[6] & also the following Papers: *What does it Signify?* Aug 31/08. *Significs*, Sept 9 *Ditto* Sept 30. *'Trans—'* Aug 14 08 *To What End?* June 8/07. *Faith v. Belief* Jan 8th. 08. *Unborn Church* Aug 20/Aug 14 08 *Communion of Saints* Nov 1.07. But you *must* not let them trouble you.

---

6. V. Welby, "Significs," *The Encyclopaedia Britannica*, 11 ed., Vol. XXV, 1911, pp. 78-81. See Appendix C.

Milford, Pa.
1909 Jan. 31

My dear Lady Welby:

I yesterday received your beautiful letter of the 21st inst. which has done me a world of good & which I shall read again and again. I have not had time to read any of the enclosures, eager as I am to get at your Britannica article; but I shall do so, I hope, in the course of this week. I must beg you to let me know if you expect the return of that MS or of any of the others.

I will notice at once two odd words I came across last evening; for if I didn't I should forget all about them, & they are rather curious. The book in which I found them was Frank Wigglesworth Clarke's "Data of Geochemistry,"[1] in which the author spoke of "*salic* rocks and *femic* rocks." I was completely at a loss to imagine what these words could mean or whence they were derived; but diligent search through the volume disclosed the chemist-author's notion of the way to form words. [Note that I am professionally a

---

1. U.S. Government Printing Office, Washington, 1908, pp. 358-359.

chemist myself, but not enough of a chemist to fathom the allusions of the two words.] I found out, at last, that "salic rocks" were rocks predominantly composed of oxygen, *silicon* (Si) and *aluminum* (Al); so that *si-al*-an or *si-al*-ian would have been better than "Salic"; while femic rocks were those in which Iron (Fe) and magnesium (Mg) predominate. If chemists had agreed upon M as the symbol of *magnesium*, as they would have done but for the necessity of distinguishing it from *manganese* (originally, the same word) this would have been intelligible, once one possessed the secret of the general method of formation; but under the circumstances "femgan" seems to me the proper word. I thought the words were interesting as specimens of the utterly un-English, and I may say un-Aryan ways of word-formation that chemists have found so well adapted to their purposes. Those two words of Frank Wigglesworth Clarke suddenly bring to my mind something that I do not believe I have thought of for half a century; how as a boy I invented a language in which almost every letter of every word made a definite contribution to its signification. It involved a classification of all possible ideas; and I need not say that it was never completed. I remember however a number of features of it. Not only must the ideas be classified, but abstract and psychical ideas had to be provided with fixed metaphors; such as *lofty* for pride, ambition, etc. Roget's Thesaurus did not exist in those days. I had no better prompter than Bishop Wilkins's "Real Character,"[2] —a book (if you have never seen it) that attempts to furnish a graphical sign for every idea. The grammar of my Language was, I need hardly say, modelled in a general way after the Latin Grammar as almost all ideas of grammar are to this day. It had, in particular, the Latin parts of speech; and it never dawned upon me that they could be other than they are in Latin. Since then I have bought Testaments in such languages as Zulu, Dakota, Hawaian, Jagalu, Magyar (Basque I have dipped into otherwise; and I learned a little Arabic from

2. John Wilkins, *An Essay Towards a Real Character, and a philosophical language.* Printed by J. M. for S. Gellibrand, London, 1668.

Edward Palmer[3] whom I knew in Constantinople & later in Cambridge). These studies have done much to broaden my ideas of language in general; but they have never made me a good writer, because my habits of thinking are so different from those of the generality of people. Besides I am left-handed (in the literal sense) which implies a cerebral development and connexions of parts of the brain so different from those of right-handed people that the sinister is almost sure to be misunderstood and live a stranger to his kind, if not a misanthrope. This has, I doubt not, had a good deal to do with my devotion to the science of logic. Yet probably my intellectual lefthandedness has been serviceable to my studies in that science. It has caused me to be *thorough* in penetrating the thoughts of my predecessors,—not merely their ideas as they understood them, but the potencies that were in them. I have neglected no school, nor any logician whose books I could lay hand upon. Thus I have gained caution in forming my own opinions & still more in condemning others; and I have produced little, and that little has been far, far more deeply considered and debated than anybody dreams of its being. Yet today half of what I have written seems to me immature and not sufficiently considered.

I place a high valuation upon my Existential Graphs, and hope you will persevere in the study of the system; and if you do so, I desire to aid you. The use of it arises from its furnishing an *icon* of thought which in formal respects is of the highest exactitude. The study of it must tend to prevent its student from rashly interfering with the arrangements of nature; and whatever man is given to doing is an arrangement of nature. Its most generally useful rules are those of Iteration (in evenly enclosed areas) and Deiteration (from oddly enclosed areas), and the Rule of the Double Cut. Though not particularly adapted to drawing conclusions, practice in so

3. Edward Henry Palmer (1840-1882), British orientalist and author of *The Arabic Manual* (1881), *A Grammar of the Arabic Language* (1874), and *Simplified Grammar of Hindustani, Persian, and Arabic* (1882). See Peirce's reference to Palmer in *Collected Papers*, 4.48 n.

applying it is the only way to acquire mastery of it. I will give a few easy examples now.

Example 1.   Given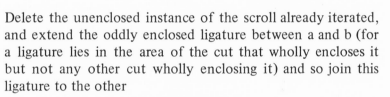

Transform to

Solution.   Iterate one scroll in the inner close of the other; thus,

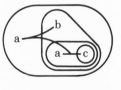

Delete the unenclosed instance of the scroll already iterated, and extend the oddly enclosed ligature between a and b (for a ligature lies in the area of the cut that wholly encloses it but not any other cut wholly enclosing it) and so join this ligature to the other

better thus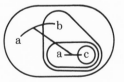

---

4. In Peirce's letter, this figure appears as , and is corrected by him in the following note: "The cross line is a slip of the pen."

Deiterate the inner *a*; thus

Remove the Double Cut

Now prove the same thing by the *Reductio ad Absurdum*; thus:
Starting with

1st Put a double cut about the b and another about the c
2nd *Twice* iterate the a within two cuts and delete the
      unenclosed a and the outer ligature. The next day try to
      do both these transformations without copying.

An iteration within the inner close of a scroll will usually
be followed by a deiteration; and for the most part there will
be two ways in which the iteration can be performed, one of
which ways yields a result while the other does not. Let us
see which is right, and work out the rule for doing it right. I
show the two ways in parallel columns.

Iterate the left hand scroll in the inner close of the right hand one	Iterate the right hand scroll in the inner close of the left hand one

 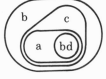   

Erase the inner *b*, this being evenly enclosed

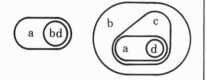

Deiterate the inner b

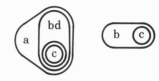

Nothing can be done toward eliminating *b* except by iterating the whole right hand scroll in the left hand one

Suppress the scroll or double-cut with the vacant outer close

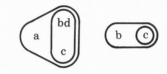

Erase the evenly enclosed bd and the unenclosed scroll to the right

You see that an erasure of an evenly enclosed graph or the insertion of an oddly enclosed graph can only diminish the *information* of a proposition. [Note by the way that the logical rule given in many logics that to increase the breadth, or extension, or denotation, or *Umfang*, of a concept is necessarily to decrease the depth, or comprehension, or signification, or "connotation," a bad term this last, or *Inhalt* of it and *vice versa*, should be that to increase the breadth of a term, of a proposition, or of an argument, is *either* to decrease its depth *or* increase its information; and to increase its depth is *either* to decrease its breadth or to increase its information; or, calling its information its "area" that breadth x depth = area.] Consequently, if an iteration is to be followed by a deiteration effecting the elimination of a partial

graph, that graph must at the outset be oddly enclosed, and
the graph in which it is oddly enclosed must be iterated into
an evenly enclosed area.

Here is another example that I will work both ways.

Iterating the left hand graph
into the innermost even enclosure of the right hand
graph

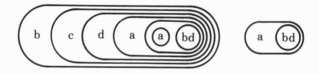

This procedure is futile; but
the insertion might be made
again thus

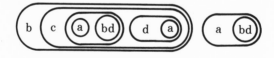

The inner b can now be got
rid of by deiteration; and
nothing but *c* will remain in
the area with c except

Now it will be just as well to bear in mind, as a general theorem that this graph equally reduces in two ways. For one way is to iterate so as to get

and erasing the last graph which is evenly enclosed, 2 de-iterations will give

& since a vacant enclosure destroys the whole area in which it is, this reduces to

 or a

The other way consists in first putting a double cut round *d* so as to get

 and then

treat (d) just as d was treated in the first way. We thus reach *a* conclusion but not so complete a one as by the method at the right hand side of the page.

Iterating in the opposite *sens* at the same time into *both* the inner closes of the left hand double scroll. [But I will scribe these two insertions in blue ink, so as to make them readily distinguishable.]

I now deiterate one b and one d:

I strike out two double cuts where the d and b have been, I omit an evenly enclosed

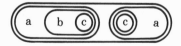 and the unenclosed graph to the right, and an evenly enclosed bd

I now put a double cut round the second c, in *red* for distinctness

I now insert b in an oddly enclosed area

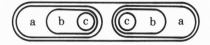

I now deiterate one of the two identical graphs, and remove the outer double cut, and so finally obtain

a (b (c))

1909 Feb 1

I will now "set you some sums to do" (in childhood's phrase) and put the solutions on the *back's* of pages 5, 4, 3.

Example 3. "There is a woman who is adored
by all catholics"
Expressing this in Existential Graphs, we have

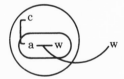

where   M-c   = M is a catholic
          M-a-N = M adores N
          M-w   = M is a woman

Iterate *w* in the inner close of the scroll and we get

"There is is [*sic*] a woman, and every catholic adores some woman who is identical with that woman"
Erase the outer w and we get

"There exists a certain object such that if there be any catholic he (or she) adores a woman, who in any case is identical with that existing object whether there be a catholic or not, although if there be no catholic the object is perhaps not a woman, (may be, in that state of things she, the object, was not grown up).

Cutting off the identity with an object existing whether there be a catholic or not, we get

"Whatever catholic there may be adores
some woman or other"

Now I suggest that you deduce by means of graphs from the proposition "There is a gentleman whose great toe nobody is in the habit of kissing, except catholics" a consequence related to it as the meaning of the last graph

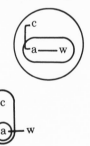

is related to that of

For solution see back of p. 5.[5]

Example 4. Let the meaning of the graph be represented by A. By working with the same general

---

5. For Peirce's solution, see the section immediately following this letter.

method as in the last example, deduce from **A** a consequent, **B**, of which **A** shall be reciprocally a necessary consequent; so that the two graphs shall be "logically equivalent." In other words their dynamical objects, that is, the imaginary state of things which they would represent if a, b, c, and d had any dynamical interpretants would be identically the same, though their immediate objects would be different. Moreover, the new graph must consist of a single enclosure (though it will necessarily have other enclosures in its area.) It is to be a compound scroll; i.e. its outer cut is to contain more than one cut included within no other cut. Also show the manner of transforming the new graph so as to recover the original one which expresses **A**. Also scribe the two corresponding direct contradictories of the two equivalent graphs.

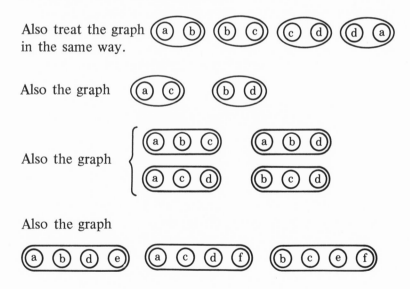

Example 5. Treat the graph

in the same manner, finding that logical equivalent of it which consists of a single enclosure having more than one enclosure in its area. You needn't go back to the fundamental rules, after theorems have been established.

Also treat the graph
in the same way.

Also the graph

Also the graph

Also the graph

Also the Graph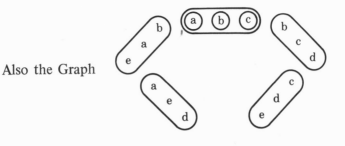

Example 6: I call your attention to the fact that $\left(\oint_b^a\right]$ asserts

that if anything is both *a*'d by anything and *b*'d by anything then that which *a*'s it and that which *b*'s it are the same

individual; and so $\left(\oint_a^a\right)$ asserts that if anything is *a* and

anything is *a* they are the same individual, or there is at most but *a* single individual that is *a*. That being evident it follows

that (removing the outer cut) $\oint_a^a$ asserts that some *a* exists

that is not some other *a*, or that there are two *a*s at least; and

so $\oint_b^a]$ asserts that something is *a*'d by something and is *b*'d

by something else; and $\oint_B^A$ asserts that there is some A that is

other than some B. I wanted to call your attention to the meaning of $-\!\!\bigcirc\!\!-$ namely "something is other than something." I will use this in the following problem.[6] I have to compose this and write down subject to incessant interruptions, and so it is likely enough that it may involve some inconsistencies. But perhaps that won't matter, as far as its value as an exercise is concerned. I will begin by supposing a dyadic

6. Here the date of the letter changes to February 13, 1909.

relationship (i.e. *fundamentum relationis*) of the greatest possible generality as far as either relate is concerned; but absolutely individual as far as both its *second breadths* are concerned. I will explain what I mean by the "second breadth" of a dyadic relation. Suppose the relation to be expressed by the transitive verb "to *l*." Then the number of individual objects each of which "*l*s" anything is the *first active breadth-multitude*, and the number of individuals each of which "is *l*'d by" anything, is the *first passive breadth multitude*. And the proportion of all individual objects that *l* anything is the *first active breadth-ratio*; and the *first active breadth-ratio* needs no explanation. The *average number* of individuals that are *l*'d by one individual that *l*'s anything is the *second passive breadth*; the average number of individuals that *l*'s one individual that is *l*'d is the *Second Active Breadth*. Now our problem shall be concerned with a transitive verb "to *x*" And the two *First Breadths* of this verb shall be the greatest possible, while the the [*sic*] Second Breadths shall be the least possible. That can be expressed by four graphs

With the aid of these I now define the meaning of another transitive verb, "to *w*." Namely,

defines "A *ws* B."

1909 Feb. 24
Ash Wednesday

I think what a lapse of time has intervened in which I have been working with might & main to get my wife rescued from her failing state of health. We must pull up stakes & go about to give her *change*. To do that we must sell this house which is any way too big for her. To accomplish that the outside of it must be made attractive. For now it looks so forlorn that nobody can be persuaded that the inside is worth looking at. Besides, its four roofs are all in need of shingling & a new verandah must replace the present one. All these things have compelled me to drop logic for the last days completely. I had intended to make the last example very elaborate & instructive. But it can wait, until I ascertain whether or not you are at all interested in my Existential Graphs.

Dear me, I won't deny I am beginning to age; but it seems to me that it is not nearly so much that it is I that have grown old as it is that the world in my day has been settling down to a state of ferocious hum-drum-acity,—a positive appetite for the humdrum. I could still enjoy an old time Roman carnival, or an old time *bal masqué* at the Paris Opera. But how did I celebrate my *mardi gras*? I read all your essay-cules.[7] I had already read your Britannica article and had learned something important from it. It is that what you are after, what you are well on the *piste* of, in your Sense, Meaning, & Significance

1909 March 14

Oh, to think that, in the Middle of March, I should not have finished a letter begun in January;—a letter to my dear Lady Welby! And, what is much worse still, that I should have let your admirable letter go all this time without one word of response, nor even acknowledgment. It has been because one thing after another has demanded my instant attention, while I was always promising myself that surely in two or three days at the utmost I should get back to this. But what have you been thinking of me? Will you really forgive me? If you knew all that I have been forced to neglect, and how terribly overworked I have been, every night falling asleep while my pen scrawled over the paper, and every morning jumping up at the alarum!

---

7. See Appendix E.

I wrote somewhat further about your Britannica article; but as I have, at odd moments, thought considerably of it since my last words, I prefer to begin that subject again. I propose to treat it with the coolest criticism, because it is worth such treatment. I confess I had not realized before reading it, how fundamental your trichotomy of Sense, Meaning, and Significance really is. It is not to be expected that concepts of such importance should get perfectly defined for a long time.

By the way, I find in my portfolio some part of a letter, if not the whole, dated December 28.[8] I suppose I sent you that. I hope so, because it seems, from the glance I cast upon [it] to be concerned with my gropings after the three kind of Interpretant. I now find that my division nearly coincides with yours, as it ought to do exactly, if both are correct. I am not in the least conscious of having been at all influenced by your book in settling my trichotomy, as nearly as it is settled; and I don't believe there was any such influence; though of course there may have been without my being aware of it. In reading your book my mind may, quite well have absorbed the ideas without my remembering it; and when I came to search for a division of the Interpretant, those ideas may have seemed to me to have been struck out by processes of thought that I thought then were presenting themselves to me for the first time, when the fact was that they were due to a bent of my thoughts which the perusal of your book had made. However, as I do not believe this did happen, I feel some exultation in finding that my thought and yours nearly agree, for I think it is because we were both trying to get at the truth; and I should not wonder if you have the same feeling. But as far as the public goes, I can only point out the agreement, and confess to having read your book.

Let us see how well we do agree. The greatest discrepancy appears to lie in my Dynamical Interpretant as compared with your "Meaning."[9] If I understand the latter, it consists in the

8. See Burks's note, *Collected Papers*, 8.342n 15.

9. Lady Welby's explanation of *Meaning* is given in her Britannica article. See Appendix C.

effect upon the mind of the Interpreter that the utterer (whether vocally or by writing) of the sign intends to produce. My Dynamical Interpretant consists in direct effect actually produced by a Sign upon an Interpreter of it. They agree in being effects of the Sign upon an individual mind, I think, or upon a number of actual individual minds by independent action upon each. My Final Interpretant is, I believe, exactly the same as your Significance; namely, the effect the Sign *would* produce upon any mind upon which circumstances should permit it to work out its full effect. My Immediate Interpretant is, I think, very nearly, if not quite, the same as your "Sense"; for I understand the former to be the total unanalyzed effect that the Sign is calculated to produce, or naturally might be expected to produce; and I have been accustomed to identify this with the effect the sign first produces or may produce upon a mind, without any reflection upon it. I am not aware that you have ever attempted to define your term "Sense"; but I gather from reading over what you say that it is the first effect that a sign would have upon a mind well-qualified to comprehend it. Since you say it is Sensal and has no Volitional element, I suppose it is of the nature of an "impression." It is thus, as far as I can see, exactly my Immediate Interpretant. You have selected words from vernacular speech to express your varieties, while I have avoided these and manufactured terms suitable, as I think, to serve the uses of Science. I might describe my Immediate Interpretation, as so much of the effect of a Sign as would enable a person to say whether or not the Sign was applicable to anything concerning which that person had sufficient acquaintance.[10]

---

10. See *Collected Papers*, 8.184. This is part of a forty-sheet letter Peirce intended to send William James (see Ralph Barton Perry, *The Thought and Character of William James*, Vol. II, Boston: Little, Brown and Co., 1935, pp. 438-439). The forty-sheet draft is in the Peirce Correspondence, Houghton Library, Harvard University (Robin *Catalogue*, L-224). Peirce also deals with this same three-part distinction in *Collected Papers*, 8.343 and 5.475-476.

My Interpretant with its three kinds is supposed by me to be something essentially attaching to anything that acts as a Sign. Now natural Signs and symptoms have no utterer; and consequently have no Meaning, if Meaning be defined as the intention of the utterer. I do not allow myself to speak of the "purposes of the Almighty," since whatever He might desire is done. Intention seems to me, though I may be mistaken, an interval of time between the desire and the laying of the train by which the desire is to be brought about. But it seems to me that Desire can only belong to a finite creature.

Your[11] ideas of Sense, Meaning, and Signification seem to me to have been obtained through a prodigious sensitiveness of Perception that I cannot rival, while my three grades of Interpretant were worked out by reasoning from the definition of a Sign what sort of thing *ought* to be noticeable and *then* searching for its appearance. My Immediate Interpretant is implied in the fact that each Sign must have its peculiar Interpretability before it gets any Interpreter. My Dynamical Interpretant is that which is experienced in each act of Interpretation and is different in each from that of any other; and the Final Interpretant is the one Interpretative result to which every Interpreter is destined to come if the Sign is sufficiently considered. The Immediate Interpretant is an abstraction, consisting in a Possibility. The Dynamical Interpretant is a single actual event. The Final Interpretant is that toward which the actual tends.

It is now a good while since I read your essay-lets. If I can recall anything in them, it must have struck me as very good or else as open to some particular criticism. When you speak in one of them of Man as *translating* vegetal and Brute strength into intellectual and spiritual vigor, that word *translating* seems to me to contain profound truth wrapped up in it. Then there was one piece dated All-Souls'[12] that I liked in

11. The following portion of the letter was written March 15, 1909.
12. Surely Peirce is referring to Lady Welby's essay "The Communion of Saints," written on All Saints' Day, November 1st, 1907. See Appendix E.

much the same way; that is, as expressing thoughts familiar to me too, but probably not to Tom, Dick, and Harry. I regard Logic as the Ethics of the Intellect,—that is, in the sense in which Ethics is the science of the method of bringing Self-Control to bear to gain our Satisfactions. If I had a son, I should instil into him this view of morality, and force him to see that there is but one thing that raises one individual animal above another,—Self-Mastery, and should teach him that the Will is Free only in the sense that, by employing the proper appliances, he can make himself behave in the way he really desires to behave. As to what one ought to desire, it is, I should show him, what he will desire if he sufficiently considers it, and that will be to make his life beautiful, admirable. Now the Science of the Admirable is *true* Esthetics. Thus, the Freedom of the Will, such as it is, is a one-sided affair, it is Freedom to become Beautiful, καλὸς κ'ἀγαθὸς: There is no freedom to be or to do anything else. Nor is there any freedom to do right if one has neglected the proper discipline. By these teachings, by showing him that a good dog is more to be respected than an improvident man, who has not prepared himself beforehand to withstand the day of temptation, I should expect to render him eager to submit to a pretty severe discipline.

One remark I approved particularly was that "Language is only the extreme form of expression" Also; "Life, itself, may be considered [I should have said *should be recognized*] as Expression."

But your method of getting at the exact meanings of words is very different from mine. I should be greatly obliged to you if you would give me a statement of what your method is, and of your reasons for adopting it; and if I may petition for still more, I should further like to know, since your Britannica article contains much less about the physiology of signs than about efforts that ought to be made for improving our language, what your method is of assuring yourself and others that any given habit of language ought to be changed, and that a given sort of effort will *pay*, that is will cause advantages greater than any other way of expending the same energy. In this connection, I will send you, if I can find one, a copy of a study I made a good many years ago of the *economics of research.*[13]

I ask these things of you because, if you have considered well your methods,—a study which I have just endeavored to show you is about what Morals amount to,—I shall certainly get some good, some practical application to my own doings from what you tell me, while in any case, it is not likely to be altogether profitless for you to set down for the benefit of another what you so often ruminate upon for your self; since one generally gains some new *aperçu* in putting one's personal meditations into shape for communication.

Your trichotomy of Sense, Meaning, Signification is a positive earnest of the value of what I ask to myself.

In order at any rate to prove my disposition to reciprocate the benefit, I will explain my own methods.

My father was universally acknowledged to be by far the strongest mathematician in the country, and was a man of great intellect and weight of character. All the leading men of science, particularly astronomers and physicists resorted to our house; so that I was brought up in an atmosphere of science. But my father was a broad man and we were intimate with literary people too. William Story the sculptor, Long-fellow, James Lowell, Charles Norton, Wendell Holmes, and occasionally Emerson, are among the figures of my earliest memories. Among them I remember the Italian Gallenga, who went by the name of Mariotte. The Quincy's we also knew very well, but not the Adams's. My mother's father had been a Senator in Washington. But his weak lungs having obliged him to retire, he set up a law school; and in the way I used to see some of the most eminent of the political people, such as Webster. Bancroft had been very intimate with my mother's family, as in his old age he was a great friend of my wife here. I used occasionally to see him; and Lothrop Motley

---

13. See *Collected Papers*, 7.139-157.

was one of our friends. My father had strong contempts for certain men whom he considered shams, and among them was Charles Sumner, who was, I must say, one of the absurdest figures of vanity I ever laid eyes on. Among the lawyers I remember Rufus Choate, Judge Story, etc. Another figure of my childhood was Emerson's friend Margaret Fuller (Countess d'Ossoli.) I was brought up with far too loose a rein, except that I was forced to think hard & continuously. My father would sometimes make me sit up all night playing double dummy till sunrise without relaxing my attention.

I was educated as a chemist, and as soon as I had taken my A.B. degree, after a year's work in the Coast Survey, I took first six months under Agassiz in order to learn what I could of his methods, & then went into the laboratory. I had had a laboratory of my own for many years & had every memoir of any consequence as it came out; so that at the end of two or three years, I was the first man in Harvard to take a degree in chemistry *summa cum laude*.

But I had already discovered that my only very unusual gift was for logical analysis. I began with German Philosophy having read hardly any of the great English school and not very much of such French writers as Maine de Biran, Jouffroy, Cousin, etc. For several years I studied the Kritik der reinen Vernunft, and knew it almost word for word, in both editions. Even now, I fancy there are few who know it better. Then I devoted myself for some years chiefly to the scholastics and after that to Locke, Hume, Berkeley, Gay, Hartley, Reid, Hamilton, etc. I had already read the most readable part of Cudworth & all Hobbes. Gradually, I gained independent views.

By this time the inexactitude of the Germans, and their tottering logic utterly disgusted me. Kant & Leibniz alone seemed to me great. I more and more admired British thought. Its one great and terrible fault, which my severe studies in the schoolmen had rescued me from,—or rather, it was because I suspected they were right about this that I took to the study of them & found that they didn't go far enough to satisfy me,—was their extreme Nominalism. To be sure *all* modern philosophers were nominalists, even Hegel. But I was quite convinced they were absolutely wrong. Modern science, especially physics, is and must be, for all the brilliant Lothringian—whose name escapes me,—says, essentially on the side of scholastic realism. So is religion; but that cannot be admitted as evidence. I set myself to finding out how it happened that all modern philosophy had put up with that dire nonsense. It did not take very long to solve that problem. It was that all the humanists were no better than *littérateurs*, with the total lack of ratiocinative power which I had seen in the literary men whom I personally had known. Such fools! On the intellectual level of the wine-tasters of Bordeaux. [By the way, I was myself for six months under the tutelage of the *sommelier* of Voisin in Paris before he sold out his great *caves*, to study the red wines of Médoc, and became quite an expert.] Now the Scotists had almost undisputed supremacy in almost all the Universities having gained it by their superiority in Logic. They therefore appeared as the old fogeys whom the Humanists had to fight. The latter called them Dunces after their master Duns Scotus. But for the first generation of the renaissance a Dunce was far from meaning or suggesting a stupid person. The title rather conveyed the idea of a man so skilled in debate on the wrong side as to be a terror to the pure humanist upon whom he might fall. So since the great adversaries of the Scotists were the Ockhamists, or terminists, who belonged to the class of *nominales*, whom the humanists called nominalists, the humanists allied themselves with the nominalists to cast the Scotists out of the Universities, & not caring a tuppence for the dispute between the two kinds of logicians they conformed to the nominalistic confession in return for the favor of that party; and so, because from that day to this scarcely anybody has examined into the real meaning or merits of the controversy & it was very easy and obvious to say that "Generals are mere words," which moreover is perfectly true in a sense, which was not the point at issue, it follows that

everybody has admitted that Nominalism was the correct
doctrine, just as everybody in England of any consequence
that I saw, in my time, publicly assented to all the mon-
strosities of the Athanasian Creed, and just as everybody who
graduated from Oxford for I know not how many centuries
swore to hate and detest one Simon, (or I forget the name)
though no English writer whom I ever consulted professed to
know for certain who the Simon he had sworn to devote
himself to putting down was. He was supposed to be some-
body who lived under the reign of King John; but nobody
knew what he had ever said or done that was amiss.

It is very easy to prove in two twos that Realism is right
and Nominalism is wrong. The realists are those who declare
that *some* generals such as are fit each to be predicated of
many subjects are Real. The nominalists said in various forms
that no general was Real. Now the word "real,"—Latin
realis—was not an old word. It had been invented during the
controversy to mean that which is not a *figment*, as of course
any word of a particular language is, or, to express the precise
meaning of it in terms intelligible today, the Real is such that
whatever is true of it is not true because some individual
person's thought or some individual group of persons' thought
attributes its predicate to its subject, but is true, no matter
what any person or group of persons may think *about* it.
Thus a dream, meaning what is dreamed is not real, because,
for example, if it be true that the dream was about hen's
eggs, it is because the action of the dreamer's mind made it to
be true. But the *fact* that A given person did dream of hen's
eggs, if it be true *is* true whether he remembers dreaming it,
or thinks he dreamed it or not. It in truth depends ⌐n the
action of his mind, but does *not* depend upon any attribution
by his mind to the *fact* that he dreamed, which is now that
whose reality is in question. All the scholastic philosophy is
full of such subtilties, and it requires *exact thinking*, which
few people except lawyers, mathematicians etc. are, in our
days trained to, in order to steer one's bark between them
without swamping it. Those humanists broke up the habit of

exact thinking throughout Europe. That of which whatever is true depends for its truth on the action of a mind is *internal* or as schoolmen said *objective* (Germans might say *subjective*). That of which the truth of whatever is true of it depends not merely on the action of a person's or a goup of persons thought but also upon their thought *about* the substance of the proposition that is true, is unreal. That which is such that something true about it is either true independently of the thought of any *definite* mind or minds or is at least true independently of what any person or any definite individual group of persons think about that truth, is real. It was Duns Scotus more than anybody else who (though he did not first invent the word *real*,) brought it into use. The word *real* had already been used for *Real property*. But that had nothing at all to do with the usual metaphysical sense which attaches to it.

Now that you see what the word *real* means, I ask you, as to the Law that every body set in motion continues to move right on at a uniform rate only modified by its coming into the spatial vicinity of some other body that acts upon it, whether supposing this Law to be true, whether it be not a *real Law*. Does it depend for its truth upon some person's *thinking* it to be true? Not so; supposing it to be true at all. To be sure, you may say, with Kant, that it is only true of Space which is a form of thought [of course *Kant* does not use "thought" in this wide sense; but in English we *do*. Germans often think the English ought to change their language to conform to German habits, but this is only an example of the extreme modesty and diffidence of which the Germans are so prodigiously vain.] But that though it makes the truth of whatever is true of the law to depend upon *thought* in general, does not make it depend upon the thought of any particular person or any particular group of persons. So if you believe that modern science has made any general discovery at all, you believe that general so discovered to be real, and so you *are a scholastic realist* whether you are aware of it or not. Not only does all *science* hang upon the

decision but so do Truth and Righteousness![14] Nominalism
and all its ways are devices of the Devil if devil there be. And
in particular it is the disease which almost drove poor John
Mill mad,—the dreary outlook upon a world in which all that
can be loved, or admired, or understood, is figment.

Oh I must skip a great deal; for I cant spend what I dont
own, which is an hour's more time for this letter!

I at first defined logic as the general science of the relation
of *symbols* to their *objects*. And I think still that this defines
the Critic of Argument which is the central part of logic,—its
heart. But studies of the limits of the sciences in general
convinced me that the Logician ought to broaden his studies,
and take in every *allied* subject that it was no business of
anybody else to study and in short, and above all, he must
not confine himself to *symbols* since no reasoning that
amounts to much can be conducted with [*sic*] *Icons* and
Indices.[15] Nor ought he to confine himself to the relations of
signs to their Objects since it had always been considered the
business of the logician and of nobody else to study
Definition. Now a definition does not reveal the Object of a
Sign, its Denotation, but only analyzes its Signification, and
that is a question not of the sign's relation to its Object but
of its relation to its Interpretant. My studies must extend over
the whole of general Semeiotic. I think, dear Lady Welby,
that perhaps you are in danger of falling into some error in
consequence of limiting your studies so much to Language
and among languages to *one* very peculiar language, as all
Aryan Languages are; and within that language so much to
words.

Now as to English Words, there are only three classes with
which I have any decent acquaintance. The first are the words
of the vernacular of the class of society in which I am
placed;—not a very cultivated class of late years but for a few

---

14. For an extended statement of Peirce's realism, see *Collected
Papers*, 5.93-119.

15. The manuscript reads "with *Icons* and *Indices*," but it is clear
that Peirce meant "without."

correspondents. The second are the words of philosophical and mathematical terminology. The third,—which can hardly be said to be English or any other Aryan speech, being of a synthetic structure much like those of the tribes of our brown "red Indians," I mean chemical words. This third class answer their purpose admirably except for their intolerable length; and they might be enormously cut down & be even more descriptive than they are. But chemists wont bother to learn a *new* vocabulary. It wouldn't pay. One route between two places may be far preferable to another; and yet, when one is more than half-way over the latter, if wont be worth while to toil back and take the former.

Well my time is up! I must tell you another time how I discover or try to discover the best use of words.

Very faithfully
C. S. Peirce

VERSO PAGES[16]

Peirce's Letter of January 31, 1909

Note to p. 6.   Solution of Example 3.

The proposition "There is a gentleman's toe that nobody but catholics are in the habit of kissing" is expressed by the graph

where X-c   means "X is a catholic"
X-k-Y   means "X is in the habit of kissing Y."
X-t   means "X is the great toe of a gentleman"

Encircling k with a double cut, we get ⎯⎯ t

---

16. The following are the solutions to examples 3, 4, and 5 which Peirce poses in his letter of January 31, 1909.

Iterating -t within 2 cuts we get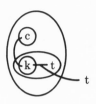

Erasing the outer t and the ligature, we get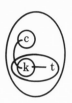

and the interpretation of this is "Nobody but a catholic is in the habit of kissing every great toe of a gentleman." We might

carelessly have concluded 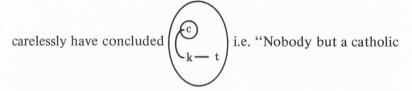 i.e. "Nobody but a catholic

is in the habit of kissing any great toe of a gentleman;" and it is important to understand precisely why that is illogical and precisely what rule it violates. For it will be observed that the most fundamental of all inferences generally recognized as such, the *modus ponens* appears from a point of view admitted in my Monist paper to be exactly analogous to the fallacious inference. You will recognize, however, that the difference is that the conditional proposition "If A, then C" may have either of two meanings, "If in the state of things which we conceive as actual A is, then (i.e. in that state of things) C is" and "In all states of things in which A should be, C would be". In the *modus ponens* we only conclude that in the actual state of things C is, and not that in every possible state of things C would be, unless the other premiss is that not only is A in the actual state of things, but it would be in every conceivable state of things. The mood Ferio is entirely analogous. Therefore, as long as the graph M is a *spot*, from S—M (M — P) we can conclude S —(P). But if M is merely the line of identity, we have no right from—(P) to conclude (-P). Now you will observe that in the rule given on pp. 536, 537 of the *Monist* of October 1906,[17] I speak of a "simple" graph. A "simple graph" is of course a graph which cannot be separated into two or more graphs. A line of identity *can* be so separated and therefore is *not* a simple graph. That rule is correct. As for the rule near the top of p. 536,[18] which ends, "This involves the Permission to distort a line of Identity, at will," it might have been improved by adding "but not the Permission to sever it." But even then, it seems to permit changing

That is from "Nothing is at once A and B unless something is C" to infer that Whatever there may be that is at once A and B is C, which the rule further down certainly does not permit. It should have been plainly declared the the Rule of Iteration and Deiteration does not apply to the line of Identity considered as a Graph.

Example 4. We have given (a) (b)   (c) (d)

We *twice* iterate one of the enclosures thus: 1st

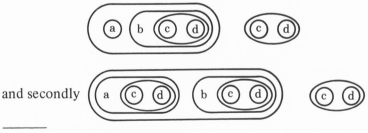

and secondly

---

17. See *Collected Papers*, 4.567.
18. See *Collected Papers*, 4.566.

Now twice iterate a and twice iterate b and delete (c) (d) by the first Permission thus

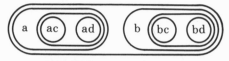

Now by the Rule of Insertion & Omission, delete the a that is alone and the b that is alone, thus

Now by Permission No. 4 get rid of the two double cuts and we finally get (ac)(ad)(bc)(bd) This is the B sought. For from it we can rededuce the A thus: Iterate the whole:

(ac)(ad)(bc)(bd) (ac)(ad)(bc)(bd) Now by the rule of Insertion & Omission, we get (a) (a) (b) (b) (c) (d) (c) (d)

Now deiterate the duplicates: which is A again.

(a) (b)   (c) (d)

The direct contradictory of A (or Ā,) is ((a) (b)   (c) (d))

That of B (or B̄) is (ac) (ad) (bc) (bd)   To derive B̄ from Ā,

we may begin with 4 iterations, thus:

We then make 8 insertions thus

We now make one deiteration thus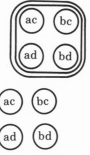

We remove the double cut & get B̄

To deduce Ā from B̄ requires *Ingenuity*. Now Ingenuity consists in a disposition to reason about what method ought to be applied to get a required result. "Not also *skill* in the performance of the reasoning?" you ask. *Skill* in anything chiefly consists in such familiarity with a kind of performance that one sees in a given case an analogy with known situations which one knows just how to handle. It is therefore a mixture of habit with analytic reasoning. But ingenuity is not required where habit suffices. Therefore, I am inclined to think that the secret of ingenuity lies in a disposition thoroughly to reason about methods of doing anything before undertaking to do it. So let us summon up our ingenuity on this problem.

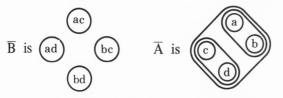

Every reasoning ought to begin by considering the general character of the problem in hand. Here it is to transform one symmetrical system of letters into another. A "symmetrical" system is a system into which all elementary parts enter in the same way. There are 4 letters, 2 of one set, 2 of another. Of 4 letters there are 6 pairs of which only 4 enter into B̄. Ā on the other hand contains only those pairs (the members of each being in special enclosures) that B̄ excludes. Represent B̄, then, by the icon $\frac{Mm\ Mn}{Nm\ Nn}$ and Ā by the icon $\frac{M;N}{m;n}$. How shall we change one into the other? By thrice performing the process of uniting the like elements of a pair of pairs with the pair of unlike elements.

The First Performance changes Mm Nm to $\left.\begin{matrix} M \\ N \end{matrix}\right\}$ m

The Second changes Mn Nn to $\left.\begin{matrix} M \\ N \end{matrix}\right\}$ n .

The Third Performance changes $\left.\begin{matrix} M \\ N \end{matrix}\right\}$ m $\left.\begin{matrix} M \\ N \end{matrix}\right\}$ n to $\left.\begin{matrix} M \\ N \end{matrix}\right\}$ $\left\{\begin{matrix} m \\ n \end{matrix}\right.$

We are therefore to seek one principle of transformation by which $\overline{(ac)}$ $\overline{(ad)}$ can be changed to a $\underline{\overline{x}}$ $\left\{\begin{matrix} c \\ d \end{matrix}\right.$, whatever sort of union it may be necessary to regard $\Big\{$ as signifying, and whatever we must regard $\underline{\overline{x}}$ as signifying.

And $\left.\begin{matrix} a \\ b \end{matrix}\right\}$ $\underline{\overline{x}}$ $\left\{\begin{matrix} c \\ d \end{matrix}\right.$ must denote $\left(\!\left(\boxed{a}\ \boxed{b}\right)\ \left(\boxed{c}\ \boxed{d}\right)\!\right)$

If you are to learn to reason, you must not content yourself with understanding the "sense" of any reasoning that may present itself but must assimilate its "meaning" and make it your own. If my reasoning turns out to be correct, it will be found that to transform $\overline{B}$ to $\overline{A}$ whatever principle of trans- formation is applied at all must be applied in 3 distinct stages. Next, let us consider what sort of transformation is required. In $\overline{B}$ there are single enclosures enclosing no others and every letter is enclosed but once. In $\overline{A}$ the one enclosure contains a second set of enclosures and each of these a third set, so that each letter is thrice enclosed. In $\overline{B}$ every letter occurs twice: In $\overline{A}$ only once. Now the order of a nest of enclosures can be raised either by iteration or by encircling a graph with a double cut. But any amount of Iteration and Deiteration performed on $\overline{B}$ must leave two letters in the area of the outermost enclosure, whereas $\overline{A}$ has no letter in that area.

Hence the double cut must be used to get $\overline{A}$ from $\overline{B}$. Therefore it must be used thrice. Moreover in $\overline{A}$ each inmost cut contains a single oddly enclosed letter while in $\overline{B}$ there are only pairs in single cuts. Hence deiteration must be used and hence it must be used thrice. But deiteration cannot be applied to $\overline{B}$ until there has first been Iteration. Hence iteration must be thrice employed. Now let us see how the principles thus deduced are to be applied.

Starting from (iu) (ju), first put a double cut round one u; thus: (iu) (j ((u))) Now iterate into an evenly enclosed area; thus: (iu) (j ((iu) (u))) That dont work because there is nothing to deiterate! Try putting the double cut around the j instead of the u; thus: (iu) (((j)) u) Now iterate, thus: (iu) (((iu) (j)) u) Now deiterate u; thus:

(iu) (((i) (j)) u)

This evidently puts us on the right track; for the last result begins to partake of the character of $\overline{A}$ and one can almost see plainly that this process applied to $\overline{B}$ will give $\overline{A}$.

Starting then with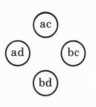

Put double cuts round letters in two different areas, the two letters being either the same, or being two that are not together in $\overline{B}$, and in the latter case they must not both be accompanied in $\overline{B}$ by the same letter. That is to say, if the a

in (ac) is one of them the other may be either of the following

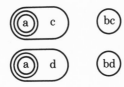 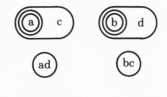

Then iterate the other enclosure so that a letter that comes to be thrice enclosed shall also be once enclosed; thus:

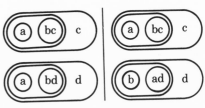

Then deiterate thus:

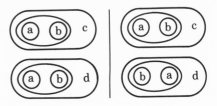

These are now just alike and I no longer need the double columns

Put double cut around one of the singly enclosed letters

Now iterate

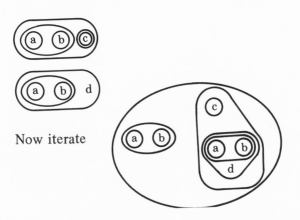

Now deiterate 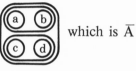 which is $\overline{A}$

Example 5 You saw, in the solution of the last example, that,

whatever graphs u v & w may be, from (u) (v) (v) (w)

follows ((uw) (v)) so that the former is what is called the

"condition" or "sufficient condition" of the latter. That it is
also called the *requisite* condition or *"conditio*[19] *sine qua*

non" is shown by simply iterating ((uw) (v)) and then from

one instance deleting the evenly enclosed *u,* and from the

other deleting the *w,* giving ((u) (v)) ((w) (v)) so that

((u) (v)) ((w) (v)) and ((uw) (v)) are logically equivalent.

Therefore, ((a) (b)) ((b) (c)) ((c) (a)) is logically equivalent to

((ac) (b)) ((c) (a)) But from this follows ((ac)(bc)(ba))

For, 1st, iterating we get ((ac) (b ((c) (a)))) and iterating

---

twice again 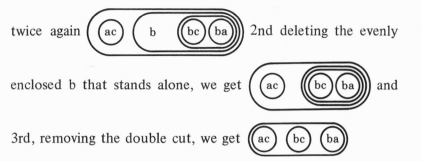 2nd deleting the evenly

enclosed b that stands alone, we get and

3rd, removing the double cut, we get

or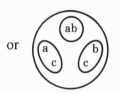

On the other hand twice iterating this, thus

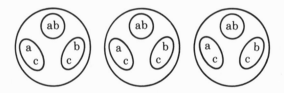

and then simply deleting evenly enclosed letters we get

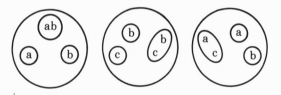

and by similar erasure we get

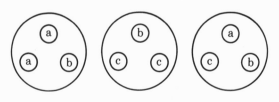

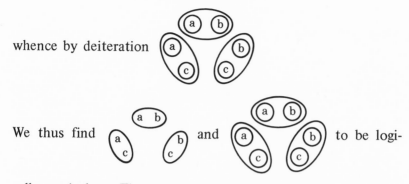

whence by deiteration

We thus find ⋯ and ⋯ to be logi-

cally equivalent. There are some numbers of letters exceeding 3 for which closely similar & symmetrical equivalences hold.

But it is not always so. Thus

is equivalent to

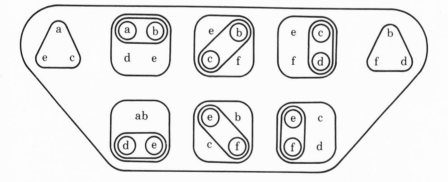

I think you will have no further possible difficulty with these examples; but on the Verso of p 1 I will give the answers to the questions.

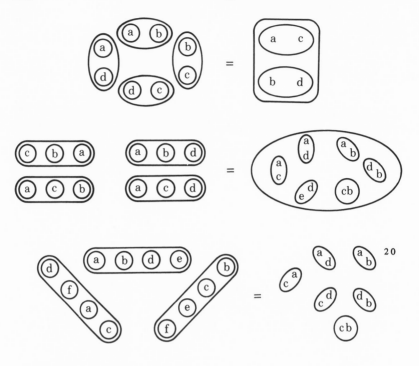

20. Peirce's solutions end here with this graph, which is crossed out in manuscript, though left unmarked here.

Duneaves, Harrow
April 09

Dear Mr Peirce[1]

Your last wonderful letter haunts me, not merely with the sense of its commanding power of thought and exposition, and its revelations of some possible developments of Significs, but also with the note of anxiety and trouble in it. I do hope that by now your skies have cleared again, that Mrs Peirce is better and life smoother.

I have been reading your deeply valued letter many times

1. This unfinished letter was enclosed in Lady Welby's letter to Peirce dated October 8, 1909.

& shall read it yet again as each time some fresh aspect of its rich suggestion opens before one.

Just now I will take the part about your father and your own early youth.

I think I told you that I was in America in 1849-50 (on 27th of this month I am 71) and it is doubly interesting to remember that while unfortunately my mother missed seeing some of the most notable of the men you name, we did go and stay with Daniel Webster & also visited Prescott the historian and knew Rufus Choate.

Other notable names I could recall if I had a copy of my mother's book here.

What you say again of your special gift being logical analysis has a special interest for me. For it seems to me that in you there must be a rare combination of that and what I would call Primal Sense. And again you must surely be conscious of a power of *constructive translation*? The ordinary analyser, logical or no, *takes to pieces* (and in the process reduces the living unit to the dust-grain!) but you create, or rather perhaps follow creative footsteps, and each, after his kind[2]

---

2. Sentence unfinished

Milford Pa.
1909 Sept 27

My dear Lady Welby:

Your most kind inquiry reached us soon after I had discovered in arranging the papers on my husband's writing table (which nobody else is allowed to do, and that I had not been able to do thoroughly for months,) a note I had written you in July for enclosure in a letter by him.

But he has been so much out of health that perhaps he may not have written at the time he proposed to do so; and you had evidently not heard from him. Knowing how much it would pain him to learn that he had been negligent of my note, I shall not mention it to him. The note was chiefly to say how much gratified we should be to receive you here if we could do justice to so honored a guest, and if the exposure and distance would permit. I have always found that among the many letters he receives there are none that seem to give him so much pleasure and refreshment as yours. My own small talents lie in quite another direction than toward philosophy; and no letter from me could be very interesting. At present, for example, most of my time is given to doing what I can for his health and to supervising some repairs of the house to make him more comfortable next winter. I learned that your health had not been good some time ago; but I hope with all my heart that by this time it is completely restored. Our daily conversation very often turns upon you, with pleasure, and there is nobody whom we so much long to meet.

With much and warm love to your Ladyship

Juliette Peirce

Harrow
Oct 8 1909

My dear Mr. Peirce

I enclose an unfinished letter written last April, which I kept back because I feared that unnecessary letters would only hinder you in the trying time I knew you were going through. So I only thanked you (from my heart) for your wonderful letter which I prize more than I can say.

I am grieved now to find, from your letter to Dr. Slaughter,[1] how much trouble you are going through, & can only hope very earnestly that you will soon be in smoother waters. I shall be anxious for better news.

I need not say how glad I am that in spite of all you are consenting to write an essay in Prof. Stout's proposed book

---

1. John Willis Slaughter (1878-?), American psychologist; author of *The Adolescent* (1910), *Social Forces in Latin America* (1912), and *East and West in China* (1927); edited *The Public* (1917-1919), and became lecturer at Rice Institute (1928). See Appendix D.

and how grateful I am for the kind words with which you give your consent.

The book has suffered one serious loss in the death of Professor Vailati last May whose death is surely felt in Italy & indeed throughout Europe.

He had been so kind a friend of mine that his death was a great shock.

I have been working continuously & very hard, and hope that the appearance of the book may definitely advance the aims of 'Significs'.

I may possibly also (though I shrink from it for many reasons) in the course of next year publish a book of some kind out of my now large collection of Papers (the last of which was written between 5 & 6 this morning).

The Encyc. Brit. has been delayed by unexpected difficulty but I hope that will appear next Spring or Summer.

I have sent in the finally revised article.

With my warmest wishes for your welfare & thanks for your unvarying sympathy & kindness I am ever

> yours most truly
> V. Welby

> Milford Pa.
> *1909 Oct. 11*

My dear Lady Welby:

I could not bear to just dot down a line or two upon a postcard to you nor to content myself with any hurried note; and in fact I did write you one long letter.[1] But my wife read it and suggested that it might bear an interpretation that had not occurred to me, and so it was not sent. The truth is that there are great obstacles to my writing. In the first place I am 70 years old and can perceive that my powers of mind are

---

1. There is a draft of a letter to Lady Welby dated September 29, 1909 in the Peirce Correspondence. Perhaps this is the letter Peirce is referring to here.

beginning to fail, and I feel that it is my most sacred of all duties to write that book which shall show that many powerful minds have held views apparently the most antipodal upon the subjects of highest concern to all men, merely because they have all alike missed that point of view which would have reconciled them all in one truth, and which will incidentally show any intelligent person how to think in such a way as to reach the truth expeditiously. Since Kant, the majority of logicians clearly sharing his opinion that the principles of reasoning had already been thoroughly investigated,—a most superficial and fatal opinion,—instead of studying their proper subject have either turned to a barren *Erkenntnisslehre* or to a study of the psychology of thought or to the attempt—like Mill,—to found logic on a baseless system of metaphysics, or to the ridiculous trifling of some other of the English logicians; and I feel that I am in possession of truth which must be put into writing before my powers quite fail. This haunts me constantly & I am now, as it were, under orders to give every minute that can be made useful to writing a *preliminary volume* on which I am now engaged which shall give a foretaste of my other & which I hope may in some way enable me to gather together the many books which I have read & whose substance I have in mind, but which of course I cannot discuss on the basis of my unaided memory & so may be enabled to resume the writing of my great book which had to be set aside because I could not refer to the books I had in mind. This preliminary volume I propose to entitle *Essays on Meaning*, where I use Meaning in a general way as it is used by persons who have not thought much about it. If it recalls your "What is Meaning?" so much the better.

Besides this my dear wife is in such a terrible state of health, particularly affecting her always very delicate though marvelously strong nerves, that that brings a great tax upon my own. And finally there are extensive repairs that *must* be made to enable us to live through next winter & I naturally have to get plans made, revised, redrawn, considered, re-

redrawn,—and though my wife attends to all the details & the ideas are wholly hers still it prevents very largely the continuity of thought requisite for the kind of work which is more particularly mine.

When I get through my work,—and often while I am still at it, I fall sound asleep so that I have no odd minutes at all. This has not prevented our talking & thinking a great deal about you at our meals; and I suppose what has set me to writing you this egotistical & complaining utterance is the desire to know about your health & what you are doing in the way of writing and so forth. I hope you will answer this in that way And believe

> me I remain
> ever very faithfully yours
> C. S. Peirce

> Duneaves, Harrow

My dear Mrs. Peirce

Though, alas, I cannot emulate the delicacy of your dainty handwriting, my grateful and affectionate thanks are due to you for your letter, and to you *both* for your generous invitation.

Alas, I can only retain working power by strict economy of strength & avoidance of extra risk.

So, though I have been more than once invited to stay with American friends, I have been compelled to forego what to me would have been a delightful experience. I would of course have specially valued an opportunity of seeing something of your husband & you, and I must be allowed to send, in return for yours, much and warm love to you both, from

> Victoria Welby

[Envelope enclosed dated October 19, 1909.]

Duneaves, Harrow
May 11th. 1910

My dear Mr. Peirce,

I have not written to you since Prof. Stout asked Dr. Slaughter to write and ask you for a Contribution to the Essays[1] which he is editing, since I wanted it to be plain that the programme was quite independent of me; and therefore communicated with none of the writers asked. Such a separate treatment of the subject by various able hands was what I had long hoped for.

But as time goes by I feel very anxious to know that all is at least as well as may be, with you and Mrs. Peirce; and much hope to hear that an Essay from you is now on its way. The others have been sent in, all but one on economics. It is a joy to me to feel that at last there will be some independent writing on my subject. I am myself arranging for another book which I hope will make my own position, in its various aspects, clearer than hitherto.

The great shock caused by the unexpected loss of our King makes itself felt in many ways and brings back to me much of my earlier life.

With warm good wishes and hoping for good news from you both

I am yours ever
Victoria Welby

_____

1. See Appendix D.

Milford Pa.
1911 Apr. 17

My Dear Lady Welby:

Your post card[1] reached me Good Friday, late in the afternoon. Owing to an appointment with a magistrate, along with two other persons, for Saturday, which occupied the whole day, this is the earliest possible moment at which I

_____

1. The postcard is not in Peirce's correspondence.

could reply. I am a little surprised that it should take so long a time for the Post Card to reach me. Although Post Cards are not here stamped with the date and hour of arrival, yet I have reason to think that no delay took place in the Milford P.O. However, I should not have mentioned this were it not that, if I read a word of your very kind and touching post card as "third," you say that that was your *third* attempt to communicate with me. I have however received nothing from you for a very long time; and therefore the question arises, which Post Office has been in fault. I do not know; but I rather incline to think that if it be either Harrow or Milford, it is the former, since I do not know of any other person named Peirce or Pierce in the vicinity of Milford, where the Post Office people are extra attentive to me, I suppose being under the delusion that I am influential in Washington.

The reasons why I have not written to you are many and physically strong. Indeed they have amounted to absolute necessity. I will mention only a few of them. I am suffering from an early old age, which has been, apparently, the case with all the males of my ancestors; and besides all my later years have been full of worries of almost every description. And this fact has made me desperately anxious to put my logical discoveries into a form in which they may be useful. In the next place, my poor wife and I have been in miserable health for the last few years and particularly since winter before last have been exhausted with more duties than we could severally fulfill and more and more so; and to these difficulties have been added vexations due to other people, continual and cruel. One of our great consolations, dear Lady Welby, has been to remind one another of you.

We have been doing all we could to try to get rid of this estate which has value enough to be a very serious consideration; but now that we no longer entertain and almost all our old friends in this country are dead, the place is nothing but a burden. Just now we are indulging in a definite though not brilliant hope of selling out at a sacrifice, when we shall wish to go abroad & perhaps settle in some French town.

I am just now trying to get a small book written[2] in which I positively prove just what the justification of each of the three types of reasoning really consists in,—absolutely refuting the two usual modes of justifying Induction,—Mill's & Laplace's;[3] and showing the real nature of Retroduction (which has usually been considered either as not reasoning at all or as a species of Induction)[4] and from the analysis so proved, I shall show that the essential articles of religious faith have a justificaton that scientific men have been too apt to pooh-pooh. I have heard nothing of that volume to which your friends were to contribute. Has it ever appeared? I must not write more today but will do so as soon as I can; & with warmest wishes of good for you from both of us I remain Dear Lady Welby

ever truly yours
C. S. Peirce

---

2. See Robin *Catalogue*, Mss. 663-670.
3. See *Collected Papers*, 2.761-772 and 5.167-170.
4. See *Collected Papers*, 2.619-644.

Duneaves, Harrow
May 2nd. 1911

My dear Mr. Peirce,

It was a real joy to get your letter at last. I had written to you several times. I have fortunately got a duplicate of the last letter and send you a rough copy.[1] I do hope you have safely received Dr. Slaughter's letter[2] and will be able to contribute a Paper for the book of Essays which is only waiting for your contribution.

Meanwhile the news I was anxious to impart when I wrote my post-card is that I have found you, I think, a disciple at Cambridge. He has been studying with care all I could show him of your writing on Existential Graphs, and is anxious to

---

1. The rough copy of Lady Welby's letter could not be found in either Peirce's or Lady Welby's correspondence.
2. See Appendix D. Slaughter's letter was dated April 25, 1911.

see your contribution to the volume of Essays which Prof. Stout is still holding back, in hopes of receiving it. The name of the recruit is C. K. Ogden,[3] and he is at Magdalene College. He enters also with enthusiasm into the possibilities of Significs.

My book[4] is nearly ready now and I shall hope soon to send you a copy of it. Meanwhile I am greatly stirred by what you tell me of the 'small book' you are writing. Do get it written and published as soon as you can! I sympathise with all my heart with your difficulties and hope they may greatly lessen if not disappear before long. You must remember that we cannot get on without work like yours. I gather from what you say that you must have sent your contribution to the 'Essays' and that it has never reached Dr. Slaughter. However he has now written to you about this. Meanwhile be sure that my thoughts have often been with you and Mrs. Peirce. I hope that wherever the cause of the hiatus in our correspondence may lie, there will be no more interruption of our communication, since I fully reciprocate the kindly warm words you and Mrs. Peirce have sent me.

Yours ever sincerely
Victoria Welby

---

3. Charles Kay Ogden (1889-1957), British psychologist and educator; inventor of "basic English," coauthor with I. A. Richards of *The Meaning of Meaning* (1923).
4. V. Welby, *Significs and Language*, Macmillan and Co., 1911.

Milford, Pa.
1911 May 20

My dear Lady Welby:

I have put off answering your last letter as well as one from Mr. Slaughter, because I could not bear to say it was impossible for me to write for the book, and yet I do not see how I can.

We have been advertising the place for sale; and if it only

were sold for half what it might be sold for if we could take our time about it, all difficulty about writing would disappear. But it is so late in the season now that I am in a dreadful state of mind about it. I must sketch my whole situation to you. I don't see any issue to it.

In the first place, my health is like this. I have days when I am in vigorous health of mind and body. But I am extremely emotional, with great self-control; so that anything which affects me has no outlet and simply shakes my whole being, so that I cannot walk across the floor and can hardly hold a pen. The same causes affect my memory so that I cannot think of the words I want to use.

I am not affected by small things; but the difficulties of my situation are not small. In the first place, my poor wife who has not only the highest sense of duty, and far too much energy for her naturally extremely delicate frame, but also a tender solicitude about me and my health, has been sinking in strength and suffering agonizing pain night & day, and I cannot blink the fact that she could not survive another winter in this house. She was constructed to be a princess and she yielded to my wishes & became the wife of a man who ought to have foreseen that it must mean ultimate penury to her.

That is almost literally our condition now. We cannot afford a servant or to obey the doctor's solemn injunctions about my wife's health. The only thing that I can do is to spend my energy in domestic details. It is what I should be doing at this moment, but that I am utterly broken up by grief so that I should probably fall if I tried to do more than I have done. I, who used to be thoroughly up in the current state of all the principal scientific problems, have not seen a new book or memoir for years. Still, I have in my head a book consisting in, 1st, a complete proof and somewhat elaborate discussion of just what it is that justifies each kind of sound reasoning.

2nd, on that basis I show first how utterly wrong were all the metaphysicians from Descartes to Hume inclusive. I show just how far Kant was right though even when right twisted up in formalism. It is perfectly true that we can never attain a knowledge of things as they are. We can only know their human aspect. But that is all the universe is for us. Reid's position was sounder, except that he seems to think Common Sense is infallible, at least for that human-phenomenal Universe which is all there is for us. This is a great mistake[.] Common Sense is to be trusted only so far as it sustains critical investigation. Of course I cannot say in short compass exactly what I mean. Moreover not all the judgments of Common Sense are easy to arrive at. I show by what method they must be ascertained; and one important result is that whatever hypothesis we *need* we ought to believe. For example, if a soldier is sure that a certain line of action is the only one that can save him & those he commands he ought to believe it *will* save him, because that belief will enhance the success or the chances of it. *Useless* doubts are worse than useless. But of course this is a path along which eggs are scattered. It is however mere meaningless pedantry to distinguish such reasoning from accepting a hypothesis because it renders phenomena intelligible. My proof of this must, I am confident, make an impression.

In the third place, I am going on to criticize a number of articles considered essential to religious faith.

There are some propositions favorable to religion which in my opinion are not to be reckoned as matters of *faith* so much as of logical *conviction*[.]

One of these is that the universe is not governed by immutable law.

The proof of this is surprizingly simple. Namely I show that if precisely the same consequence always resulted from the same cause there could be no real progress. Now there is real progress. Every science proves it, and we must believe that the world is governed by a living spirit.[1]

I further show that even if it were true that every physical

---

1. In this connection, see *Collected Papers*, 6.35-65.

event were wholly caused by a physical event exclusively, as far as *immediate* action is concerned, nevertheless that would leave room for immaterial beings to act upon matter & the converse.

I show that all the old metaphysicians such as Hume support their scepticism by virtually assuming, (when they say, as they perpetually are saying, "But it does not follow," etc.) that the only kind of valid inference is deductive. Now the only justification of Deduction is that its conclusions never assert anything that was not asserted in the Premisses. A perfectly analogous fallacy is involved in supposing the universe governed by immutable law, according to which no element could appear in the effect that was not in the cause. Now I propose to show just what "free will" really consists in and how it acts; and how that renders our conduct analogous to the manner in which growth takes place in plants & animals.

I feel confident that the book would make a serious impression much deeper and surer than Bergson's which I find quite too vague.[2]

But how is it ever to get written? How am I to find leisure to write even the article I want so much to contribute to your volume?

For the last three years I have not had sight of a new book. Evidently I can be of no use except in my family duties;—things which I gladly do under the circumstances but which it seems ought to get done in some less costly way.

I can only say that I will write you an article if I possibly can. I desire to please you most earnestly. But I cannot be hopeful about it.

C. S. Peirce

P.S.

Having written this letter in order to make clear how my not having written (and expressing myself is so little natural

---

2. *Creative Evolution*. The French edition was published in 1907.

to me that my Hibbert Journal[3] article occupied me exclusively for two months, and after all was not generally understood, while the writing of it was an expense to me that weighed upon my conscience,)—as I say I wanted to explain how my not having written does not argue my not ardently desiring to say what would, I hope, increase the general sense of the importance of your message to the world,—and its opportuneness, too. Now when the letter was written, I feared that, in my eagerness to make what I have just said evident, the letter might have the air of soliciting some aid. The word "penury" is probably an exaggeration. We are able for the present to obtain what is ordinarily dispensible to sustain life without running into debt. But there is no doubt that, in my wife's state of health, the hard life is killing her *fast*. Therefore it becomes my first desire, as well as my first duty, to work at nothing which does not ameliorate her condition. It is obvious, for example, that it was a wicked thing for me to work two months for fifty dollars, since life could not be sustained at that rate.

I have no doubt my book would make an impression in scientific circles; and every little helps in the development of logical views. You may be sure I feel that strongly. But in my situation it would be my duty to take care of my wife's health, if it put back the clock of progress for longer than it will.

I may however spend a few minutes in explaining a bit more clearly what I *mean* by saying that if the universe were governed by immutable law there could be no progress. In place of the word progress I will put a word invented to express what I mean, to wit, *variescence*, I mean such a change as to produce an uncompensated increment in the number of independent elements of a situation. No doubt one might suppose that all the apparent new elements, whenever there is growth or development or evolution of any kind, really were present in all their diversity from the first, though

3. Peirce's article for the *Hibbert Journal* was "A Neglected Argument for the Reality of God." See *Collected Papers*, 6.452-485.

in a form not open to our observation. But what I propose to show is that such gratuitous hypothesis is not logically defensible; but but [*sic*] that on the contrary the hypothesis of *variescence* is signally the one that sound logic points out.

Another example of scientific bad logic has been the favor shown to the hypothesis of *telepathy* as explaining a whole lot of easily observed, though infrequent, phenomena. Now telepathy in the sense of a direct action of one embodied spirit on another (which is what it *conveys*, let it be defined as vaguely as it may) is an extremely plausible hypothesis,—none is more so, in any field. But the argument against its producing effects capable of being observed more easily than is, e.g. the pressure produced by an incident light-ray is perfectly overwhelming; and it is much more plausible that such effects are due to the action of disembodied spirits. It is true that there are difficulties in supposing that there are any disembodied spirits,—and perhaps an absolutely unembodied spirit may be impossible. But physics is almost every year,— especially the theory of the ether,—making finer kinds of matter than that of the 60 odd elements more and more credible. You know Thomson's or Thompson's—I forget the spelling—theory that atoms are vortices in a fluid.[4] Very likely that may be true or some modification of it may be. But if it be true, analogy would suggest that that underlying fluid really consists of separate bodies, and that those atoms of the second class were in their turn vortices of a second class in a second underlying fluid, itself composed of atoms of a third class, and so on, *endlessly*.

Very well, there would be, then, not 64 or whatever the number of chemical elements is this afternoon—but an endless series of kinds of plausible matter in which to embody spirits.

Mind, I don't propose to ask anybody to believe seriously in any hypothesis without serious inductive support; but I do say that scientific men—many, I guess most, of them—are in a state of unconscious,—or unaware—belief in the *falsity* of such

4. J. J. Thomson, "On Bodies Smaller Than Atoms," *Popular Science Monthly*, Vol. 59, August 1901, pp. 323-335.

hypotheses, which state of mind is just as illogical as it would be to lean toward believing them. Indeed, it is scientifically much worse, since the latter state of mind, if its substance be false, is bound to get refuted; while the former may go on forever obstructing research into such matters. *Nobody will try new experiments without a leaning to an unsupported hypothesis.* The people who pooh, pooh such hypotheses make up the class that is most efficient in blocking the wheels of science.

But my dear Lady Welby I am taking up your time and mine with speculation. Once more good bye for this time. So once more most faithfully (& without misinterpretation I am confident,) C. S. Peirce

1911 May 22

Milford, Pa.
1911 May 25

My dear Lady Welby:

My wife having urged me to it, I think that if you and the others who are concerned in getting out the famous volume care to wait for what cannot be positively promised, I will do my best to send you in two months,—or better say three,—the first part of the book I want so much to write.[1] This part deals with the kinds and degrees of assurance that the different kinds of reasoning afford and with the special difficulties that affect that assurance and the means of overcoming them,—I mean strictly logical difficulties. For instance, in the theory of numbers, hardly anything can be proved without resort to the principle that whatever is true of a given integer number and which is also true, if of any integer number, then of the next higher one, is true of all integer numbers as high or higher than the given number. But *why* should this be true? Some books say it is because, 1st, of any two different integers one is higher than the other, and 2nd, every integer

---

1. See Robin *Catalogue*, Ms. 669.

number has a next higher one. But that is not sufficient; nor would it be made so by adding that every integer is next higher than some other. It is necessary to define the relationship between integers more exactly. If one added that between any two integers there is but a *finite number* of integers, that no doubt is what is wanted; only the word *finite* requires a formal definition. [Of course, you must not talk of a finite number (i.e. an *integer* that is finite) in *defining* an integer.][2] We get that by introducing the abstraction "property" or "predicate." Thus, it suffices to say that if of different integers the lower has a "property" that the higher has not, then there must be an integer as high as *that lower* one, but lower than the higher one, that possesses the property, while the integer next higher than it does not. That illustrates a class of difficulties in mathematics which are overcome by introducing suitable abstractions into definitions. One has in effect defined a "finite series" by means of that word "property" or "predicate." It furnishes a definite *hold* to the mind. That illustrates the kind of considerations that I should notice in my essay on "Assurance through Reasoning."[3]

I mention it, as enabling you perhaps to decide *pro* or *con* upon whether or not it will be worth waiting for without a positive assurance. This would be the easiest thing for me to write, and therefore presumably the best I could write; and it would be unquestionably very useful. Then I should want to use the essay afterward in my own book which I cannot, however, complete until I can procure a few books, of which the new Encyclopaedia Britannica will be first & foremost; for I am so greatly hampered by want of information about the researches since I have been deprived of books, that I feel it won't do for me to appear before the public until I catch up; and that is the reason I take the assurance through reasoning as the only subject on which I can now venture. [Of course

2. In manuscript, the bracketed sentence appears in the margin with no insertion mark. Brackets are added.

3. See *Collected Papers*, 3.562. Also, Robin *Catalogue*, Mss 669-670.

the time for subscribing to the Britannica will have expired before this reaches you; so that my lamentation cannot be misunderstood.][4] I could not venture one step beyond that; and perhaps I am foolhardy to attempt even that. To tell you the plain truth I know I have thoughts that would be of great use to the world and that nobody is likely for a very long time to reach the same truths; and yet owing to my obscurity and lack of information I had better seek the tomb as quietly as possible.

As for my example about the soldier, don't mistake the point. His confidence may *cause* his success. But that is not what I mean. His confidence is a reason for thinking that he will succeed: it is a sign of that sort of spirit that does succeed. As for me I am long past the military age. I came within an ace of teaching men something to their profit. But certain misfortunes have prevented my keeping up to the times. I will write you the "Assurance from Reasoning" if you desire it, and that will be my last unless by good luck we should sell this estate. It would fetch with patience near forty thousand dollars, and it is ridiculous for us to live in such a place.

Ever very faithfully
C. S. Peirce

---

4. In manuscript, the bracketed sentence appears in the margin with no insertion mark. Brackets are added.

Milford, Pa.
1911 June 3

My dear Lady Welby:

Your word of cheer by cable[1] which would have made you *really* "dear" to our hearts if you had not already been so, did me particularly ever so much good; not that Juliette was not fully as much touched by it as I. Only she was not herself, I think, so despondent as I, and certainly had no suspicion of the

---

1. No cable could be found in Peirce's correspondence.

state of my feeling, since I knew she had enough to bear on her own score,—and far more than she ought,—without worrying about me.

A curious event that was taking place in our household prevented my looking at my mail; so that I did not see your dispatch until it was too late to acknowledge it that day. I will tell you what happened. You know, or rather you don't know, that along sometime since the middle ages, I was for a year or two in charge of the Coast Survey Office, and that circumstance made me well acquainted with all the particularly clever instrument-makers in the country. (Besides, among the various operations for the proper conduct of which I was responsible was an Instrument Shop where new kinds of instruments of geodesy, astronomy, & micrometry had to be built. So you will easily understand that I came to have a tolerably thorough acquaintance with the nature of the species so many individuals of which I had to deal with as instrument mechanics.) Well, day before yesterday, Juliette being away, a man in one of those long grey linen coats they call "dusters" and a hat that looked as if it had lain on a dust heap several years made his appearance and wished to view the house & the place. For there is a board out directing people to inquire within about buying. I took him over the house with which he was frankly delighted; and his remarks indicated a positiveness & a kind of taste that is by no means usual. But I could not show him over the grounds & so invited him to sit down & wait for Mrs. Peirce. So he began to talk & I saw at once that he was so skilled an instrument maker that I must have known him, for he was about my age. I was much attracted to him & so was Juliette when she got home. But I had seen that there was a mystery about him & felt pretty sure he hadn't a dollar. He was such a sympathetic person that one hated to be any ruder to him than was necessary, yet Juliette became timid when it turned out he had escaped from the state Insane Asylum at Middletown, N.Y. and though we are in a different sovereign state, Pennsylvania, so that no N.Y. official would dare arrest him here yet he was evidently terrified at the idea of leaving until it was quite dark. In the morning he was the first object we saw yesterday, he took breakfast with us, showed better than ordinary good manners,—really delicate manners,—and a little later his son appeared with the hostess of a little inn where the father had passed the night before I saw him, & after a very touching but long discussion carried him off to New York City. That is why I could not write until today. For they did not get away until the mail had gone; and then we were quite done up.

So your cable came at a moment to do us both even more good, perhaps, than it would if we had been quite in our "assiettes." It was so very good of you, dear Lady Welby.

C. S. Peirce

Milford, Pa.
June 20, 1911

Dear Lady Welby,

Your cablegram of June 2 came to hand. It promised a letter.

I replied warmly to it.

No letter from you has since been received by me.

The piece for your book is getting written, but not so fast as it would progress had I the least idea whether it was wanted or not. My last letter to you stated my uncertainty on this point.

With warmest good wishes believe me faithfully yours.

C. S. Peirce

I am in the same state of depression due to my being cut off from all knowledge of recent scientific work in branches to which I must refer in my piece for your book as well as in the book I have interrupted in order to write for yours.

June 27 1911
Duneaves, Harrow

My dear Mr. Peirce

I have been very unwell & much hindered in writing or I
would have written sooner to tell you what Prof. Stout now
says. He thinks it "very important" (which indeed it is) that
your Essay should appear in his collection.

I am therefore writing to Mr. A. Sidgwick[1] & Mr. Jourdain[2] (who want their contributions published soon) to ask
them to wait till you are ready. Prof. Stout is overwhelmed
with work at present but hopes to write a preface to the
book later. So please set to work on yours at once and don't
let *anything* worry or discourage you!

I have a feeling that things are going to be better for you
all around: "it is a long lane that has no turning" says the
proverb!

I only wish I could be of more use. Please tell Mrs. Perice I
should love to hear from her. I quite understand her
anxieties!

We *all* have them when we are devoted to anyone.

I am sending you my book.[3] But it is only a *plea* for what
the next & last volume will I hope prove beyond cavil to be
our greatest, most immediate, most pressing need.

Ever faithfully yours
Victoria Welby

---

1. Alfred Sidgwick (1850-?), British logician and philosopher; author
of *The Application of Logic* (1910), *The Use of Words in Reasoning*
(1901), and *Distinction and the Criticism of Belief* (1892). The latter
book was reviewed by Peirce in the *Nation*.

2. Philip Edward Bertrand Jourdain (1879-1919), mathematician and
scientist; author of *The Nature of Mathematics* (1912) and *The Philosophy of Mr. B*rtr*nd R*ss*ll* (1918).

3. *Significs and Language.*

Milford Pa.
1911 July 25

My dear Lady Welby:

It is dreadful that I could not answer your letter sooner, but I could not,—owing to my own condition of health & that of my dear wife,—unless I disappointed you and myself about the essay for the book or else held out hopes which I had no right to be confident that I could fulfill. But now Mrs. Peirce has got some help,—not much, I fear, and I have in the last week or so,—whether by virtue of the greatest heat I have experienced in 40 years *at least*, (some year of the 60's); and I am confident I shall be able to send Dr. Slaughter my copy.[1] I ought to write to him & say so; and I will try to get time to look up his address etc.[2]

I *wanted* to write an abstract of my entire system of logic. But in order to make sure of being within the limits of space and time, and to be readable—or as nearly so as I can ever hope to be,—I must limit myself to *Logical Critics*; that is to the *quality* & *grade* of assurance that the three classes of reasoning afford.

I have been greatly concerned dear Lady Welby to learn of your failure of strength; and my wife has been as much so as I. But I must catch the mail. Believe me it has been a long time since I have done *any* work (not calling what I do for Juliette by that name) that has not been done to please you or to further the common cause which moves you & me both.

Most earnestly yours
C. S. Peirce

Juliette wishes to be affectionately remembered to you, but her condition is such that her *writing* must be postponed a bit yet.[3]

---

1. See Appendix D.
2. So far as is known, Peirce never sent a manuscript to Dr. Slaughter.
3. This is the last letter of Peirce's in Lady Welby's file.

Morar-Inverness-shire
August 10, 1911

My dear Peirce,[1]
Your kind letter was very welcome. I have reported to Professor Stout just what you are now proposing to do; and I feel confident that it will be what he wants. As Dr. Slaughter is now in S. America and may not be here again for a long time, any communication from you to Prof. Stout should be addressed to him direct . . .

I thank you warmly for your most kind words and Mrs. Peirce for her touching message. With my love please tell her how much I sympathize with her.

You will be glad to hear that there are already some reviews as good as I could expect, and prospect of others.

I am hoping to gather strength for the most important of my books (so far as!) giving both witness to and universal application of Significs.

––––––––

1. From a draft version of a letter to Peirce in Lady Welby's correspondence.

Duneaves, Harrow
December 31, 1911[1]

Dear Mrs. Peirce
I am getting to be very unhappy at hearing nothing from your husband for so sadly long a time: and it is a great disappointment not to hear anything of the promised contribution to Prof. Stout's book of Essays for which we have so eagerly looked.

I am afraid it means that Mr. Peirce is ill or suffering.

Forgive me these confessions, for you and your husband and all the great honour he has done me have been so much to me!

––––––––

1. The following appears, in Lady Welby's own hand, at the beginning of this letter: "I am just beginning the crucial effort of my life."

It would be a joy to hear and a double joy to find that the promised Essay was on its way. With affectionate wishes for you both

> I am your faithful friend
> Victoria Welby

> Duneaves, Harrow
> *Feb. 25. [1912]*

Dear Mrs. Peirce,

My mother in law (Victoria, Lady Welby) (who is laid up with serious illness following on influenza) is anxious that I should write & thank you for your kind letter. She was much distressed to hear of your husband's state of health, and also very much concerned about your own. I must tell you that she had great trouble a fortnight ago with aphasia & loss of power in the right hand. This is now very much better, and her brain is perfectly clear. The weakness is great, and the real trouble that we have to combat is extreme depression, and the persisting idea that she ought not to be kept alive, & that there is now nothing for her to live for.

Her voice is very weak, and it is not always easy to catch what she says—but it is *at times* much clearer, and she is really every day regaining a little strength, & the Dr. says there is no real reason why she should not get back to her former state of health. Should you again write to her, will you say anything you can to hearten her up into believing she can recover, without ignoring the fact that she *is* very far from well at present.

> Yours sincerely,
> Maria L. H. Welby

APPENDIXES

Appendix A

Charles S. Peirce's Review of Lady Welby's
What is Meaning? The Nation 77
(15 Oct 1903), 308-309.

What is Meaning? By V. Welby.
Macmillan Co. 1903 8vo, pp. 321

The Principles of Mathematics. By Bertrand Russell.
Vol. I. Cambridge (Eng.): University Press; New York:
Macmillan 1903. 8vo, pp. 534.

Two really important works on logic are these; or, at any rate, they deserve to become so, if readers will only do their part towards it. Yet it is almost grotesque to name them together, so utterly disparate are their characters. This is not the place to speak of Mr. Russell's book, which can hardly be called literature. That he should continue these most severe and scholastic labors for so long, bespeaks a grit and industry, as well as a high intelligence, for which more than one of his ancestors have been famed. Whoever wishes a convenient introduction to the remarkable researches into the logic of mathematics that have been made during the last sixty years, and that have thrown an entirely new light both upon mathematics and upon logic, will do well to take up this book. But he will not find it easy reading. Indeed, the matter of the second volume will probably consist, at least nine-tenths of it, of rows of symbols.

Lady Victoria Welby's little volume is not what one would understand by a scientific book. It is not a treatise, and is free from the slightest shade of pedantry or pretension. Different people will estimate its value very differently. It is a feminine book, and a too masculine mind might think parts of it painfully weak. We should recommend the male reader to peruse chapters xxii. to xxv. before he reads the whole consecutively, for they will bear a second reading. The question discussed in these chapters is how primitive men ever came to believe in their absurd superstitions. This has generally been supposed to be the simplest of questions. Lady Victoria does not deign to mention La Fontaine's pretty fable (the sixth of the ninth book; the whole of it is worth rereading if you have forgotten it) of the sculptor and his statue of Jove:

> "L'artisan exprima si bien
> Le caractère de l'Idole,
> Qu'on trouva qu'il ne manquoit rien
> A Jupiter que la parole.

> "Même l'on dit que l'ouvrier
> Eut à peine achevé l'image,
> Qu'on le vit frémir le premier,
> Et redouter son propre ouvrage.
>   . . . .
> "Il étoit enfant en ceci:
> Les enfants n'ont l'âme occupée
> Que du continuel souci
> Qu'on ne fâche point leur poupée.

> "Le coeur suit aisément l'esprit.
> De cette source est descendue
> L'erreur Payenne qui se vit
> Chez tant de peuples répandue.
>   . . . .
> "Chacun tourne en réalités
> Autant qu'il peut ses propres songes.
> L'homme est de glace aux vérités;
> Il est de feu pour les mensonges."

La Fontaine's theory is somewhat complex, and allows more to the artistic impulse than modern ethnologists have done. They make mythology rather an attempt at a philosophical explanation of phenomena. But the authoress shows by a painstaking analysis that all such theories—La Fontaine's and the new current ones alike—are fatally irreconcilable with those traits of the primitive mind that have struck Tylor, Spencer, and ethnologists generally, as the deepest graven. In place of them she offers a hypothesis of her own, and the reader is tempted to lose patience with her for regarding it only as provisional, so strongly does it recommend itself, until she presents quite another view which one must admit has its plausibility.

The greatest service the book can render is that of bringing home the question which forms its title, a very fundamental question of logic, which has commonly received superficial, formalistic replies. Its vital and far-reaching significance has been even more ignored than usually happens with matters of universal and ubiquitous concern. To direct attention to the subject as one requiring study, both on its theoretical and on its practical side, is the essential purpose of the work. But in doing this the authoress had incidentally made a contribution towards the answer to the question, in pointing out three orders of signification. She has wisely abstained from any attempt at formal definitions of these three modes of significance. She tells us what she means only in the lowest of those three senses. To have gone further would have shunted her off upon a long and needless discussion.

One can see, though she does not remark it, that her three kinds of meaning correspond roughly to Hegel's three stages of thought. Her distinction, too, partly coincides with what was long ago said,[1] that to understand a word or formula may, in the first place, consist in such familiarity with it as will enable one to apply it correctly; or secondly, may consist in an abstract analysis of the conception or understanding of its intellectual relations to other concepts; or, thirdly, may consist in a knowledge of the possible phenomenal and practical upshot of the assertion of the concept. We might point out other interesting affiliations of her thought, sufficient to show that she must be upon the right track.

Lady Victoria, however, does not wish the matter to be agitated in the logician's study alone. She urges that people do not sufficiently take to heart the ethics of language. She thinks that modern conceptions call for a modern imagery of speech. But we fear that she does not realize how deep the knife would have to go into the body of speech to make it really scientific. We should have to form words like those the chemists use—if they can be called words. In particular, she preaches making logic—"significs," she calls it, but it would be logic—the basis or core of education. All those ideals deserve to be pondered. The book is very rich in illustrations drawn from contemporary writing.

---

1. Peirce made a similar distinction in January 1878. See *Collected Papers*, 5.388-410.

Appendix B

Irwin C. Lieb on Peirce's Classification of Signs

Lieb's account of Peirce's division of signs was appended to the earlier edition of Peirce's letters to Lady Welby (Irwin C. Lieb, *Charles S. Peirce's Letters to Lady Welby*, New Haven: Whitlock's, Inc., 1953). For a more recent study of Peirce's classification of signs see: Gary Sanders, "Peirce's Sixty-Six Signs?" *Transactions of the Charles S. Peirce Society*, Winter 1970, Vol. VI, No. 1, pp. 3-16. Sanders concludes, after his own careful analysis, that the "attempt to distinguish sixty-six classes may be ill advised."

According to Peirce, a sign is properly categorized by the third of his three *modalities of being*. It is something which brings an object into relation with an interpretant. A sign consequently exhibits each of the three modalities: it is *something* in itself, in connection with a second, and as a mean between a second and a third.

The triadic character of signs provides the three divisions which Peirce most fully explored: 1. Signs in Themselves; 2. Signs in Connection with Objects; and 3. Signs as Representations for Interpretants. Each of these divisions contains all the categorial varieties. Signs in themselves may be qualities, facts, or of the nature of laws or habits. Signs may be connected with their objects in virtue of similarity, non-cognitive relations, or in virtue of habits (of use). Finally, in relation to interpretants, signs may represent their objects to be qualities, facts, or laws.

In catalogue, these trichotomous divisions are:

Category or Modality	1. Signs in Themselves	2. Connections of Signs with Objects	3. Representations by Signs for Interpretants
a. First, Quality	a. Qualisign	a. Icon	a. Rheme
b. Second, Fact	b. Sinsign	b. Index	b. Proposition
c. Third, Law	c. Legisign	c. Symbol	c. Argument.

160

Not any combination of these varieties is, according to Peirce, a possible sign; for what a sign represents its object to be will depend partly upon the connection of the sign and its object, and the sort of connection will itself depend partly upon the character of the sign. Restrictions have therefore to be introduced. Peirce provides them with the remark that "It is evident that a possible (a first) can determine nothing but a Possible, it is equally so that a Necessitant (a third) can be determined by nothing but a Necessitant". With these restrictions, instead of 27 sorts of signs, the three trichotomies above provide for only 10 classes of signs. These are the classes which Peirce enumerates in the postscript to his October 12, 1904 letter:

	Divisions 1. 2. 3.	Name (or Abbreviation of the name) of the Sign	Example
1.	a a a	Qualisign	A feeling of 'redness'
2.	b a a	Iconic Sinsign	An individual diagram
3.	b b a	Rhematic Indexical Sinsign	A spontaneous cry
4.	b b b	Dicent Sinsign	A weathervane
5.	c a a	Iconic Legisign	A diagram abstracting its individuality
6.	c b a	Rhematic Indexical Legisign	A demonstrative pronoun
7.	c b b	Dicent Indexical Legisign	A street cry
8.	c c a	Rhematic Symbol	A common noun
9.	c c b	Dicent Symbol	A proposition
10.	c c c	Argument	A syllogism.

With the recognition that a sign has two *objects* (the Immediate and the Dynamoid Objects), and that there are three interpretants (the Destinate, Effective, and Explicit Interpretants) additional trichotomous divisions are required. In all, according to Perice, there are ten: 1. Signs in Themselves; 2. Immediate Objects in Themselves; 3. Dynamoid Objects in Themselves; 4. Destinate Interpretants in Themselves; 5. Effective Interpretants in Themselves; 6. Explicit Interpretants in Themselves; 7. Connections of Signs with Dynamoid Objects; 8. References of Signs to Effective Interpretants; 9. Representations by Signs for Explicit Interpretants; and 10. Assurances of Interpretants by Signs.

In Catalogue, these are the ten trichotomies, along with the several names that Peirce attached to the varieties:

1. Signs in
   Themselves
   a. Qualisign (Tone,
   b. Mark)
   b. Sinsign (Token,
   Replica)
   c. Legisign (Type)

2. Immediate Objects
   in Themselves
   a. Descriptive
   b. Designative
   c. Copulant

3. Dynamoid Objects
   in Themselves
   a. Abstractive
   b. Concretive
   c. Collective

4. Destinate Inter-
   pretants in Them-
   selves
   a. Hypothetical
   b. Categorical
   c. Relative

5. Effective Interpre-
   tants in Themselves
   a. Sympathetic
   b. Percusive
   c. Usual

6. Explicit Interpre-
   tants in Themselves
   a. Gratific
   b. Practical
   c. Pragmatistic

7. Connections of
   Signs with Dyna-
   moid Objects
   a. Icon
   b. Index
   c. Symbol

8. References of Signs
   to Effective Inter-
   pretants
   a. Suggestive
   b. Imperative
   c. Indicative

9. Representations by
   Signs for Explicit
   Interpretants
   a. Rheme (Seme)
   b. Dicent (Pheme)
   c. Argument (Delome)

10. Assurances of Interpretants
    by Signs
    a. Assurance by Instinct
    b. Assurance by Experience
    c. Assurance by Form (Habit)

When Peirce writes of 28 classes of signs in his letter of December 23, 1908, he makes it clear that he means those classes of signs which are possible given the first six of the trichotomies above. He says that "... the Dynamoid Object determines the Immediate Object, which determines the Sign itself, which determines the Destinate Interpretant (,) which determines the Effective Interpretant (,) which determines the Explicit Interpretant. . . .". The 28 classes of signs, then, will be those with the following constituent features:

	Divisions					
	3.	2.	1.	4.	5.	6.
1.	a	a	a	a	a	a
2.	b	a	a	a	a	a
3.	b	b	a	a	a	a

4.	b	b	b	a	a	a
5.	b	b	b	b	a	a
6.	b	b	b	b	b	a
7.	b	b	b	b	b	b
8.	c	a	a	a	a	a
9.	c	b	a	a	a	a
10.	c	b	b	a	a	a
11.	c	b	b	b	a	a
12.	c	b	b	b	b	a
13.	c	b	b	b	b	b
14.	c	c	a	a	a	a
15.	c	c	b	a	a	a
16.	c	c	b	b	a	a
17.	c	c	b	b	b	a
18.	c	c	b	b	b	b
19.	c	c	c	a	a	a
20.	c	c	c	b	a	a
21.	c	c	c	b	b	a
22.	c	c	c	b	b	b
23.	c	c	c	c	a	a
24.	c	c	c	c	b	a
25.	c	c	c	c	b	b
26.	c	c	c	c	c	a
27.	c	c	c	c	c	b
28.	c	c	c	c	c	c

The order of determination of these divisions is explicit, and it accords with Peirce's definition of 'a sign'. In adding the four additional trichotomies, the same relative order must therefore be preserved. Yet it may seem an open question whether the divisions numbered 7, 8, 9, and 10 are to follow the six above, whether they are to precede them, or whether the four divisions are to be inserted between the six above. Divisions 7 and 9, however, must follow the six above if the 10 classes of signs which Peirce most fully explored are to have the features he attributed to them. Divisions 8 and 10 must also follow the six above if there are finally to be 66 classes of signs.

The relative order of the last four divisions, then, adopting Peirce's usual pattern of enumeration, is 7, 8, 9, and 10. So that, most likely, the order of determination to which Peirce subscribed is: the Dynamoid Object determines the Immediate Object, which determines the Sign itself, which determines the Destinate Interpretant, which determines the Effective Interpretant, which determines the Explicit Interpretant, which determines the Connection between Sign and Object, which determines the Reference of Sign and Effective Interpretant, which determines the Representation by a Sign for an Explicit Interpretant, which determines the Assurance a Sign provides for an Interpretant.[1]

Upon this order of determination, Peirce's 66 sorts of sign have the following features:

	Divisions									
	3	2	1	4	5	6	7	8	9	10
1.	a	a	a	a	a	a	a	a	a	a
2.	b	a	a	a	a	a	a	a	a	a
3.	b	b	a	a	a	a	a	a	a	a
4.	b	b	b	a	a	a	a	a	a	a
5.	b	b	b	b	a	a	a	a	a	a
6.	b	b	b	b	b	a	a	a	a	a
7.	b	b	b	b	b	b	a	a	a	a
8.	b	b	b	b	b	b	b	a	a	a
9.	b	b	b	b	b	b	b	b	a	a
10.	b	b	b	b	b	b	b	b	b	a
11.	b	b	b	b	b	b	b	b	b	b
12.	c	a	a	a	a	a	a	a	a	a

---

1. This order of determination is not followed in the comprehensive account of Peirce's classification of signs given by Professors Paul Weiss and Arthur Burks in "Peirce's Sixty-Six Signs" (*The Journal of Philosophy*, Volume XLII, No. 14). They take the order of determination by divisions to be 1, 2, 3, 4, 5, 6, 7, 8, 9, 10; while the order above is 3, 2, 1, 4, 5, 6, 7, 8, 9, and 10. The differences between these orders derive from different opinions of the determination of signs and objects. The evidences which support the classification given by Weiss and Burks are Peirce's many claims that, in the triadic relation of representation, a sign is first, an object second, and an interpretant third. The evidences which support the second order of determination, however, seem stronger. They are: 1) Peirce's explicit statement of the order of the first six trichotomous divisions; 2) Peirce's definition of 'a sign' as "anything which is so determined by something else, called its Object, and so determines an effect upon a person, which effect I call its Interpretant, that the latter is thereby mediately determined by the former"; 3) Peirce's commitment to a realism which requires that *cognition conform to things, not things to cognition*; and 4) the view that although a sign is the first, and consequently the most *complicated*, item in the triadic relationship of representation, its position as first does not specify the *kind* of sign it may be.

The differences in these orders of determination affect the features of 21 of the 66 classes of signs. [Lieb]

13.	c	b	a	a	a	a	a	a	a	a
14.	c	b	b	a	a	a	a	a	a	a
15.	c	b	b	b	a	a	a	a	a	a
16.	c	b	b	b	b	a	a	a	a	a
17.	c	b	b	b	b	b	a	a	a	a
18.	c	b	b	b	b	b	b	a	a	a
19.	c	b	b	b	b	b	b	b	a	a
20.	c	b	b	b	b	b	b	b	b	a
21.	c	b	b	b	b	b	b	b	b	b
22.	c	c	a	a	a	a	a	a	a	a
23.	c	c	b	a	a	a	a	a	a	a
24.	c	c	b	b	a	a	a	a	a	a
25.	c	c	b	b	b	a	a	a	a	a
26.	c	c	b	b	b	b	a	a	a	a
27.	c	c	b	b	b	b	b	a	a	a
28.	c	c	b	b	b	b	b	b	a	a
29.	c	c	b	b	b	b	b	b	b	a
30.	c	c	b	b	b	b	b	b	b	b
31.	c	c	c	a	a	a	a	a	a	a
32.	c	c	c	b	a	a	a	a	a	a
33.	c	c	c	b	b	a	a	a	a	a
34.	c	c	c	b	b	b	a	a	a	a
35.	c	c	c	b	b	b	b	a	a	a
36.	c	c	c	b	b	b	b	b	a	a
37.	c	c	c	b	b	b	b	b	b	a
38.	c	c	c	b	b	b	b	b	b	b
39.	c	c	c	c	a	a	a	a	a	a
40.	c	c	c	c	b	a	a	a	a	a
41.	c	c	c	c	b	b	a	a	a	a
42.	c	c	c	c	b	b	b	a	a	a
43.	c	c	c	c	b	b	b	b	a	a
44.	c	c	c	c	b	b	b	b	b	a
45.	c	c	c	c	b	b	b	b	b	b
46.	c	c	c	c	c	a	a	a	a	a
47.	c	c	c	c	c	b	a	a	a	a
48.	c	c	c	c	c	b	b	a	a	a
49.	c	c	c	c	c	b	b	b	a	a
50.	c	c	c	c	c	b	b	b	b	a
51.	c	c	c	c	c	b	b	b	b	b
52.	c	c	c	c	c	c	a	a	a	a
53.	c	c	c	c	c	c	b	a	a	a
54.	c	c	c	c	c	c	b	b	a	a
55.	c	c	c	c	c	c	b	b	b	a

56.	c	c	c	c	c	c	b	b	b	b
57.	c	c	c	c	c	c	c	a	a	a
58.	c	c	c	c	c	c	c	b	a	a
59.	c	c	c	c	c	c	c	b	b	a
60.	c	c	c	c	c	c	c	b	b	b
61.	c	c	c	c	c	c	c	c	a	a
62.	c	c	c	c	c	c	c	c	b	a
63.	c	c	c	c	c	c	c	c	b	b
64.	c	c	c	c	c	c	c	c	c	a
65.	c	c	c	c	c	c	c	c	c	b
66.	c	c	c	c	c	c	c	c	c	c

Appendix C

Victoria Lady Welby on "Significs"
The Encylcopaedia Britannica, Vol. XXV, 1911, pp. 78-81.

SIGNIFICS. The term "Significs" may be defined as the science of meaning or the study of significance, provided sufficient recognition is given to its practical aspect as a method of mind, one which is involved in all forms of mental activity, includng that of logic.

In Baldwin's *Dictionary of Philosophy and Psychology* (1901-1905) the following definition is given: —

"1. Significs implies a careful distinction between (a) sense or signification, (b) meaning or intention and (c) significance or ideal worth. It will be seen that the reference of the first is mainly verbal (or rather sensal), of the second volitional, and of the third moral (e.g. we speak of some event 'the significance of which cannot be overrated,' and it would be impossible in such a case to substitute the 'sense' or the 'meaning' of such event, without serious loss). Significs treats of the relation of the sign in the widest sense to each of these.

2. A proposed method of mental training aiming at the concentration of intellectual activities on that which is implicitly assumed to constitute the primary and ultimate value of every form of study, i.e. what is at present indifferently called its meaning or sense, its import or significance. . . . Significs as a science would centralise and coordinate, interpret, inter-relate and concentrate the efforts to bring out meanings in every form and, in so doing to classify the various applications of the signifying property clearly and distinctly."

Since this dictionary was published, however, the subject has undergone further consideration and some development, which necessitate modification given. It is clear that stress needs to be laid upon the application of the principles and method involved, not merely, though notably, to language, but to all other types of human function. There is need to insist on the rectification of mental attitude and increase of interpretative power

167

which must follow on the adoption of the significal viewpoint and method, throughout all stages and forms of mental training and in the demands and contingencies of life.

In so far as it deals with linguistic forms, Significs includes "Semantics," a branch of study which was formally introduced and expounded in 1897 by Michel Bréal, the distinguished French philologist, in his *Essai de sémantique*. In 1900 this book was translated into English by Mrs. Henry Cust, with a preface by Professor Postgate. M. Bréal gives no more precise definition than the following:—

"Extraire de la linguistique ce qui en ressort
comme aliment pour la réflexion et—je ne
crains pas de l'ajouter—comme règle pour notre
propre langage, puisque chacun de nous collabore
pour sa part à l'évolution de la parole humaine,
voilà ce qui mérite d'être mis en lumière, voilà
ce qui j'ai essayé de faire en ce volume."

In the *Dictionary of Philosophy and Psychology* Semantics is defined as "the doctrine of historical word-meanings; the systematic discussion of the history and development of changes in the meanings of words." It may thus be regarded as a reform and extension of the etymological method, which applies to contemporary as well as to traditional or historical derivation. As human interests grow in constantly specialized directions, the vocabulary thus enriched is unthinkingly borrowed and reborrowed on many sides, at first in definite quotation, but soon in unconscious or deliberate adoption. Semantics may thus, for present purposes, be described as the application of Significs within strictly philological limits; but it does not include the study and classification of the "Meaning" terms themselves, nor the attainment of a clear recognition of their radical importance as rendering well or ill, the expressive value not only of sound and script but also of all fact or occurrence which demands and may arouse profitable attention.

The first duty of the Significian is, therefore, to deprecate the demand for mere linguistic reform, which is indispensable on its own proper ground, but cannot be considered as the satisfaction of a radical need such as that now suggested. To be content with mere reform of articulate expression would be fatal to the prospect of a significantly adequate language; one characterized by a development only to be compared to that of the life and mind of which it is or should be naturally the delicate, flexible, fitting, creative, as also controlling and ordering, Expression.

The classified use of the terms of expression-value suggests three main levels or classes of that value—those of Sense, Meaning, and Significance.

(a) The first of these at the outset would naturally be associated with Sense in its most primitive reference; that is, with the organic response to environment, and with the essentially expressive element in all experience. We ostracize the senseless in speech, and also ask "in what sense" a word is used or a statement may be justified.

(b) But "Sense" is not in itself purposive; whereas that is the main character of the word "Meaning," which is properly reserved for the specific sense which it is *intended to convey*.

(c) As including sense and meaning but transcending them in range, and covering the far-reaching consequence, implication, ultimate result or outcome of some event or experience, the term "Significance" is usefully applied.

These are not, of course, the only significal terms in common use, though perhaps sense and significance are on the whole the most consistently employed. We have also signification, purport, import, bearing, reference, indication, application, implication, denotation and connotation, the weight, the drift, the tenour, the lie, the trend, the range, the tendency, of given statements. We say that this fact suggests, that one portends, another carries, involves or entails certain consequences, or justifies given inferences. And finally we have the *value* of all forms of expression; that which makes worth while any assertion or proposition, concept, doctrine or theory; the definition of scientific fact, the use of symbolic method, the construction of mathematical formulae, the playing of an actor's part, or even art itself, like literature in all its forms.

The distinctive instead of haphazard use, then, of these and like terms would soon, both as clearing and enriching it, tell for good on our thinking. If we considered that any one of them were senseless, unmeaning, insignificant, we should at once in ordinary usage and in education disavow and disallow it. As it is, accepted idiom may unconsciously either illuminate or contradict experience. We speak, for instance, of *going through* trouble or trial, we never speak of *going through* well-being. That illuminates. But also we speak of the Inner or Internal as *alternative* to the spatial—reducing the spatial to the External. The very note of the value to the philosopher of the "Inner" as opposed to the "Outer" experience is that a certain example or analogue of enclosed space—a specified inside—is thus not measurable. That obscures. Such a usage, in fact, implies that, within enclosing limits, space sometimes ceases to exist. Comment is surely needless.

The most urgent reference and the most promising field for Significs lie in the direction of education. The normal child, with his inborn exploring, significating and comparing tendencies is so far the natural Significian. At once to enrich and simplify language would for him be a fascinating endeavour. Even his crudeness would often be suggestive. It is for his elders to supply the lacking criticism out of the storehouse of racial experience, acquired knowledge and ordered economy of means; and to educate him also by showing the dangers and drawbacks of uncontrolled linguistic, as other, adventure. Now the evidence that this last has virtually been hitherto left undone and even reversed, is found on careful examination to be overwhelming.[1] Unhappily what we have so far called education has, anyhow for centuries past, ignored—indeed in most cases even balked— the instinct to scrutinise and appraise the value of all that exists or happens within our ken, actual or possible, and fittingly to express this.

Concerning the linguistic bearing of Significs, abundant evidence has been collected, often in quarters where it would least be expected—

1. Of general unconsciousness of confusion, defeat, antiquation and inadequacy in language.

2. A. Of admission of the fact in given cases, but plea of helplessness to set things right. B. Of protest in such cases and suggestions for improvement.

3. Of direct or implied denial that the evil exists or is serious, and of prejudice against any attempt at concerted control and direction of the most developed group of languages.

4. Of the loss and danger of now unworthy or misfitting imagery and of symbolic assertion, observance or rite, once both worthy and fitting.

5. Of the entire lack, in education, of emphasis on the indispensable means of healthy mental development, *i.e.* the removal of linguistic hindrances and the full exploitation and expansion of available resources in language.

6. Of the central importance of acquiring a clear and orderly use of the terms of what we vaguely call "Meaning"; and also of the active modes, by gesture, signal or otherwise, of conveying intention, desire, impression and rational or emotional thought.

7. Finally and notably, of the wide-spread and all-pervading havoc at present wrought by the persistent neglect, in modern civilization, of the

---

1. It would be impossible of course in a short space to prove this contention. But the proof exists, and it is at the service of those who quite reasonably may deny its possible existence. [Lady Welby]

factor on which depends so much of our practical and intellectual welfare and advance.

As the value of this evidence is emphatically cumulative, the few and brief examples necessarily torn from their context for which alone room could here be found would only be misleading. A selection, however, from the endless confusions and logical absurdities which are not only tolerated but taught without correction or warning to children may be given.

We speak of beginning and end as complementary, and then of "both ends"; but never of both beginnings. We talk of truth when we mean accuracy: of the literal ("it is written") when we mean the actual ("it is done"). Some of us talk of the mystic and his mysticism, meaning by this, enlightenment, dawn heralding a day; others (more justly) mean by it the mystifying twilight, darkening into night. We talk of the unknowable when what that is or whether it exists is precisely what we cannot know—the idea presupposes what it denies; we affirm or deny immortality, ignoring its correlative innatality; we talk of solid foundations for life, for mind, for thought, when we mean the starting-points, foci. We speak of an eternal sleep when the very *raison d'être* of sleep is to end in awaking—it is not sleep unless it does; we appeal to a root as to an origin, and also figuratively give roots to the locomotive animal. We speak of natural "law" taking no count of the sub-attentive working in the civilized mind of the associations of the legal system (and the law court) with its decreed and enforced, but also revocable or modifiable enactments. Nature, again is indifferently spoken of as the norm of all order and fitness, the desecration of which is reprobated as the worst form of vice and is even motherly in bountiful provision; but also as a monster of reckless cruelty and tyrannous mockery. Again, we use the word "passion" for the highest activity of desire or craving, while we keep "passive" for its very negation.

These instances might be indefinitely multiplied. But it must of course be borne in mind that we are throughout dealing only with the idioms and habits of the English language. Each civilized language must obviously be dealt with on its own merits.

The very fact that the significating and interpretative function is the actual, though as yet little recognized and quite unstudied condition of mental advance and human achievement, accounts for such a function being taken for granted and left to take care of itself. This indeed, in pre-civilized ages (since it was then the very condition of safety and practically of survival), it was well able to do. But the innumerable forms of protection, precaution, artificial aid and special facilities which modern civilization implies and provides and to which it is always adding, have entirely and dangerously changed the situation. It has become imperative to realize the fact that through disuse we have partly lost the greatest as the most universal of human prerogatives. Hence arises the special difficulty of clearly showing at this stage that man has now of set purpose to recover and develop on a higher than the primitive plane the sovereign power of unerring and productive interpretation of a world which even to a living, much more to an intelligent, being, is essentially significant. These conditions apply not only to the linguistic but to all forms of human energy and expression, which before all else must be significant in the most active, as the highest, sense and degree. Man has from the outset been organizing his experience; and he is bound correspondingly to organize the expression of that experience in all phases of his purposive activity, but more especially in that of articulate speech and linguistic symbol. This at once introduces the volitional element; one which has been strangely eliminated from the very function which most of all needs and would repay it.

One point must here, however, be emphasised. In attempting to inaugurate any new departure from habitual thinking, history witnesses that the demand at its initial stage for unmistakably clear exposition must be not only unreasonable but futile. This of course must be typically so in the case of an appeal for the vital regeneration of all modes of Expression and especially of Language, by the practical recognition of an ignored but governing factor working at its very inception and source. In fact, for many centuries at least, the leading civilizations of the world have been content to perpetuate modes of speech once entirely fitting but now often grotesquely inappropriate, while also remaining content with casual changes often for the worse and always liable to inconsistency with context. This inevitably makes for the creation of a false standard both of lucidity and style in linguistic expression.

Still, though we must be prepared to make an effort in assuming what is virtually a new mental attitude, the effort will assuredly be found fully worth making. For there is here from the very first a special compensation. If, to those whose education has followed the customary lines, nowhere is the initial difficulty of moving in a new direction greater than in the one termed Significs, nowhere, correspondingly, is the harvest of advantage more immediate, greater, or of wider range and effort.

It ought surely to be evident that the hope of such a language; of a speech which shall worthily express human need and gain in its every possible development in the most efficient possible way, depends on the awakening and stimulation of a sense which it is our common and foremost interest to cultivate to the utmost on true and healthy lines. This may be described as the immediate and insistent sense of the pregnancy of things, of the actual bearings of experience, of the pressing and cardinal importance, as warning or guide, of that experience considered as indicative; a Sense realized as belonging to a world of what for us must always be the Sign of somewhat to be inferred, acted upon, used as a mine of pertinent and productive symbol, and as the normal incitant to profitable action. When this germinal or primal sense—as also the practical starting-point, of language has become a reality for us, reforms and acquisitions really needed will naturally follow as the expression of such a recovered command of fitness, of boundless capacity and of perfect coherence in all modes of expression.

One objection, however, which before this will have suggested itself to the critical reader, is that if we are here really dealing with a function which must claim an importance of the very first rank and affect our whole view of life, practical and theoretical, the need could not have failed long ago to be recognised and acted upon. And indeed it is not easy in a few words to dispose of such an objection and to justify so venturesome an apparent paradox as that with which we are now concerned. But it may be pointed out that the special development of one faculty always entails at least the partial atrophy of another. In a case like this the principle typically applies. For the main human acquirement has been almost entirely one of logical power, subtle analysis and co-ordination of artificial means. In modern civilization the application of these functions to an enormous growth of invention of every kind has contributed not a little to the loss of the swift and direct sense of *point*: the sensitiveness as it were of the compass-needle to the direction in which experience was moving. Attention has been forcibly drawn elsewhere; and moreover, as already pointed out, the natural insight of children, which might have saved the situation, has been methodically silenced by a discipline called educative, but mainly suppressive and distortive.

The biological history of Man has been, indeed, a long series of transmutations of form to subserve higher functions. In language he has so far failed to accomplish this. There has even in some directions been loss of advantage already gained. While his nature has been plastic and adaptive, language, the most centrally important of his acquirements, has remained relatively rigid, or what is just as calamitous, fortuitously elastic. There have been notable examples—the classical languages—of the converse process. In Greek and Latin, Man admirably controlled, enriched, varied, significated his expressions to serve his mental needs. But we forbear ourselves to follow and better this example. All human energies have come under orderly direction and control except the one on which in a true sense they all depend. This fatal omission, for which defective methods of education are mainly responsible, has disastrously told upon the mental advance of the race. But after all we have here a comparatively modern neglect and helplessness. Kant, for instance, complained bitterly of the defeating tendency of language in his day, as compared with the intelligent freedom of the vocabulary and idiom of the "classical" Greek, who was always creating expression, moulding it to his needs and finding an equally intelligent response to his efforts, in his listeners and readers—in short, in his public.

Students, who are prepared seriously to take up this urgent question of the application of Significs in education and throughout all human spheres of interest, will soon better any instruction that could be given by the few who so far have tentatively striven to call attention to and bring to bear a practically ignored and unused method. But by the nature of the case they must be prepared to find that accepted language, at least in modern European forms, is far more needlessly defeating than they have supposed possible: that they themselves in fact are continually drawn back, or compelled so to write as to draw back their readers, into what is practically a hotbed of confusion, a prison of senseless formalism and therefore of barren controversy.

It can hardly be denied that this state of things is intolerable and demands effectual remedy. The study and systematic and practical adoption of the natural method of Significs can alone lead to and supply this. Significs is in fact the natural response to a general sense of need which daily becomes more undeniably evident. It founds no school of thought and advocates no technical specialism. Its immediate and most pressing application is, as already urged, to elementary, secondary and specialised education. In recent generations the healthy sense of discontent and the natural ideals of interpretation and expression have been dis-couraged instead of fostered by a training which has not only tolerated but perpetuated the existing chaos. Signs, however, are daily increasing that Significs, as implying the practical recognition of, and emphasising the true line of advance in, a recovered and enhanced power to interpret experience and adequately to express and apply that power, is destined, in the right hands, to become a socially operative factor of the first importance.

LITERATURE.—Lady Welby, "Sense, Meaning and Interpretation," in *Mind* (January and April 1896), *Grains of Sense* (1897), *What is Meaning?* (1903); Professor F. Tönnies, "Philosophical Terminology" (Welby Prize

Essay), *Mind* (July and October 1899 and January 1900), also article in *Jahrbuch,* &c., and supplements to *Philosophische Terminologie* (December 1906); Professor G. F. Stout, *Manual of Psychology* (1898); Sir T. Clifford Allbutt's Address on "Words and Things" to the Students' Physical Society of Guy's Hospital (October 1906); Mr. W. J. Greenstreet's "Recent Science" articles in the *Westminster Gazette* (November 15, 1906, and January 10, 1907). (V. W.)

Appendix D

J. W. Slaughter to Peirce

The following letters from J. W. Slaughter and the prospectus which accompanied the first of them are filed with the correspondence with Lady Welby in Mrs. L 463 of the Peirce Papers. They refer to a collection of essays on significs to which Peirce was asked to contribute. As the correspondence shows, Peirce was never able to complete his essay. The book was never published.

19, Gray's Inn Residences,
Holborn, W.C.
August 20th/09

Dear Sir,

I wrote to you some months ago but fear my letter has failed of its destination. My object was to secure your cooperation in the venture described in the enclosed memorandum. Professor Stout very much hopes that you will find it possible to contribute an essay, and indeed, feels that the book would be incomplete without it. The length of the essay must suit the wishes of the contributor but should be within nine or ten thousand words. It is hoped that the book may be ready for publication in January. You will be glad to know that Lady Welby continues well; she is at present in Scotland.

Yours faithfully,
J. W. Slaughter

Essays on Significs[1]

It is proposed to bring together a number of representative studies of a critical and constructive character bearing upon the group of topics which Lady Welby has so long endeavoured to bring into prominence. The word

---

1. This is the "memorandum" enclosed with Slaughter's letter.

which she has fixed upon as covering the whole range of these questions is "Significs"—the study and use of signs in all their bearings. For this purpose it is desirable to approach and appeal for co-operation to those who have shown sympathy for her general aims. As indicating the kind of subjects that will come within the scope of the volume, the following suggestions are offered.

1. The Analogical Extension of Interpretation from one Field of Experience to another.
2. Value and Purpose as Factors in Significance.
3. The Function of Metaphor in Thought.
4. The Figurative Element in the Conception of Space and Time.
5. The Relation of Mathematical Symbolism to Significance.
6. The Sources of Obscurity and Ambiguity in the Use of Words.
7. The Extent of Voluntary Control over Language.
8. The Means of Developing in Children a true Insight into the Nature and Use of Language.

Further suggestions as to desirable subjects will be welcomed.

The Essays will be edited by Professor Stout, The University, St. Andrews, and Dr. Slaughter, Elmwood, Bickley, Kent.

4, Harcourt Buildings
Temple, E. C.
April 25th, 1911

Dear Dr. Peirce,

I am venturing to write again regarding the volume of Essays which friends of Lady Welby are contributing. We now have all the materials except your contribution, and are greatly hoping that your health has permitted you to prepare a paper. If so, we shall be glad to receive it soon, in order to get the volume through the press some time this summer. If you require some further time, we can proceed with the printing, being certain that your contribution will come.

Yours truly,
J. W. Slaughter

Appendix E

Essays by Lady Welby

The following essays were written by Lady Welby. They are reproduced here from the copies she sent to Peirce. It was Lady Welby's practice to formalize her thoughts in the form of brief essays and send them to her correspondents. The two included here are representative of the ideas she was working on during the time of her correspondence with Peirce. They also reveal her own rather unique interest in significs.

All Saints' Day, November 1st, 1907.

The Communion of Saints.

Why do I insist that 'Psychical Research' must begin at the other end, else it will be sanctioning and encouraging the very evil it has been initiated to exorcise by explaining?

Taking 'sainthood' as one mode of expressing the highest type attained by the true human being as moral,—that is, social,—and tracing it back through all grades or spheres of the Natural world known to us, what is the first character of what we rightly call holiness, that is, whole-ness?*

That of unbroken communication, rising into full and conscious communion and creating combined thought and action in flawless harmony with the universe.

In this sense we find our first sainthood in what we negatively call the Inorganic world. The 'crystalloid', the 'mineral', the material, the mechanical world is 'saintly', i.e. true to what is the most and the best possible to

---

* As in many like cases we have here sadly missed a psychological lesson in the traceable derivation often curiously recent of a term. [Lady Welby]

it. The physio-chemist will own that this wholeness, this sainthood, never fails him: he can trust it to the uttermost, else his work would collapse.

Well, the true human saint is the Man in whom good is an absorbing passion, whom you can trust to the uttermost end, who not only never would but never could fail you, because his life and hope are bound up in yours and your needs are his. Defects he may have of many kinds: but his very flaws are loyal to that which answers to what we call 'natural law', to the Order of the Universe.

The flaw in the 'diamond' is as true and loyal as the 'precious stone' in which it appears. The only sinner would be the flaw which under given conditions failed to appear, as would be the diamond which failed in such facet to reflect the spectrum.

While, therefore, there is here the sharpest possible distinction and spatially, it may be, separation, there is nowhere 'self-centred' and self-contained isolation. And still less is there any attempt at mutual defeat or exclusion or paralysis, among even the most sharply contrasted forms of energy, such as those called 'positive and negative' electricity. The centripetal and centrifugal are only the contraction and expansion of one 'activity', which in some sense, subtle or obvious, is in communication and co-operation with all others. All orders of motion act 'in concert' with all others. Thus you get the first level of the 'communion of saints'. Physical science is engaged in investigating the conditions, range, results, of this inorganic or lower 'communion', and in producing 'new' forms of it, with 'new' consequences; sometimes it may be destructive or explosive, sometimes formative, even 'creative', but it is always true to the natural order.

It is hardly necessary here to trace precisely the same 'sainthood' in the vital loyalty to the organic order. You may not understand, but you can always depend upon, the fidelity of Life to its own canons and its own norm. It will always act up to its own, its 'true' ideal, in the many and various grades and types of this.

But Life introduces us to what as yet we vaguely and confusedly call 'consciousness', sensation, feeling, mind, and so on, ending in that devouring vortex which we call our 'self' and allow to dominate us and destroy the natural sainthood of self-gift. Hitherto this fresh factor of 'awareness' has been the very means of our discovery of all that seems 'below' or 'previous to' it. By what power therefore are we in turn to investigate 'mind', as 'mind' investigates motion, matter, and life? It is clear that Motion and Matter cannot plan and effect research into 'themselves'; cannot observe and report upon dynamical or statical phenomena; cannot form assumptions or conclusions, cannot even experiment.

This applies also to Life. But mind* (as we conceive it) at once proceeds to violate this elementary logical sequence by professing to do this very thing and calling it Psychology.

For who or what is the impartial, the thorough, the critical, the scientific, the expert observer of the 'psyche'?

The Psyche!

Now it is surely here obvious that we are using the word 'psyche' in two senses:

(1) As what we (in some sense) Have.

(2) As what we (in the fullest sense) Are.

We *have* children. But except in a secondary and somewhat strained sense we do not even say though they emanate from us, that we *are* those children. So with 'our' hands, eyes, etc. I submit that it is vitally, logically, and ethically necessary that we choose out and devote some word exclusively to what in the fullest sense of Identity we *are*, and leave all other words,—such as person, mind, soul,—for what, broadly and in some sense we *have*. For in the present confusion between Us and what is Ours—between primary and secondary Identity—the Communion of Saints in the mental and intellectual world, real though it be, is from the outset thwarted and sterilised. It is directed into impotent controversy, each mind being cut off from others and only partially, by the acquired means of language, able at will to exchange standpoints with them. The world of mind and thought becomes a sort of caricature of space, wherein every position like every direction was protesting that all others were wrong or mistaken: or if that illustration be too abstract, like a man who, standing on one side of an object, were unable to 'go round' and stand with equal ease on the other, and spent his time in arguing with some one already on the other side (and in the same 'Alice in Wonderland' condition) that *his* position was a 'false' one. Yet the fact that the communion is real is made conspicuously evident by the common possession and use of the subtle network of the logical along the lines of which alone, as in a sustaining and protective framework, we can coherently or productively *think*.

This ever-increasing lack, then, of that dynamic unity and flawless communication (involving changes e.g. of position in a spatial continuum) which naturally results from the wholeness—the soundness—of nature through all and uttermost diversity, brings us to the enormous *promise* of the community of human sainthood and the Communion of Saints, to which All Saints' Day witnesses.

---

* As I long ago tried to point out in a very crude paper called the 'Mental Brain.' [Lady Welby]

There we have, at least in the emotional, moral, religious world, the symbolic recognition of a possible recovery of that perfect communication of which in the 'inorganic' world, human society is becoming, through the extensions of 'wireless' telegraphy and telephony, etc., so much more and so vividly conscious. The Communion of Saints is made possible by a logical and ethical—by a divinely human 'ether.'

It is only the 'personal' world and the conceptual or thought-world which remain relatively paralysed by an unnatural isolation. Here throughout the world the communion of saints is as yet little more than a dead letter. Each one of us is shut up within his own personality. And each type of sainthood involves a theory or a 'belief' or a doctrine, which tends to cut it off from all others and leave it stranded in an isolated group, on a mental island inaccessible not only to the rest of humanity, but to all other saintly groups.

This then is my reason for feeling so strongly as I do, that all Research into that region, whatever it be, which lies beyond or within the narrow belt of human response which we call normal experience, must, if it is to be really effective and fruitful in deepening, widening and enriching a sane and healthy outlook, *begin at the other end*. By this beginning at the other end I mean the systematic collection of the fast increasing evidence not only of biological but also of physical, chemical, and electrical science as to the reality of worlds of potential experience beyond our present 'touch'. I mean the patient and untiring labour of tracing this up through the living world to its human consummation, and learning at each stage of our climb the really natural conditions, not of the Occult but rather of the Implicit: not of the dangerous region which is frontier of the morbid and fanatical and for which our disloyal because deceptive craving must be inhibited, but of the blessed region of the orderly and revealing, *explaining* clearness, of which we have the only safe analogy in the laboratories of physical, chemical, electrical, biological science and in the strict analysis and tentative generalizations of the true Mathematician and Statistician.

Starting from this end, our Psychical Research will give us a reversed view of what, betraying our own false position, we call the Occult, and associate with Mystery and Mysticism. We henceforth turn our back on that; and enter the converse world of inexorably simple and emphatically orderly, consistent investigation. The atmosphere of our laboratory of research glows it is true with a severer light, and dream-certainties cannot live in it for a moment. Their tremendous power is at last undermined, while the glory of natural reality, as we can bear it, presses in.

Then there will be no longer question of any alternative between the revelations of science and the intimations of emotion: between what we realise through experimental process and logical proof, and what we realise, not by congenital or acquired 'belief' but by that attribute which is common to all that is best in human nature, by the Faith which connotes unreserved loyalty at all costs to inexorably tested fact and to true and pure motive, natural and divine.

We need not fear to lose by this anything really precious to any man. The highest like the humblest of our aims and aspirations are included in a communion which embraces all that is good in each man and in all. And this then, in the truest sense of the words, is the Communion of Saints.

August 31st. 1908

What Does It Signify?

In defining the subject, range, and practical relevance of Significs, this question, here put in no careless or impatient sense, is more than suggestive. Though a popular phrase, it confesses and accentuates a profound, elementary, universal need, and the sternest and most inexorable of demands.

Every existent, every proposition, every movement, every object, every incident or occurrence, every fact and every fancy, every presentation or representation of any kind; all that for any reason or in any way arouses attention or claims interest, excites response or suggests inference, must be subjected to this introductory and exhaustive test.

First of all, what does it signify?

For unless in some sense or degree it *signifies*, we may ignore it; it is indeed waste of energy to consider it. In some sense and however remotely or indirectly, it must concern us all, be it only as somewhat to be denied, ignored, or neglected. However abstract or conjectural, even however irrational, it must needs have some bearing on our knowledge if not on our status or our conduct. It must concern if only some or even but one, of us. The barest gabble, the most purposeless antic, the wildest folly, the idlest dream must at least *signify* in some context, reference, direction,—sense. Many things may be senseless; many things are meaningless,—that is, outside the purview of Intention, still more of deliberate Purpose and Design; many things may be un-important. But when we say that anything is in-significant we ourselves are at least ambiguous. For not only every fact or thing if it be one, or if we take it for one, somehow signifies, but nothing thus can be insignificant except in the sense 'of no account in certain contexts'; negligible for a purpose in hand, ignorable. Even thus its very predication acknowledges its signifying quality: the crassest mistake or merest omission must signify if only the absence or lack of somewhat.

It will thus be clear that the question so constantly asked when some unusual occurrence or condition is brought to our notice, and we do not see how it affects or need interest us—the question, What does it Signify? has the widest of applications. For the one function really elementary and universal in a world which for us in an inexhaustible mine of Signs, is to Signify; not merely in the conventional sense of affecting or modifying our personal or social requirements or welfare, but in that of Indication. In this sense, on this ground, nothing is for us any more complete in itself than the marks now made on this paper and grouped into words and sentences. They 'embody' and thus designate or suggest, denote or connote, indicate or imply notions or ideas, assumptions, 'trains of thought', results emotional or logical, imaginative or actual. They symbolise at least the presumably or conjecturally existent.

When in infancy we begin to question and to distinguish and name the excitants wherewith life surrounds the responsive sense-complex which we call the nervous system: when 'mind' at its first budding prompts the little one to ask What, How, Why, and so on, there you have the irrevocable confession, repeated with fresh and urgent emphasis by the leaders and pioneers of the race, that every impulse and impression, every appearance or stimulus to attention and action is *significant*; not of course necessarily in the sense of being especially and notably important or far-reaching and momentous (in predictable or measurable consequence) but in the barest indicative or implicative sense.

Surely therefore it follows that Significs, the study of that of which all experience is the Sign: Significs, which seeks to clear our ideas of what that experience brings, offers, bestows upon us; Significs, which must be not only the best of all scouts but also the best of all watchmen to tell us "what of the night"—of the shadows baffling and misleading us and the stars serene above them—is a very immediate and practical concern of everyone [*sic*] of us, at all times and in all places. The really strange thing is thus, not that we should discover this ingenerative factor and act upon our discovery now, but that Man should ever have overlooked or ignored a study so vitally central and so certain to enhance the value of all other studies to which he is impelled or can undertake, and of every possible form of healthy action, invention, industry, business, as well as all art, speculation, poetry; in short the value of all his interests and activities.

It is perhaps in education and in ethics and economics—in all that Sociology may include,—that the need and lack of Significs is most evident. The hitherto 'insoluble' questions of social welfare, with all the misery and conflict, bitterness and tragedy involved in them, are partly at least entailed by our want of grip on the germinal elements of the whole evolution of what we call civilization. The really first questions are rarely asked, and when they are they lack the true inspiration and context and remain barren. We need, again, flashlights on the social 'situation' and its problems; but we want them from many quarters, and that they should be met with such response that a general illumination shall be the result. We need to rise out of a state of interminable bickering and recrimination, all the more dangerous when it is too superficially logical and too dignified and apparently weighty to be recognised under such names. We need to begin at real beginnings and to ask the most 'previous' of all questions. Our attention, trained conventionally to act keenly or dwell persistently in some directions or on some grounds only, must be trained naturally to fix on *all* that first and most needs it, and especially to matters which for assignable reasons have been missed at least in some practical contexts as in theoretical explorations, but which are in fact often the unrecognised original sources of many of our worst failures and most crying evils.

At present it is no wonder that any suggestion that a fresh form of training, point of view, subject of study, is needed, should seem but as one more 'visionary' panacea for irremediable troubles. Yet the very number and insistence of the problems which beset us in the most prosaically practical of lives may suggest, does suggest, that there is something wrong somewhere. In the homely image of the 'screw loose' we do sometimes show a dim consciousness not only that all is not as it should be, but not as it *shall* be, *must* be, if social calamity or even ruin is to be averted.

If our inherited forms of education—now happily everywhere criticised and freely condemned—had not helped to stultify us in our most growing and explorative years: if, instead, the most had been made of our significating and interpretative powers: if we had been incited to make suggestions, however raw, and encouraged to express unusual ideas and ask apparently unanswerable questions: if our teachers, themselves trained in Significs, had in their turn done the same thing on a reasoned and experienced footing, how much higher the average level of ability would have been! A new Wonderland with the birth-mark of orderly knowledge, verified reality, upon it; a new Open Gate to the Borderlands of experience, would be ours. We should gain a test and mastery of the 'occult' which would bring much from shadow-land to light-land. But at present we must begin both lower down and higher up and further in, to find in baffling or illusive mysteries the organic and embryonic simplicities.

Appendix F

List of Drafts by Peirce in the
Peirce Correspondence

In the Peirce Correspondence in Houghton Library, Harvard University, there are a number of drafts by Peirce. As mentioned earlier, it was Peirce's practice to write drafts of his letters to Lady Welby before sending them. Peirce kept a number of these drafts along with other material related to his correspondence with Lady Welby. Some of the drafts are of letters which were actually sent; some contain ideas which Peirce evidently wanted to keep for future reference. The longest draft, for example, reflects Peirce's efforts to work out a classification of Signs. It is obvious that Peirce wanted to keep these drafts for future reference.

The following is a list of these drafts with some indication of their contents. In most cases, they are dated, and where not dated, an effort has been made to date them by reference to content and to letters actually sent.

(1) 2 pages. Draft of a letter from Peirce to Lady Welby dated May 4, 1904. This is an earlier draft of a letter Peirce sent dated May 7, 1904. (see p. 19.) In the draft, Peirce mentions his Metric System paper, and remarks: "My Metric System paper has developed a very fundamental difference between us. You are a rationalist and a radical; while I am a conservative of the most convinced kind."

(2) 14 pages. Draft of a letter to Lady Welby dated October 1904. Apparently an early version of the letter Peirce sent to Lady Welby dated October 12, 1904. (See p. 22.) This is one of the most important letters in the correspondence, and the one in which Peirce carefully outlined his theory of signs for Lady Welby. There are some differences between the draft and the letter sent, but the content of the two is substantially the same.

(3) 2 pages. Parts of a letter presumably written in December of 1904. In one place, Peirce refers to his brother as Assistant Secretary of Foreign Affairs, who ". . . has the appointment of consuls in his hands. . . ." There is a similar comment in the letter he sent dated December 16, 1904. (See p. 46.) On one of the draft pages he makes the following remark: "My dear Lady Welby—*Entre nous*, I am seriously thinking of selling this place at once and accepting a consulate in the tropics. I feel that life in the open air is my wife's only chance, and then the care of this rambling house is too much for her, especially as a speck of dust deranges her equanimity. Besides, small as the salary of an American consul is, I imperatively need the money. . . ."

(4) 8 pages. Undated draft of a letter to Lady Welby. The draft can be dated after November 20, 1904, since the opening sentence refers to Lady Welby's essay on time. This essay was sent to Peirce in her letter of that date. (See p. 37.) In the draft, Peirce also makes the following remark: "I have just been giving to our National Academy of Sciences an outline of a very elaborate study that I have been making of the logical analysis of the idea of space the accuracy of which is perhaps in some part confirmed by my being able to deduce from it many new and important geometric theorems." Peirce read a paper entitled "Topical Geometry" before the National Academy of Science at the meeting held November 15-16, 1904. This is most likely the outline he is referring to. The draft was probably written in early December of 1904.

(5) 7 pages. Draft pages which can also be dated somewhere around December of 1904. One page begins: "As for your Ladyship's Essay on Time, you probably sent it to me because I mentioned that I had been at work on Time & I might have added on space." This corresponds to a similar comment in Peirce's December 16, 1904 letter. (See p. 46.)

(6) 18 pages. Draft of a letter to Lady Welby written in July of 1905. (A copy of this draft has been included in Appendix G.) On page 15 of the draft, Peirce comments: "Oh, I am writing dreadful twaddle, garrulous chat; but it is our July weather which dries up or drenches one, as inconvenience may dictate." On page 5 of the draft, he refers to "Mr. Russell's suggestion that there is a *Fourthness, Fifthness*, etc." Lady Welby had made copies of Peirce's October 12, 1904 letter and sent them to Russell and J. Cook Wilson. She sent copies or extracts of Russell's comments to Peirce on two different occasions: November 20, 1904 and January 7, 1905. There are two letters in Lady Welby's correspondence from Russell which refer to Peirce's notion of Firstness, Secondness, and Thirdness: one is dated November 14, 1904 and the other is dated

December 27, 1904. In view of Peirce's reference to Russell's comments, this draft would have been written in July of 1905.

(7) 9 pages. This draft is dated July 16, 1905. Peirce notes that he has been rereading Plato's *Theaetetus*. His comments particularly refer to the notion of Socratic irony and Socratic induction. In the draft, he digresses with a discussion of his own notion of Abduction. He remarks: "There are three kinds of reasoning only. Namely, on first coming to a problem we must study the data and derive from them by thought a theory. This theory has some chance of being correct, in consequence of the fact that the human mind is a product of Nature and therefore its ways have some affinity with Nature's ways. This kind of reasoning by which theories are formed under the inspiration of the facts I call Abduction because I think there is *evidence* to warrant the assumption that the scamp Apellicon by a blundering insertion f a single wrong word in Chapter 25 of the same book gave ἀπαΐωΐή an entirely different meaning from that intended by Aristotle." The draft is incomplete.

(8) 52 pages. A rather long draft dated March 9, 1906. The draft is ostensibly a long commentary on a poem Lady Welby sent to Peirce ("A Confession in Doggerel," published in *The University Review*, Vol. II, No. 10). The draft is interesting not so much for his analysis and comments on the poem, as because it contains some interesting biographical information about Peirce. (A portion of this draft has been included in Appendix G.)

(9) 33 pages. A number of draft pages on signs written between December 14 and 28, 1908. The draft pages bear various dates: December 23, 1908, December 24, 1908; "Christmas Day, 1908." There is one passage similar in content to the opening paragraph of the letter he sent to Lady Welby dated December 14, 1908 which would indicate that some of the drafts might have been written at least that early. At any rate, all of this material seems to be related to the letter Peirce sent to Lady Welby bearing the dates December 14, 1908 and December 23, 1908. (See pp. 66-85.) From the drafts, it is evident that Peirce was working on a rather extensive classification of signs. One page, for example, is headed "The Trichotomies of Signs (as apprehended 1908 Dec 24)"; another "The Ten Main Trichotomies of Signs (as they were apprehended by me 1908 Dec. 24.)." Most of the material in these drafts has been published in *Collected Papers*, 8.342-379.

(10) 11 pages. Draft pages of a letter Peirce sent to Lady Welby dated January 31, 1909. Seven of the pages are dated in the upper left-hand corner. All of these drafts appear to be discarded pages from the letter on Existential Graphs. (See pp. 94-130.)

(11) 13 pages. In her letter of January 21, 1909, Lady Welby sent Peirce several essays. (See p. 94.) These drafts contain Peirce's comments on these essays. They are dated February 9, 1909, March 14, 1909, and August 14, 1908. The latter date, however, is the date of one of Lady Welby's essays entitled "Trans–." Peirce used the date and title for the heading on one of the draft sheets. In the drafts, Peirce comments on the following essays: "Trans–," "To What End," "Communion of Saints," "Faith vs Belief," and on her *Encyclopaedia Britannica* article on "Significs."

(12) 11 pages. Draft of a letter to Lady Welby dated September 29, 1909. The letter begins with an apology for not having written in reply to her letter. The cause of the delay, he notes, is the "need of repairs on the house to make it habitable for next winter and the consequent need of getting together a considerable sum of money." Apparently, the letter was never sent.

(13) 3 pages. Two drafts of letters from Juliette Peirce to Lady Welby written in Peirce's hand. Neither is dated.

(14) 3 pages. Loose sheets, undated, of calculations. None of these calculations seem to have any relation to Peirce's correspondence with Lady Welby. One sheet has the following comment: "The artist in definition likes, after he has worked out the principal features of his design, to assemble them and hold a sort of rehearsal."

Appendix G

Peirce to Lady Welby (Draft). July 1905

The following is a copy of a letter Peirce wrote but apparently never sent to Lady Welby. It was written presumably in July of 1905. (See p. 186.) Page 3 of the draft has not been found.

My dear Lady Welby

I have been overhauling my classification of signs with the result of throwing the matter into a state of confusion which I hope with time will heal up into some connective tissue. My three categories appear always more and more clear to me. These resulted from two years incessant study in the direction of trying to do what Hegel tried to do. It became apparent that there were such categories as his. But bad as his are, I could substitute nothing radically better. Alongside of these, however, which may be called material categories, there are formal categories, corresponding to his three grades of thought. These are certainly as much more important as all classifications according to structure are than classifications according to material. Taking the *phaneron,* by which I mean whatever is before the mind in any way whatever & regardless of whether it be fact or fiction, let us begin by considering whether it be possible that there are indecomposable elements of the *phaneron* which have different grades of structure, some being such as they are (that is, as they seem, for we are speaking of *phanera*) in themselves regardless of anything else,—*Primans,* We may call them; others being such as they are as second to something,—*Secundans*; others such as they are as *Tertians*, etc. If there be a *Priman* it can have (i.e. can appear to have) no parts. For if it had, it would not be such as it is regardless of these parts. For the same reason, different Primans cannot differ in any respect, that is by having in themselves different characters. They cannot have. . . . .[1]

---

1. Text incomplete due to missing manuscript page.

189

Next let us suppose there are indecomposable elements of the phaneron which occur only (and therefore *can* occur only since the phaneron comprises all that can be conceived, thought or distinguished in any way,) as paired with other elements; so that they are Secundan [I don't know whether *secundanus* occurs in any classical writing or not; but it is *per se* just as good a word as the familiar *tertianus* and *quartanus*.] These, then, though indecomposable, are of a higher st[r]ucture than the Primans, just as a garret is higher than a rez-de-chaussée, in what it supposes. An effort is an example. For an effort without resistance would be as great an absurdity as a contradiction in terms, though the Logic-books do not say so.

Next, for *Tertians*. It is evident that if there are any triadic relations at all, there must be indecomposable triads, that is, triads not definable in monadic and dyadic terms alone. For a triad that is so definable is a compound. Now composition is itself a triadic relation, $a + b = c$.

Mr. Russell's suggestion that there is a *Fourthness, Fifthness*, etc. is natural, when one does not stop to think what we are driving at. We are seeking the grades of structure of *indecomposable* elements of the phaneron. Now to say that there is a relation between four objects A, B, C, D is the same as to say that there is an object, M, so related to C and for D that A is in the given relation to B and for M. (I use the two prepositions merely to suggest variety in the relations.) Thus to say that A gives up B to C in exchange for D is to say that there is a surrender of D by C which takes place in consideration of the reciprocal surrender of B by A. Thus, the tetradic relation is resolved into two triadic relations. [It is true that an accurate analysis of the exchange would show it to be considerably more complex than I have represented it to be. But the point is evident in the abstract.] The whole thing is this

λ is an exchange of property between A and C
l is a transposition of ownership of B and D
L is an accomplishment of λ through l

μ is the surrender by A of B
m is the surrender by C of D
M is the performance of μ in reciprocal consideration of M

ν is the acquisition by A of D
η is the acquisition by C of B
N is the performance of ν in reciprocal consideration of N

L is carried out by the union of M and N.

It is thus evident that a tetradic relation is reducible to at most ten triads, a pentadic relation to at most a hundred triads, a hexadic relation into at most a thousand triads, an enneadic relation into at most a million triads; and so there is no such thing possible as elementary Fourthness, Fifthness, etc.

If you will allow me to use the phrase "in general (mathematically speaking)" to mean, "truly (unless something prevents its being so)" as when we say "a quintic equation is in general insoluble by radicals," then I can say

In general (mathematically speaking) a definite Secundan is also a Priman abstractly considered; and a definite Tertian is doubly a Secundan. That is, if A gives B to C, A enriches C, and A parts with B. Also in general (mathematically speaking) if there is a dyadic relation between A and B, either A or B is more specially Priman and the other Secundan. That is, one is the *agent* or determining factor, the other the *patient*, or determined factor. (Of course in innumerable cases there is no truth in this.) Also in a triadic relationship, a definite one of the three subjects is Priman and a definite other is Secundan. This depends upon how the relation is thought; but a triadic relation is usually a truth of thought, and there is a certain naturally Primary way of thinking of it. In the vast majority of languages there is one most natural way of expressing a dyadic relation of the ordinary type, which puts one subject in the Nominative case and the other in the Accusative, as "he loves her," which is simpler than "She charms him," though probably not so true. And in expressing an ordinary triadic relation there is a most natural expression which places a given one of the three subjects in the Nominative, a given other in the Accusative, and the third in the Dative.

He gives them to her

rather than He presents her with them

or She receives them from him

or She has to thank him for them

or They endebt her to him

or They _____ him for her.

Now the Nominative is the Priman case, the Accusative the Secundan, the Dative the Tertian.

Even in logical algebra where these shades of meaning are irrelevant, when the Subjects are expressed by selectives, their order becomes significant thus

"Any man praises some horse to any woman" i.e. If there is a man, then there is a horse and if there is a woman that man praises that horse to that woman

"Any man to any woman praises some horse" i.e. If there is a man and there is a woman then there is a horse and the man praises that horse to that woman.

"Some horse any man praises to any woman" i.e. There is a horse and if there is a man and a woman the ʿman praises the horse to the woman

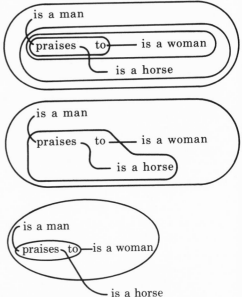

So then anything (generally in a mathematical sense) is a Priman (not a priman *element* generally) and we might define a sign as follows:

A "sign" is anything, A, which,

(1) in addition to other characters of its own,

(2) stands in a dyadic relation, γ, to a purely active correlate, B,

(3) and is also in a triadic relation *to* B *for* a purely passive correlate, C, this triadic relation being such as to determine C to be a dyadic relation, ς , to B, the relation ς corresponding in a recognized way to the relation γ .

In the which statement the sense in which the words active and passive are used is that in a given relationship considering the various characters of all or some of the correlates with the exclusion of those only which involve all the correlates and are immediately implied in the statement of the relationship, none of those which involve only non-passive correlates will by immediately essential necessity vary with any variation of those involving only passive correlates; while no variation of characters involving only non-active elements will by immediately essential necessity involve a variation of any character involving only active elements. And it may be added that by active-passive is meant active and passive if the entire collection of correlates excluding the correlates under consideration be divided into two parts and one part and the other be alternately excluded from consideration; while *purely* active or passive means active or passive without being active-passive.

This definition avoids the niceties for the sake of emphasizing the principal factors of a sign. Nevertheless, some explanations may be desirable. But *first* for the terminology. I use 'sign' in the widest sense of the definition. It is a wonderful case of an almost popular use of a very broad word in almost the exact sense of the scientific definiton. It was so used even in classical Latin, in consequence, I fancy, of the logical researches of the Epicureans. The stoics being nominalists as well as the Epicureans, fell into line on this point, though in those later days they had no such breadth of conception as was needed to give the word its proper breadth. In modern days Condillac helped to preserve that breadth intact. I formerly preferred the word *representamen*. But there was no need of this horrid long word. On the contrary, it requires some stretching to cover such imperative ejaculations of drivers, as, "Hi!" or "Hullah," which was in my boyhood's days the signal to get out of the way of a coaster's sled on Boston Common, where I suppose coasting has long since been prohibited. My notion in preferring "representamen" was that it would seem more natural to apply it to representatives in legislatures, to deputies of various kinds, etc. I admit still that it aids the comprehension of the definition to compare it carefully with such cases. But they certainly depart from the definition, in that this requires that the action of the sign as such shall not affect the object represented. A legislative representative is, on the contrary, expected in his functions to improve the condition of this constituents; and any kind of attorney, even if he has no discretion, is expected to affect the condition of his principal. The truth is I went wrong from not having a formal definition all drawn up. This sort of thing is inevitable in the early stages of a strong logical study; for if a formal definition is attempted too soon, it will only shackle thought. Oh, I am writing dreadful twaddle, garrulous chat; but it is our July weather which dries up or drenches one, as inconvenience may dictate. I thought of a representamen as taking the place of the thing; but a sign is not a substitute. Ernst Mach[2] has also fallen into that snare.

---

2. Ernst Mach (1838-1916), an Austrian physicist; author of *Die Mechanik in Inher Entwicklung* (1883) (The Science of Mechanics, 1893), *Erkenntnis und Irrtum* (1905), Space and Geometry (1906), etc.

The dictionary is rich in words waiting to receive technical definitions as varieties of signs. The word *seme*, Greek σημεῖον or σῆμα, is probably not in the English Dict'y. But it is a good word, brief, general, and unmistakable,—unless one were to mistake it for Italian.

Ma se le mie parole esser den seme

that will only make them better σημεία. "Token" is our good old Gothic word, though generally something material, or at least individual, while a "type", on the contrary,—literally, = French *coup*,—is of the nature of a form, an impression. The idea seems to prevail that the Greek word is often used by Plato in the sense of a sculptor's model. I have my doubts whether Greek sculptors of that age used models as ours do. I think the canon and their memory guided them mainly. At any rate, Plato rarely if ever used the word in any such sense. There is a place in the Republic filling 42 pages of the Teubner (C. F. Hermann) edition (Vol IV pp 58-99) in which Plato uses the word no less than 17 times, in every possible sense. Among these there are perhaps two or three instances where it means something to be imitated, though not certainly. They are not the instances cited by L & S. But if you look through his works for places in which he would be expected to use the word in that sense, it is very strikingly absent. I infer, therefore, that to his sense of the word, it was somewhat of a stretch so to use it. It usually means a character with the idea of being quite roughly like something, or the rough impression that experience of a thing leaves upon the mind.

Then we have *mark, note, trait, manifestation, ostent, show, species, appearance, vision, shade, spectre, phase*

Then, *copy, portraiture, figure, diagram, icon, picture, mimicry, echo*

Then, *gnomon, clue, trail, vestige, indice, evidence, symptom, trace*

Then, *muniment, monument, keepsake, memento, souvenir, cue*

Then, *symbol, term, category, stile, character, emblem, badge*

Then, *record, datum, voucher, warrant, diagnostic*

Then, *key, hint, omen, oracle, prognostic*

Then, *decree, command, order, law*

Then, *oath, vow, promise, contract, deed*

Then, *theme, thesis, proposition, premiss, postulate, prophecy*

Then, *prayer, bidding, collect, homily, litany, sermon*

Then, *revelation, disclosure, narration, relation*

Then, *testimony, witnessing, attestation, avouching, martyrdom*

Then, *talk, palaver, jargon, chat, parley, colloquy, tittle-tattle,* etc.

Peirce to Lady Welby (Draft, pages 24-30).
March 9, 1906 (L-463)

The following is a portion (pages 24 to 30) of a draft letter of 52 pages from Peirce to Lady Welby, dated March 9, 1906. (See p. 187.)

I should like to write a little book on 'The Conduct of Thoughts' in which the introductory chapter should introduce the reader to my existential graphs, which would then be used throughout as the apparent subject, the parable or metaphor, in terms of which everything would be said,—which would be far more scientific than dragging in the "mind" all the time, in German fashion, when the mind and psychology has no more to do with the substance of the book than if I were to discourse of the ingredients of the ink I use. If the average logician had anything like the comparatively exalted understanding of an average earth-worm, such a book would not be needed. The mere description of Existential Graphs would [be] sufficient.

Existential graphs are to be conceived as scribed upon the different leaves of a whole book. This whole book represents the thought (upon a given subject) of one mind. Each leaf represents a single stage of that thought. In the beginning, the successive leaves must represent strictly successive states of thought—I speak of, *logical* succession. But afterward when the minute anatomy of the thinking process has been mastered by the reader one can successively enlarge the intervals of development between the states of thought that successive leaves represent.

The blank leaf itself is the quasi-mind. I almost despair of making clear what I mean by a "quasi-mind;" But I will try. A *thought* is not *per se* in any mind or quasi-mind. I mean this in the same sense as I might say that Right or Truth would remain what they are though they were not embodied, & though nothing were right or true. But a thought, to gain any active mode of being must be embodied in a Sign. A thought is a special variety of sign. All thinking is necessarily a sort of dialogue, an appeal from the momentary self to the better considered self of the immediate and of the general future. Now as every thinking requires a mind, so every sign even if external to all minds must be a determination of a quasi-mind. This quasi-mind is itself a sign, a determinable sign. Consider for example a blank-book. It is meant to be written in. Words written in that in due order will have quite another force from the same words scattered accidentally on the ground, even should these happen to have fallen into collections which would have a meaning if written in the blank-book. The

language employed in discoursing to the reader, and the language employed to express the thought to which the discourse relates should be
kept distinct and each should be selected for its peculiar fitness for the
purpose it was to serve. For the discoursing language I would use English,
which has special merits for the treatment of logic. For the language
discoursed about, I would use the system of Existential Graphs throughout
which has no equal for this purpose.

I use the word *"Sign"* in the widest sense for any medium for the
communication or extension of a Form (or feature). Being medium, it is
determined by something, called its Object, and determines something,
called its Interpretatnt or Interpretand. But some distinctions have to be
borne in mind in order rightly to understand what is meant by the Object
and by the Interpretant. In order that a Form may be extended or
communicated, it is necessary that it should have been really embodied in
a Subject independently of the communication; and it is necessary that
there should be another subject in which the same form is embodied only
in consequence of the communication. The Form, (and the Form is the
Object of the Sign), as it really determines the former Subject, is quite
independent of the sign; yet we may and indeed must say that the object
of a sign can be nothing but what that sign represents it to be. Therefore,
in order to reconcile these apparently conflicting Truths, it is indispensible
to distinguish the *immediate* object from the *dynamical* object.

The same form of distinction extends to the interpretant; but as
applied to the interpretant, it is complicated by the circumstance that the
sign not only determines the interpretant to represent (or to take the form
of) the *object*, but also determines the interpretant to represent the sign.
Indeed in what we may, from one point of view, regard as the principal
kind of signs, there is one distinct part appropriated to representing the
object, and another to representing how this very sign itself represents that
object. The class of signs I refer to are the dicisigns. In "John is in love
with Helen," the object signified is the pair, John and Helen. But the "is in
love with" signifies the form this sign represents itself to represent John
and Helen's Form to be. That this is so, is shown by the precise
equivalence between any verb in the indicative and the same made the
object of "I tell you." "Jesus wept" = "I tell you that Jesus wept."

There is the *Intentional* Interpretant, which is a determination of the
mind of the utterer; the *Effectual* Interpretant, which is a determination
of the mind of the interpreter; and the *Communicational* Interpretant, or
say the *Cominterpretant*, which is a determination of that mind into which
the minds of utterer and interpreter have to be fused in order that any

communication should take place. This mind may be called the commens. It consists of all that is, and must be, well understood between utterer and interpreter at the outset, in order that the sign in question should fulfill its function. This I proceed to explain.

No object can be denoted unless it be put into relation to the object of the *commends*. A man, tramping along a weary and solitary road, meets an individual of strange mien, who says, "There was a fire in Megara." If this should happen in the Middle United States, there might very likely be some village in the neighborhood called Megara. Or it may refer to one of the ancient cities of Megara, or to some romance. And the time is wholly indefinite. In short, nothing at all is conveyed until the person addressed asks, Where?—"Oh about half a mile along there" pointing to whence he came. "And when?" "As I passed." Now an item of information has been conveyed, because it has been stated relatively to a well understood common experience. Thus the Form conveyed is always a determination of the dynamical object of the *Commind*. By the way, the dynamical object does not mean something out of the mind. It means something forced upon the mind in perception, but including more than perception reveals. It is an object of actual *Experience*.

The system of Existential Graphs (at least, so far as it is at present developed) does not represent every kind of Sign. For example, a piece of concerted music is a Sign; for it is a medium for the conveyance of Form. But I know not how to make a graph equivalent to it. So the command of a military officer to his men: "Halt!" "Ground Arms!" which is interpreted in their action, is a Sign beyond the competence of existential graphs. All that existential graphs can represent is *propositions*, on a single sheet, and arguments on a succession of sheets, presented in temporal succession.

If you take in all that I have said and what I am just about to say, you will begin to get an insight into the marvellous perfection and minute truth and profundity of this system.

Logicians who analyze a proposition into "terms" and a "copula" are guilty of overlooking the truth I have just enunciated, that it is out of the nature of things for an object to be signified (and remember that the most solitary meditation is dialogue,) otherwise than in relation to some actuality or existent in the commend. A common noun is by no means an indispensible part of speech. Indeed, there are few languages, outside the modern European languages, in which this part of speech is so fully developed as in them. All the Aryan languages have this part of speech. But in Greek one can say 'A man is an animal' without using any verb; and this shows that the nouns themselves have a trace of the verb-character. In the Shemitic languages almost all nouns have the form of derivatives of verbs. In Arabic and (in a somewhat different way) in Old Egyptian the "substantive verb" may be replaced by a pronoun, which proves that the nouns themselves have a share of predicative force. In most of the non-inflectional languages there are no fully developed common nouns, and a language like Basque (which has few verbs) is most exceptional. My analysis of 'A man is an animal' is as follows. I am looking, at present, at this paper. Then, to me, the proposition is: 'Something is coexistent at once with this paper and with Something that is at once a man and is an animal'. Now if I throw off the coexistence, (the being at once this and that), the paper, and the man, what will remain will [be]

Something is animal

If I throw off from this the "Something is" still what remains is

Something is an animal,

because the conception "Something is" is continuous. That is, it is the same as "Something is something that is," or "Something is Something that is Something that is," and so on *ad infinitum*. But you will say, "Surely there is a concept of *an animal* without any verb." No doubt there is. But, in my opinion, instead of being simpler than, it is only a complication of, the concept 'Something is an animal,' and it would be easy to defend this by a redoutable argument. However, I wont make so much of a small matter. Let it go that so it may be considered. Since "is" is a continuous conception in the above sense, it is appropriately represented in Existential graphs by a plain line _____ Here is the above proposition

⌠ a man
⌡ an animal

But Note Well that as yet the question whether a proposition to be asserted is to be simply scribed on that sheet or how otherwise it is to be attached to the sheet.

I insert in this diagram nothing but the paper, because that is sufficiently represented by the thing being written on this paper, which *shows* I must be thinking that the man is in the same universe as the paper. However I could scribe

$$\text{─}\hspace{-2pt}\left(\begin{array}{l} \text{a man} \\ \text{an animal} \end{array}\right.$$

Introducing the graph of teridentity ─(or ⊃ etc. Quateridentity is obviously composed of two teridentities.

I.e. ┼ is ⅄ or ✕ or ⤬ or ⋈ but teridentity cannot be formed out of binidentity _____ where two lines merely make one longer line.

Here let me point out what we mean in logic by *equivalence* and by *composition*.

If one rheme, or verb, would be true in every conceivable case in which the other would be true, and conversely, then and only then those two verbs are *logically equivalent*. For logic has in view only the possible truth and falsity of signs.

To say that a rheme is *logically composed* of two rhemes is to say that the first rheme is logically equivalent to the composite of the other two.

If follows in the first place that every line of identity ought to be considered as bristling with microscopic points of teridentity; so that _____ when magnified shall be seen to be ─₊₊╳╳₊₊₊╳╳╳₊╳╳╳─

In the second place it follows that using "coexistence" in such a sense that it is mere otherness, then since if anything is not coexistent with itself the same is equally true of anything else, to say that _____ a bird, i.e. that there is a bird, is equivalent to

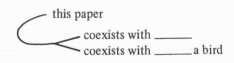

Whence it follows that a very appropriate symbol for tercoexistence, that is, for

$$\text{─────}\hspace{-4pt}<\hspace{-2pt}\begin{array}{l} \text{coexists with} \rule{1.5em}{0.4pt} \\ \text{coexists with} \rule{1.5em}{0.4pt} \end{array}$$

is simply any blank point of the sheet so that

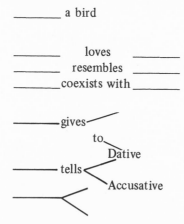

⎧ a bird
⎩ coexists with ＿＿＿ a fish

is equivalent to

＿＿＿ a bird
＿＿＿ a fish

But the latter mode of writing is somewhat of the nature of an abridgment.

We can next say that every logical concept has a definite valency in the chemical sense

＿＿＿＿ a bird   is a monad like hydrogen, lithium, potassium, iodine (?)

＿＿＿＿ loves ＿＿＿＿   are dyads like glucinum, oxygen,
＿＿＿＿ resembles ＿＿＿＿   sometimes sulphur, and perhaps
＿＿＿＿ coexists with ＿＿＿＿   tungsten

＿＿＿ gives ⟨to⟩ Dative   are triads like boron, yltrium, some-
＿＿＿ tells ⟨Accusative   times nitrogen, phosphorus, vana-
＿＿＿ ⟨   dium

All tetrads etc are compounds. There are no medads like argon and xenon except the absolute Truth. But loosely we may take a complete proposition for a medad.

The only way in which concepts can be connected or compounded (without the addition of other concepts) is by bringing the lines of identity attached to them into abuttal, or by something which is virtually that. For we have seen that

＿＿＿ a bird
＿＿＿ a fish

is really

⎧ a bird
⎩ coexists with ＿＿＿ a fish

So far all the conventions of the system seem almost forced upon us. But now we come to the sole feature of the system which may be strongly suspected of being arbitrary. Namely, all the objects of graphs, or propositions, are of two classes. Every object is either asserted as an *actuality*, i.e., as an *object of* positive *knowledge* or it is merely suggested as a *possibility*, or as an *object of ignorance* i.e., an object of whose *existence* the *proposition written* leaves us ignorant. Let us write the objects of knowledge on the recto of the sheet and appropriate the verso to indications of objects of ignorance.

But our objects of knowledge are limited. We cannot insert one without some evidence. We can erase any without incurring responsibility.

Our objects of ignorance are an infinite multitude and we cannot exclude any without evidence while we can insert any we like, since it is merely to represent ourselves as ignorant.